DATE DUE

JUN 0 3 1989	~~Full occ Plate~~	
MAY 1 2 '89	~~Seu 7-14-28~~	
	4 wks use	
APR 1 0 '90		
APR 9 '90		
DEC 06 '91		
DEC 8 91		
MAY 1 4 '92		
APR 2 1 '92		
MAR 2 8 '98		
MAR 31 '98		

THE ART OF FAILURE

Conrad's Fiction

THE ART
OF FAILURE

Conrad's Fiction

SURESH RAVAL

Professor of English,
The University of Arizona

Boston
ALLEN & UNWIN

London   Sydney

Allen & Unwin, Inc.,
8 Winchester Place, Winchester, Mass. 01890, USA

Allen & Unwin (Publishers) Ltd,
40 Museum Street, London WC1A 1LU, UK

Allen & Unwin (Publishers) Ltd,
Park Lane, Hemel Hempstead, Herts HP2 4TE, UK

Allen & Unwin (Australia) Ltd,
8 Napier Street, North Sydney, NSW 2060, Australia

First published in 1986

Library of Congress Cataloging in Publication Data

Raval, Suresh
    The art of failure.
Bibliography: p.
Includes index.
1. Conrad, Joseph, 1857–1924 – Criticism and interpretation.
2. Failure (Psychology) in literature.
I. Title
PR6005.04Z7864   1986   823'.912   85–15116
ISBN 0-04-800039-6 (alk. paper)

British Library Cataloguing in Publication Data

Raval, Suresh
    The art of failure: Conrad's fiction.
1. Conrad, Joseph – Criticism and interpretation
I. Title
823'.912   PR6005.04Z/
ISBN 0-04-800039-6

Set in 10 on 11 point Garamond
and printed in Great Britain by
Biddles Limited, Guildford, Surrey

The only indisputable truth of life is our ignorance. Besides this there is nothing evident, nothing absolute, nothing uncontradicted; there is no principle, no instinct, no impulse that can stand alone at the beginning of things and look confidently to the end . . . The only legitimate basis of creative works lies in the courageous recognition of all the irreconcilable antagonisms that make our life so enigmatic, so burdensome, so fascinating, so dangerous— so full of hope.

Joseph Conrad

Only because of the hopelessness is hope given to us.
Walter Benjamin

For Frances

Contents

Acknowledgments

I wish to thank my colleagues L. D. Clark and Gerald McNiece for comments on parts of the manuscript. I think Douglas Canfield, Herbert Schneidau, and Edgar Dryden, who read my very first attempt on Conrad, can stand for all my friends and colleagues to whom I owe gratitude for their interest and support. Professor Ian Watt's advice and comments on an earlier version gave me the confidence necessary to finish this book, and Professor Jacques Berthoud's comments gave me the basis for undertaking final revisions. Claude Rawson's generosity and support far exceed anything I can say here by way of gratitude.

For permission to reprint, my thanks go to the Editors of *Nineteenth-Century Fiction*, in which my essay on *Victory* originally appeared, in 1980; and to the editors of *ELH—A Journal of English Literary History*, in which my essay on *Lord Jim* originally appeared, in 1981. The piece on *Victory* is slightly revised; the one on *Lord Jim* is substantially revised and expanded.

To Carolyn Slaughter I owe gratitude for help with proof-reading. To Jill Weber and Judy Johnson I owe thanks for expert typing.

To Frances, to whom the book is dedicated, I owe a debt too extensive to be easily specified. She read the penultimate version and helped me to rethink it at several crucial stages.

Suresh Raval

References to Conrad's works are to the *Complete Works of Joseph Conrad*, 26 vols, Kent Edition (New York: Doubleday, 1926). Page numbers in parentheses in this study refer to the Conrad novel under discussion.

Introduction

I

Of all the statements Conrad has made in his essays, notes, and letters, none has attracted the critical attention given to this statement in the celebrated preface to *The Nigger of the "Narcissus"*: "My task which I am trying to achieve is, by the power of the written word, to make you hear, to make you feel—it is before all to make you *see*. That—and no more, and it is everything" (xviii).[1] The metaphor of perception, strongly marked in the phrase "to make you *see*", gives rise to the speculation that Conrad's poetic is essentially imagist. This speculation is in accord with what some critics have called the primarily impressionist method of his fiction.[2] Imagism and impressionism derive from similar theories of how to capture the "real" in art, and there is no doubt that a preponderance of statements in the preface suggests a commitment to the process of perception rather than to a finished work of art allowing for disinterested contemplation.

My own insistence, however, on the connection between artistic creativity and "seeing" in Conrad underscores the problematical nature of understanding that is central to all his major fiction. Conrad's statement that the artist heroically struggles to render "the truth, manifold and one, underlying . . . every aspect" (xv) seems to involve a metaphysical insight into the nature of reality, but is in fact a commitment to the romantic conceptions of sincerity and authenticity of artistic expression. This commitment would seem to place him within the tradition of romanticism rather than within the tradition that derives from the imagist aesthetic elaborated by T. E. Hulme, Ezra Pound, and others early in this century.[3] "The artist", states the preface, "descends within himself, and in the lonely region of stress and strife, if he be deserving and fortunate, he finds the terms of his appeal" (xv–xvi). Consequently, specific moments in Conrad's fiction appear to possess the vividly striking qualities of an image, but, when carefully probed, those moments increasingly reveal the multiple and contradictory features which somehow resist both the translucent clarity of an image and the determinacy of a specific and fixed meaning.

1

Conrad does say, in the preface, that if the artist is successful in his task, which is "to make you *see*", the vision "shall awaken in the hearts of the beholders that feeling of unavoidable solidarity; of the solidarity in mysterious origin, in toil, in joy, in hope, in uncertain fate, which binds men to each other and mankind to the visible world" (x). This statement is more an expression of an idealistic hope than a critically compelling observation of the complex workings of the novels which deal with multiple and discordant realities of human experience. Consequently, the sincerity and authenticity of artistic expression insisted on in the preface imply a conception of human experience which transcends any merely fanatic commitment by a given protagonist in Conrad's fiction to his specific ideals and projects. Jim's sincerity and authenticity, for instance, are explored in a way that enables Conrad simultaneously to celebrate them as exemplary and tragic and to castigate them as aberrant and self-destructive. Conrad's project of making his readers *see* is a project of exploring a variety of contexts in which a particular character's historical, social, or personal experience becomes so bewildering that only by questioning our habitual modes of understanding can that experience be made accessible to us. Thus it is that Conrad writes "Realism, Romanticism, Naturalism, even the unofficial sentimentalism . . . all these gods must abandon the artist . . . to the stammerings of his conscience and to the outspoken consciousness of the difficulties of his own work" (xxi). The various narrators who appear in his novels often struggle with the inadequacy of language, striving for a sense of clarity which at times turns out, by their own admission, to be unattainable or illusory. And, for the same reason, everywhere in his major fiction one finds the attempt to remove what Victor Shklovsky calls the "automatism of perception",[4] not merely from the minds of the readers but also from the minds of the narrators who cannot be too sure they have escaped it.

Conrad's fiction, then, dramatizes those moments of experience which sometimes force his main characters, sometimes his narrators, and always his readers, to ask whether they can be trusted to understand what has been brought to their critical attention. It deals with issues in the context of a historical—political—social world in which understanding is a problem, our knowledge of ourselves and of the world questionable, and our language inadequate to grasp the experience which makes up our cultural and spiritual life. Conrad's fiction is concerned with the larger cultural issues which are always embodied, in his treatment of them, in individual human situations and actions. Consequently, artistic and philosophical concerns become deeply intertwined, though not in the sense that we are made to puzzle over a metaphysical enigma. For, as one probes Conrad's most crucial novels, there occurs a compelling and distressing engagement of the mind which cannot be reduced to simply the peculiar pleasure of art.

Part of the difficulty of Conrad's fiction—a difficulty which is integral to its power—stems from his relentlessly skeptical attitude toward both language and fiction. This skepticism perhaps explains why Conrad felt rudderless and adrift when writing fiction. He writes, in the "Familiar Preface" to *A Personal Record*, about the dangers of freedom inherent in writing fiction:

> In that interior world where his thought and his emotions go seeking for the experience of imagined adventures, there are no policemen, no law, no pressure of circumstance or dread of opinion to keep him within bounds. Who then is going to say Nay to his temptations if not his conscience? (xviii)

Conrad knew that the freedom of the creative imagination carries with it liabilities no serious artist could afford to forget. Several critics as well as Conrad himself tell us about the terrible agonies he suffered during his most creative years, caused by his suspicion of the very act of writing fiction and by his feeling that he could not possibly say what he wanted to say.[5]

The problem of understanding, as I see it in Conrad's fiction, does not primarily concern the self-consciousness which is a characteristic feature of what has come to be known as post-modernist fiction. Nor is it concerned with what has become a major tenet of recent criticism, which holds that literature carries no more authority than any other mode of expression, though it bears the mark of its own invented nature more self-consciously than do other modes of expression.[6] Indeed, self-consciousness in Conrad's fiction often engenders moral paralysis in his characters and prevents them from knowing how to act intelligently without illusion or false hope, though sometimes it performs the dramatic work of exploring the actions and attitudes generated by high ideals held by someone like Lord Jim, or the sudden bleak insights of someone like Kurtz in *Heart of Darkness*. Conrad's most compelling novels are not self-sustaining epistemological narratives, unconnected with the dialectic of social and personal life. His fiction is almost always concerned with problems of a social, historical, and moral nature, and with institutions that constitute, sustain, and complicate forms of life in society.

Conrad criticism characteristically probes his work for ambiguities and paradoxes and their relation to the moral implications for human action. The consequence of this sort of inquiry has been that some critics see a pervasively dark and nihilistic attitude in nearly all his major fiction,[7] whereas other critics see a robust common sense which helps restrain and qualify the nihilistic vision of life.[8] Indeed, these two views have so persistently dominated

3

Conrad criticism that even recent studies lead to further disclosures of either irony and nihilism or sanity and moral toughness in Conrad's work.[9] There are, of course, recent studies that employ methods of historical and ideological analysis with great skill, and depart from the usual concern with the exploration of either irony or moral affirmation.[10] Conrad, it seems to me, was fascinated by the contradictions in human affairs, and in his major fiction persistently dramatized their implications for social and personal life. "It would take", he said, "too long to explain the intimate alliance of contradictions in human nature which makes love itself wear at times the desperate shape of betrayal."[11] His concern with contradictions and their impact on actual human conduct led Conrad to make an enduring and fundamental critique of the central concepts and institutions of Western culture. These contradictions are not simply matters of logical or epistemological impasse; they point to dilemmas which lie at the heart of our social-political life.

I attempt to interpret several of Conrad's major novels and to articulate the subtlety and richness of his treatment of our social-political institutions and of the forces that complicate and distort our private and public life. Before beginning, I need to clarify certain matters of procedure and method. I shall explain, first, my method, and then the background of social-political thought against which Conrad's fiction acquires its rich and multifaceted reflection on the forces operating in history and society; and, finally, I shall explain my reasons for beginning with *Heart of Darkness* and state my main conclusions about Conrad's fiction.

II

My interpretations are not done in strict adherence to any general principles. I eschew general principles because, while they often seem plausible in extremely broad terms, responses to specific literary works are always more pertinent. It is on the basis of these responses that we make general observations which then require considerable self-reflection to ensure that they will illuminate rather than obfuscate the total configuration of a novel. When criticism, as I have argued elsewhere, is performed in terms of specific absolute premises, one's conclusions are entailed in the premises.[12] Such a reading of a literary work cannot be construed as an experience of the work, but simply as a form of discourse that takes its task to be that of providing confirmation of one's assumptions. Criticism must develop a sense of the complexity of its operations which requires assimilation, rethinking, and modification of what is valuable in contemporary thought, in order that it may combine interpretation with critical reflection, and literary analysis with a probing of its implications.

Thus, for example, those who treat Conrad as a strictly nihilistic writer do so because they implicitly give credence to the idea that morality ought to have a foundation, that otherwise the very idea of morality is meaningless. When they find no such foundation in Conrad, they immediately label him a nihilist, not because they mean to condemn him, but because they wish to characterize his metaphysics. Conrad, however, as I read him, does not allow for such a broad description. This sort of description derives from abstracting general statements from Conrad's letters and novels which seem to give a sense of his consciousness or his narrative strategies.[13] This is not to deny the usefulness of Conrad's letters, prefaces, and essays; it is simply to suggest the importance of hermeneutic tact without which literary criticism becomes a barren enterprise.

Hermeneutic tact is a developed critical ability, the result of discipline, experience, historical and philosophical perspicacity, and one cannot always be sure that one possesses it. Hermeneutic tact consists of knowing when and how to use specific analytic strategies in interpreting a literary work. To know how to use a strategy is to have some sense of when it becomes misleading or overdetermining and hence trivializing or oversimplifying. To possess hermeneutic tact is already to know that one needs to engage in a process of critical reflection on methods and doctrines one finds interesting, rather than taking their truthfulness or value to be unquestionable. This underscores the importance of dialogical relation with the community of critics and scholars in the field. Hermeneutic tact is as necessary in the writing of literary criticism as it is in the writing of a literary work, and it is necessary in philosophy and in all other fields of inquiry where there is room for uncertainty, ambiguity, and error, because of the multiplicity of divergent and sometimes conflicting possibilities one may encounter. To the extent that one is aware of this ever-present liability to uncertainty and error, one hopes one's critical practice has benefited from what others have done in the field.

My method is eclectic in the sense that this study, while examining thematic and structural interrelations among Conrad's fiction, attempts to clarify what I take to be powerful reflections on man, history, politics, and society. It insists on the importance of focusing on the experience of reading Conrad, and considers the dimension of social-political criticism in Conrad's fiction to be a crucial element in this experience. Thus, for example, Conrad's fiction does not strictly belong to the tradition of the novel of character, but rather attempts a radical questioning of that tradition. Such questioning, however, cannot be done without the exploitation of that tradition's resources. So I consider it necessary, at times, to attempt a character-analysis in order to show the forces that Conrad finds working against both romantic and realistic conceptions of the individual in society.

Similarly, I think, Conrad's treatment of the epistemological impasse that some of his narrators experience is usefully analyzed by deconstructive analysis. My use of deconstruction, however, is restricted, since I do not employ it in order to determine the total reading of a novel. My reading does not turn everything into an endless, intricate interlocking of textuality. I try to employ self-interpretive elements in Conrad's fiction to elucidate and interpret the meaning and implications of the fiction. These elements include dramatization of and commentary on the nature of language, self, and community, as well as moral and political questioning of the stances adopted by the various narrators and protagonists in his fiction. These self-interpretive elements put in question any particular doctrine, and their questioning of all doctrines lends the fiction a power which enables Conrad's art to subject to serious critique even the most important contemporary methods of criticism. The questions Conrad's fiction poses, and the manner in which he continues his skeptical questioning of our values and the ways they do and do not link up with our practice, are profoundly moral, forcing us to reflect on the ambiguities and contradictions of our social-political life. Thus I believe the epistemological impasse that Conrad's narrators, and sometimes his protagonists, experience takes on far greater significance when placed in the context of conditions of their social existence which lead to the impasse.

This study, then, is informed by certain important propositions about literature and criticism, which are best summarized in this way: Criticism is a language-game in the sense that it is a form of cultural life. In so far as it is a form of life, it cannot be identified strictly with the act of interpretation alone; it is a form of doing, which is to say it is connected to human action in fundamental ways. In characterizing criticism in this manner I mean to suggest that criticism must not be construed as something occurring in and confined to language, and therefore as having no other relations and implications. When criticism is so confined to language, critics turn their practice and theory into a form of linguistic solipsism, and deny those elements of critical practice which show criticism to be a form of moral discourse. It is moral in the sense that what one does in one's practice (as well as theory) has implications which link one to, or separate one from, the lived relations in one's personal and social transactions. But it is not moral in the sense that criticism sees its task to be one of providing a social or political program for reform or revolution in society. Its morality inheres in its capacity to grasp

6

and elucidate those complications and dilemmas, such as Conrad's art presents, which are not reducible to tidy logical resolutions or theoretical systems. This is why criticism, like art, is a form of cultural life not to be subjected to the demands of systematic categories or theories. Criticism includes a host of flexible, tentative, and analogical procedures; when one tries to force these procedures into the limits of a strict theory, one predetermines critical practice and drains it of its vitality. This is not to say that theories and theoretical elements do not, or cannot, play a useful role in criticism. As we shall see, Conrad's fiction explores and questions various forms of theoretical obsessions which control and often destroy the lives of his protagonists.

III

The questions explored in Conrad's fiction concern the nature of social and political institutions and their impact on the history of society and on the conduct of many of his protagonists. Avrom Fleishman, who has usefully placed Conrad's political fiction within the organicist tradition originating in Burke, has argued that Conrad "celebrates the values of the *Volk*, its traditional manners and moral ties, and suggests the weight of national history in shaping, almost determining, human action".[14] Fleishman correctly suggests that Conrad shares an organicist view with George Eliot about the "tragic consequences of an organicism, disregarded by previous writers: since men are rooted in the past and bound by irrational ties of society and kinship, there is very little that can be done at the level of public policy to change their deepest values and habits".[15] Conrad amplifies, in Fleishman's view, George Eliot's attitude while sharing her conservatism.

I think Fleishman's characterization of Conrad's politics is correct and indeed important in capturing the dimension of organicism in Conrad's best essays such as "Autocracy and War" as well as in his major fiction.[16] But it underestimates Conrad's conception of skepticism and its implications for both politics and the historical process. A probing of Conrad's skepticism shows that no other novelist in English deals with contradictions that plague not only lives of individuals but also individuals in their relation to their community. Moreover, the fiction shows the community, even in the West, to be marked by fatal contradictions that its idealism can neither overcome nor conceal. Thus, if there are organicist strains in the major fiction, they exist in an antithetical relation with those that seriously question the values underlying organicism. For Conrad's political fiction seems to suggest that even those (like Charles Gould in *Nostromo*) who hold organicist values in order to bring about definite improvements in their society take recourse to means that go against those values.

In spite of moments which suggest the importance of the organicist ethics, Conrad's fiction raises fundamental questions concerning the status of this ethics. Consequently, Fleishman's remark that the "moral crises of Conrad's heroes are object lessons in the failure of individualism"[17] needs to be placed in the larger context of the heroes' communities, whose internal contradictions generate the self-defeating forms of individualism such as the ones represented by Kurtz, Jim, Decoud, Nostromo, Razumov, and the Professor. Thus, rather than achieving "his recovery . . . through immersion in the political and social life of a native community",[18] Jim remains, in the dream-world of Patusan, a creature of another world, cut off from both Jewel and the natives. The argument that Decoud overcomes his dilettantism by devising a strategy of provincial separatism and is thus at the center of a revolution neglects the motivating forces of his love for Antonia, which pay little attention to the implications of cutting off a nation and its people from the resources of their richest province. At the very moment of his revolutionary ideology, Decoud remains a quintessentially ironic individualist, one whose response betrays a lack of experience of deep communal bonds. It is easy for Decoud to think instinctively in terms of his ingrained ironic individualism, which is itself formed by his conception of one's irrevocable isolation from others. What appears, then, to be his horror of isolation is in fact the lack of experience on Decoud's part as a social being, one that can sustain him during the depredations of loneliness on the island.

Conrad shows, I think, an acute insight into the subtle strategies by which both idealists and demagogues use words, often unwittingly, as instruments of coercion and constraint, deception and self-deception, as tools of intimidation and submission, as signs of compromise and contempt. These and other aspects of the relation between language and power, self and community, intention and action are explored in Conrad's fiction. The organicist politics and ethics are often enough projected as values which eventually will bring wholeness and harmony within both individual and community, but these politics and ethics are mere idealistic projections of those whose very determination to retain power shows the inner perversion of their idealist fancies. And these organicist projections are often at the basis of a protagonist's failure to grasp the historical process and political forces that inevitably undermine any simple picture of equality and justice brought about through the intervention, for instance, of a supposedly noble capitalist venture.

It is here that a basic grasp of Hegel and Marx is relevant to an understanding of Conrad's fiction. Hegel can certainly be placed more easily within the organicist tradition, since he was the most important influence on English philosophical idealists such as Bernard Bosanquet and F. H. Bradley, who worked out organicist conceptions of politics and ethics in late nineteenth-century England. Hegel's conceptions of reason and history are nevertheless more complex than those central to organicist politics and ethics such as those of Edmund Burke and others. Marx, on the other hand, represents a strand of thought which radically challenges organicist and idealist politics and ethics. Conrad's relation to nineteenth-century political thought, however, is to be understood not by determining whether he had read Hegel, Marx, and others, but by developing a grasp of the views about man, society, and history implicit in his major fiction.

For both Hegel and Marx, what happens in history is not only understandable but also justifiable. They believed in the perfectibility of man and conceived of history as a process governed by definite laws. They differed on the question of how such perfectibility is realized, and on the question of the nature and implications of the laws governing history. For Hegel, world history reveals the plan of providence; at any given stage of history, the community of men is in conformity with reason at that stage. Hegel thus conceives of history as a succession of communities which in later stages embody more and more adequately the Idea. Men are caught in a drama they do not understand; but, as Hegel argues, philosophy can explain this drama, though only after any particular moment of it has played itself out. Thus philosophy can disentangle the knot of history and show the workings of reason. Men, in other words, are the agents of *Geist*. Even if they claim to have some idea of what they are doing, thay cannot understand the deepest truth underlying their actions. Hegel calls it the *cunning of reason* that the Idea, operating through history, uses man's passions for its own ends. Hegel believed, moreover, that the "History of the world is none other than the progress of the consciousness of Freedom".[19]

Marx rejects Hegel's notion of the cunning of reason, and substitutes for it the notion of a species nature of men. As long as men exist in class society, they remain, he argues, in conflict with their inner nature as generic men. As long as this contradiction persists men cannot think clearly about themselves and their actions. By overcoming this contradiction, they can become self-conscious and classless. As Marx argues:

Hegel is not to be blamed for depicting the nature of the modern state as it is, but rather for presenting what is as the essence of the state. The claim that the rational is actual is contradicted precisely by an irrational actuality, which is everywhere the contrary of what it asserts and asserts the contrary of what is.[20]

For Marx, Hegel has spiritualized man, whereas what is needed is a recognition of the nature of man in terms of his material existence, which is necessarily a social-political existence.

Hegel's *Philosophy of Right*, argues Marx, conceives of social and political institutions as particular manifestations of the Idea in various phases of its determination. When social reality is conceived in this way, it is exempted from any critique that would effect its transformation. In Hegel social reality is given a mystical status, and only the workings of the Hegelian dialectic are thought capable of contemplating change. Marx, on the other hand, seeks to discover the laws which control the rise, development, and decline of a given form of social production and its eventual replacement by a higher form of social production.

Hegel was, of course, critical of the increasing homogenization of modern society; he condemned the drive to absolute freedom characteristic of various forms of romantic individualism; and he showed an uncanny insight in seeing that the attempt to overcome all differentiation results in the dictatorship of a revolutionary elite. His insight, moreover, that the self is the product of community rather than being prior to it is incontrovertible—a conclusion that Marx found crucial to any reflection on society. Marx is right, however, in arguing that Hegel's notion of the community depends on the ontology of *Geist*, and is finally reactionary since it shows no real insight into modern man's aspiration for democratic freedom and equality.[21] In contrast to Hegel's and Marx's optimism, Conrad expresses in the major fiction his characteristic skepticism, though it does not prevent him from recognizing the meaning and value of hope in the life of both individuals and community. The power of Conrad's fiction resides, however, in its dramatization of a profoundly felt criticism of various forms of political and social life evolved in modern times. It is in this criticism that Conrad's standards of value are to be found, standards by which he measures the complexity of man's social, political, and personal existence.

IV

In this study I attempt to interpret *Heart of Darkness*, *Lord Jim*, *Nostromo*, *The Secret Agent*, *Under Western Eyes*, and *Victory*. There are, of course, other works which I could have included, but they do not seem to me to deepen our insight into the characteristic Conradian preoccupations which I attempt to explore here. Let me illustrate this point with some remarks on Conrad's first two novels, *Almayer's Folly* and *An Outcast of the Islands*, and on *The Nigger of the "Narcissus"*, a work of undeniable significance.

Almayer's Folly and *An Outcast of the Islands* bear all the marks of popular romance, but they are inevitably colored by Conrad's preoccupation with the problem of human isolation. The romantic tale of Dain and Nina (Almayer's daughter) is complemented by Almayer's dream of eventually inheriting Captain Lingard's wealth and finally settling down in a mansion in Amsterdam. But these elements of popular romance are no more than a plot of desire, one whose inner content turns out to be Almayer's overwhelming sense of failure culminating in his disintegration. Indeed, elements of ordinary banal reality are so constantly present in both novels that the plot of romance remains only a form of deferred wish-fulfillment. Despite some moments of remarkably realized dramatic scenes, both novels are marked by a writing that is persistently morbid, gloomy, and at times interminably and pointlessly descriptive. Conrad is not able to resolve, in the first two novels, the problem of tone. His narrator is often not in control of his material; sometimes his language becomes morbid to the point of becoming indistinguishable from the experience of Almayer's and Willems's disintegration. In the early novels, the focus on isolation and disintegration prevents Conrad from exploring the implications of imperialism for the natives and rulers, and he falls rather easily into the genre of colonial adventure romance, taking recourse to the glib mythology of the East as alien, brooding, evil. Sometimes Almayer's and Willems's racism becomes indistinguishable from the narrator's own attitude, which is in fact quite different. Difficulties of this nature seem to suggest that, though he has at his disposal enormously problematical material, Conrad does not yet possess sufficient technical and artistic insight to transform it into realized art.

The weakness of the first two novels, however, should not obscure the strengths of Conrad's treatment of the conflicting psychologies of the natives and Europeans, and of the main protagonists' daydreams of wealth and power. Conrad's tendency to develop particular characters in terms of genetic analysis shows itself from his first novel. Almayer's parents' home in Java is described in this way: "his father grumbled all day at the stupidity of native gardeners, and the mother from the depths of her long easy-chair bewailed the lost glories of Amsterdam, where she had been brought up, and her position as the daughter of a cigar dealer there"(5). Almayer's colonial upbringing is at the root of his gross confusion of dream and reality, power and authority, and at the root also of his failure to grasp the cultural and historical displacement that so distorts his aspirations. Almayer is an impotent Kurtz who lives vicariously in the world of fantasy and desire, an

11

entrapment that becomes complete when he turns into an opium addict.

Almayer's problems are dramatized against the background of Captain Lingard's extraordinary success, which has made him, in the manner of a typical colonial adventure hero, "father" to the Malays. As Captain Lingard would later tell Willems, "My word is law—and I am the only trader" (*An Outcast of the Islands*, 5). Lingard finally disappears, leaving Willems to disintegrate on the island, while engaging of course in various intrigues for gaining wealth and power. Conrad's instinct for the twisted love between Malayan women and white men is unfailing: the mutual incomprehension of each other's motives and attitudes, the impossibility of effective communication between them, the radical divergence between their conceptions of social and personal life take the form of mutual racial hatred. Conrad's treatment of all of these characters is nicely captured in Nina's denunciation of Almayer and Captain Lingard, and in Aissa's bitter remark that Europe is "a land of lies and of evil from which nothing but misfortune ever comes to us—who are not white" (*An Outcast of the Islands*, 144). With moments like these Conrad has begun a serious critique of European civilization and its social-political institutions which gave rise to colonial empires in Asia, Africa, and America. The critique gains in perspective and depth when Conrad is able to develop morally and politically compelling delineations of social and historical forces that complicate the actions and attitudes of particular human beings.

In his first two novels, then, though he has found his true subject, Conrad does not yet know how to develop an authentic narrative stance and an adequate voice for storytelling. With *The Nigger of the "Narcissus"*, however, there occurs a sudden readjustment in his resources of storytelling, and he is able to write a deeply felt work. It is a narrative of great simplicity and directness, but with a complexity deriving from both the manner of dramatizing experience and the implications underlying that experience. The story is a direct expression of the values Conrad cherished as a sailor. He considered sailing a fine art "made up of accumulated tradition, kept alive by individual pride, rendered exact by professional opinion, and like the higher arts . . . spurred on and sustained by discriminating praise".[22] And he conceived of work as man's salvation: "A man is a worker. If he is not that he is nothing . . . For the great mass of mankind the only grace that is needed is steady fidelity to what is nearest to hand and heart in the short moment of each human effort."[23] At the explicit narrative level Conrad focuses on a seafaring experience apparently in order to celebrate these values, represented in a bygone era of maritime greatness and its tradition of uncompromising fidelity to work. At a deeper level, however, where Conrad's fiction characteristically works, this story explores the forces of disintegration and demoralization that erupt, almost from the beginning, in the lives of the crew members, and undermine the very ideals on which the possibility of their collective survival depends.[24]

Conrad's tendency to focus so exclusively on the absolute values of solidarity, service, and discipline makes him blind to his wrenching of seamanship from its larger context where the seamen serve the merchant navy of a colonial power. His metaphysical interests here take over, culminating in a brilliant celebration of the tradition of seamanship even as it bears the marks of Conrad's melancholy sense that this tradition is nearing its end:

> The men like Singleton had been strong, as those are strong who know ·
> neither doubts nor hopes. They had been impatient and enduring,
> turbulent and devoted, unruly and faithful . . . they had been men who
> knew toil, privation, violence, debauchery—but knew not fear and had
> no desire of spite in their hearts. Men hard to manage, but easy to inspire;
> voiceless men—but men enough to scorn in their hearts the sentimental
> voices that bewailed the hardness of their fate. It was a fate unique and
> their own; the capacity to bear it appeared to them the privilege of the
> chosen. Their generation lived inarticulate and indispensable, without
> knowing the sweetness of affections or the refuge of a home—and died
> free from the dark menace of a narrow grave. They were the everlasting
> children of the mysterious sea. Their successors are the grown-up children
> of a discontented earth. They are less naughty, but less innocent; less
> profane, but perhaps also less believing; and if they have learned how to
> speak they have also learned how to whine. But the others were strong
> and mute; they were effaced, bowed and enduring, like stone caryatides
> that hold up in the night the lighted halls of a resplendent and glorious
> edifice. (25)

Singleton and Allistoun embody Conrad's ideal of the seaman celebrated in this passage. While they may be, as the narrator says, violent, uncouth, or drunken, they are, in the context of their work, equal to the elemental force of the sea which they fear and yet courageously face; they transform their fear into a collaborative effort. They resemble the elemental force of the sea to the extent they remain unself-conscious. Their unself-consciousness does not imply, however, that they exist in some kind of primal harmony with the sea. They, rather, instinctively feel that they work in a medium—the sea—which is brutally indifferent to their fate. Their work becomes a refuge against the corrosive effects of self-consciousness. Thus, if Donkin embodies verbal facility and its perversion that supposedly attends his political thinking,

Singleton embodies an essential purity born of a lack of self-consciousness and verbal facility.

The new generation of sailors, on the other hand, has become egoistic, and has driven a wedge between themselves and the work they do. As a result, they get mired in self-alienation, since the work they do does not exercise any critical pressure on the conceptions by which they define themselves and their relation to the work they are expected to do. The conceptions they hold make it virtually impossible for them to work without doubts. They are, consequently, engaged in an activity for which they lack justification. Thus the solidarity they show in their sympathy for Wait is spurious because it is more a product of their own fear than a compassionate understanding of the terror and loneliness that Wait, a black man, experiences in *Narcissus*. The crew's sympathy for Wait is an expression of "the latent egoism of tenderness to suffering" (138). The fact that many of the crew members remain immersed in their egoism is starkly illustrated in the whole gamut of their ambivalent and contradictory responses to Wait trapped and howling in the cabin. "The agony of his fear wrung our hearts so terribly that we longed to abandon him, to get . . . back on the poop where we could wait passively death in incomparable repose" (67). At the moment of Wait's final release from the cabin, the crew in their frenzied effort barely miss killing him with a crowbar. When he is finally rescued, he seems "as quiet as a dead man inside a grave" (69), and the rescuers feel "like a lot of men embarrassed with a stolen corpse" (71). Thus the whole range of feelings and activities prompted, however unwittingly, by Wait proves to be devastating: "We suspected Jimmy, one another, and even our very selves. We did not know what to do . . . It was a weird servitude" (43). There has occurred, in effect, a complete turning around of the crew's allegiance; if the tradition of seamanship demands an exacting servitude to the ship, the crew's interest in Wait, itself a form of corrosive self-interest, has bound them in demoralizing servitude to him.

The narrative does, of course, portray the experience of fellowship realized at the moment of the greatest challenge *Narcissus* faces during the storm. It makes possible a spontaneous overcoming of the self-consciousness that otherwise plagues the crew before and after the storm. Singleton, sitting at the wheel for thirty hours, is an image of "the dumb fear and the dumb courage of men, obscure, forgetful, and enduring" (90). Captain Allistoun shows a steadfastness and clarity of judgment that help him resist even his first mate's plea to cut the mast when the ship is turned on her side. Finally, when the storm is over, both Singleton and Allistoun virtually collapse. Conrad's treatment of the storm, then, is an exhilarating if also bewildering account of the experience of solidarity. But he also characteristically focuses on the crew's reflective relation to their experience of the storm. When the storm is over, the crew members feel that their action has been heroic, that they are heroes: "We boasted of our pluck, of our capacity for work, of our energy . . . we remembered our danger, our toil—and conveniently forgot our horrible scare" (100). Thus the crew members' understanding of the nature of their work remains as impoverished as before the storm, and the extraordinary fellowship the storm had engendered is soon forgotten.

Singleton does no doubt embody Conrad's vision of authentic seamanship. Yet the picture of complete immersion in the labor and pain of hard work, however illustrative of the value of the work-ethic, evokes a vision of total abnegation of the self. While Conrad seems to idealize Singleton, the modern reader is likely to question the meaning of such abnegation, of such assumption of selflessness before the might of nature, and he may wonder about the self that may be realized as the result of such abnegation. For all the admirable ascetic stoicism of Singleton, the modern reader may not share the instinctive conviction, constitutive of his very mode of being in his world, that one wrests meaning from life by an unswerving allegiance to the tireless and ultimately futile labor in a medium that is indifferent or, rather, hostile to human existence.

Viewed in this context, Donkin appears to be no more than a parody of the social reformer. The portrayal of Donkin represents Conrad's skepticism toward the idea and idealogues of social reform, but it does not show any deep insight into the impetus toward social reform or political radicalism. Conrad's interest here seems to be in imagining and probing the psychology of someone like Donkin and its implications for certain values which make possible the collaborative effort of men aboard a ship. Donkin is thus presented as an embodiment of a certain psychological type that exploits and divides, and generally thrives on, feelings of discontent others may be experiencing. The ideals of solidarity, service, and discipline, however, are here so absolute in Conrad's treatment that he must conceive of the seamen in complete isolation from their social and personal existence. The story nevertheless contains polyphonic and antithetical strains, and Donkin carries within himself the ethos of an age which manifests itself in the concern over rights of individuals to form labor unions and to help decide conditions of their labor.

The Nigger of the "Narcissus" is Conrad's symbolic allegory that both dramatizes the value of solidarity and celebrates the tradition of a fast-disappearing era of seamanship. This allegory coexists, however, with elements of strife and disharmony, omens of the disintegration of the seafaring tradition that Conrad deeply cherished. The celebration of solidarity involves an idealization of seamanship which Conrad knows can never be an adequate metaphor for life on land.[25] Yet with his first major work Conrad has begun to suggest questions which are too large and too complex to explore in the limited context of the values necessary for collective survival aboard a ship. He has, for instance, raised questions concerning the nature and implications of self-consciousness in the context of a larger community within which one has one's identity; the problem of self-justification and its relation to duties and obligations; the implications of strife and discord for the values the community cherishes; the nature of language and its relation to intention and action.

The emphasis above on the elements of contradiction is intended to identify some of the concerns that will preoccupy Conrad in his major fiction. If, for example, in *The Nigger of the "Narcissus"* Conrad deplores the facility to talk, he will develop, in nearly all his major novels, a more complex perspective on language and its relation to intention, action, and the ability to talk. Moreover, the portrayal of James Wait, who is in some ways enigmatic and becomes the object of obsessive interest and analysis for others, signals Conrad's own preoccupation with the problem of interpreting human action and experience, one that will take on overwhelming value in both *Heart of Darkness* and *Lord Jim*. My reading of Conrad's fiction attempts to examine his treatment of the values cherished and projects undertaken by specific characters and their community, and the consequences of their endeavor to realize those values and projects. This will involve a consideration of (1) their real reasons underlying the projects, (2) the historical and cultural forces that help determine the fate of the projects, and (3) the implications of their possible failure. My purpose is to reflect on what can, and what cannot, be said within the limits of a given Conrad novel, and to examine the enabling contradictions which make a particular novel possible.

Conrad was a political conservative with a profound grasp of the radical Marxist insight that matter has primacy over mind, that the history of ideas in human social organization is a history of changes in the ideas men hold brought about by material interests. Just as Marx sought to disclose the truth concealed in religious suffering, Conrad sought to disclose the truth concealed in the pursuit of absolutist notions of self, freedom, and community. The cardinal difference separating Conrad from both Hegel and Marx is that, whereas they believed, in different ways, in the possibility of creative freedom for the human community as a whole, Conrad despaired of it. Conrad would consider it absurd to think, as Hegel and Marx did, that there operates a telos through history, that its implications are world-historical, and that it operates for the eventual well-being of the community as a whole.

Conrad's vision has nothing eschatological about it; he would consider the contingencies operating through history so overwhelming that any theoretical vision of hope is naïve. His skepticism, however, is intended to subject the workings of our social-political institutions to serious moral scrutiny. Conrad's fiction seems to me to question general theoretical principles such as those of Hegel and Marx, though he would agree with a cardinal tenet of Hegel and Marx that man's life is primarily a form of political existence, that the self is the product of community. And he would agree with them that the notion of absolute freedom is inherently meaningless, only promoting various forms of anarchism and nihilism unconnected with any real change in society.

Conrad's major fiction shows an awareness that his own conservatism can work only in historical periods when relative general prosperity predominates or conceals social and personal suffering. Conrad thus understood the importance of revolution but despaired of its satisfactory realization, for men inspired by the thought of revolution lose their idealism in the process of revolution itself and often destroy the ideals they wish to realize. Conrad's conservatism, then, is a retreat into stability and order, though he has no illusions about this stability and order. Understanding as a form of therapeutic release is impossible for the major protagonists of nearly all his novels. Moreover, it seems to me an integral feature of Conrad's skepticism that he knows his dismantling of ideological fanaticism is no guarantee that even his readers will be free of extremist tendencies. Thus his fiction, far from celebrating some form of achieved understanding, keeps returning to a certain feeling of despair as the inalienable element within understanding. This seems to me to be the most compelling feature in Conrad's fiction. He never allows this skepticism to degenerate into moral nihilism, even as he questions the viability of any absolute political or social program that one might espouse.

The writing of this book has involved a prior theoretical interest that draws on contemporary literary criticism and implicitly on contemporary philosophical thought.[26] It is my feeling that Conrad criticism has not yet come to terms with the novelist's profound accommodations of some central elements of both romanticism and Greek tragedy to the experience of the modern. It is here that rhetorical criticism must combine forces with philosophical criticism, and neither must construe its value to reside in making presumed valid distinctions—since Conrad's fiction would seem to show them to be tame and at times irrelevant—but in seeking to show a complex and ambiguous yet powerful relation between art and sincerity. It is in forging this relation that Conrad's art refuses to offer comforting certitudes, and it is his persistent and unsettling treatment of this relation that distinguishes his art from the early modern masters such as Eliot, Yeats, Pound, and perhaps even Joyce, and accounts for his continuing contemporary interest.

CHAPTER ONE

Marlow and the Experience of Storytelling: *Heart of Darkness*

While *The Nigger of the "Narcissus"* is largely a celebration of work in which the discontents of civilization are held in check through action informed by courage and discipline, *Heart of Darkness* questions the sustaining assumptions of civilization. The novel, as I shall try to show, reworks the constitutive features of both allegory and the traditional act of storytelling—a reworking that makes accessible to language a monstrous dimension of experience, though language itself lacks the self-confidence necessary to enact a drama of affirmation. Indeed, I shall suggest that the novel's importance is in its disclosing the ideal of affirmation to be an aberrant expectation, dear to the genre of romance.

The modernist quality of *Heart of Darkness* inheres, of course, in its subversion of the paradigm of romance. The famous Congo river, discovered by Livingstone and explored by Stanley, serves as a symbolic element in this modernist allegory of imperialism. Unlike his contemporary romancers of the imperialist Holy Grail—Stevenson, Rider Haggard, and Jules Verne among others—Conrad divests the river of its recognizable historical outposts.[1] I want to focus on certain important features of Marlow's journey, ending after Kurtz's death with his own return home and his meeting with the Intended, in order to explore his judgment of the Congo experience. I mean to explain why Marlow's judgment, not reducible to the recovery—or the nostalgia for recovery—of a lost moral essence, inheres in the relation of his story to his mode of storytelling. If Marlow's judgment, woven into the texture of the story he tells, doesn't have the shattering precision of Kurtz's final cry, it nevertheless shares the anguish and despair our reading of Kurtz's final moments will disclose.

I

Except for two brief interruptions, the narrator who opens *Heart of Darkness* disappears after making an intriguing remark about Marlow's mode of story-telling, and reappears at the end to conclude his verbatim transcription of Marlow's story. His retrospective remark deserves to be considered in a later context where Marlow's telling of the story and the understanding he acquires will reflect light on the first narrator's remark. For now the beginning of Marlow's narrative calls for some reflection. "And this also has been one of the dark places on the earth" (48). This is Marlow's first statement in *Heart of Darkness*, and the history it evokes resonates with metaphysical implications. The use of *also* here adumbrates a genealogy which, though obscure at first, suggests the complex entanglements of the past with the present, entanglements to be explained in the rest of Marlow's prologue. But the prologue, as we shall see, cannot explain them; it can only complicate the desire for explanation. It will require the whole force of the story for the enigmatic first sentence to lose its "alienating" quality and to appropriate for its "impropriety" a proper meaning. That Marlow utters the sentence with an air of obsessiveness suggests that it leads to the heart of his experience.

Marlow's prologue is a compound of history and metaphysics. His thoughts go back to the early Romans nearly two thousand years ago. If history is construed, as Marlow seems to construe it, as pervasive darkness with isolated moments of light, the early Romans are not remote but are our contemporaries, for "darkness was here yesterday". There follows a classic Marlovian encapsulation: the Roman invaders are "dying like flies" (49) in a land where there is "precious little to eat fit for a civilized man, nothing but Thames water to drink" (49). Taken in its retrospective context, this statement is quite uncanny. Did the ancient Romans behave like the pilgrims, like so many barbarians gone crazy, unable to show restraint or withstand the ordeals of the climate? Or did they, like the cannibals in Marlow's boat, show restraint and resist the savage impulses gnawing within? Marlow can provide no answer here, though we must look to his own words for clues. Marlow, perhaps in a sudden access of good feeling, says: "They were men enough to face the darkness" (49). This seemingly positive statement remains vague in its implications, and it goads one into asking more questions. How did they face the darkness? Were they vanquished by it? The confident assertiveness of Marlow's words seem to suggest they were not. For what does facing the darkness mean? Did they perhaps surrender themselves to the wilderness? Were they like Kurtz, or like the pilgrims, or like Marlow himself? We cannot be certain, though Marlow utters his statement with certainty.

The conjectural bit of psycho-biography that follows Marlow's statement may provide some clue. The ancient Roman who came here had "to live in the midst of the incomprehensible, which is also detestable". This incomprehensible "has a fascination, too, that goes to work upon him. The fascination of the abomination—you know, imagine the growing regrets, the longing to escape, the powerless disgust, the surrender, the hate" (49). The ancient Roman might be taken for an emblematic figure of Kurtz, though from the perspective of a naïve reading of the story we do not quite know what to make of the knot of feelings attributed to the Roman; the feelings compel our anticipation and interest, but do not yield up their meaning. They set up, as it were, a strange framework of questioning and meditation within which Marlow's story might unfold. And they suggest, in their ambiguity, the complex feelings that impel Marlow to tell his story. The prologue is integral to the story, and its modes of assertion and ambivalence prefigure those of the story to follow.

Marlow's disturbing remarks are followed by a sudden reassuring remark that "none of us would feel exactly like this" (50). He says his listeners are protected from the Roman's shattering experience because they and their contemporary British/European society are devoted to the blessed ideal of efficiency. This remark seems not to be meant ironically; otherwise it could have nothing reassuring about it. Yet the miracle that the ideal performs, of protecting one from a primal, ego-shattering experience, is surely too great for it to perform. Consequently, Marlow hastily revises his short Roman history, attributing monstrosities to the ancient Romans from which, presumably, the (British) colonists are free. The Romans' brute force, "robbery with violence, aggravated murder on a great scale, and men going at it blind" (50)—a rapid summary, one might say, of Spengler's account of modern history—set them apart from the colonists, whose activities are ostensibly redeemed by "an unselfish belief in the idea" (51). But Marlow's earlier observation has already erased the difference he labors here to articulate: "The conquest of the earth, which mostly means the taking it away from those who have a different complexion or slightly flatter noses than ourselves, is not a pretty thing when you look into it too much" (50–51). This brief statement contains the whole force of Nietzsche's *Genealogy of Morals*; as Marlow puts it: "your strength is just an accident arising from the weakness of others" (50). The idea of conquest, whether Roman or British, loses its romantic halo; it is no better than a criminal wresting of possessions and freedom from those who happen to be weak.

Marlow's prologue, then, returns us to his opening statement: "And this also has been one of the dark places on the earth." Yet the prologue is marked by gestures of reassurance. Marlow, for instance, says: "We live in the flicker—may it last as long as the old earth keeps rolling! But darkness was here yesterday" (49). "Darkness" presumably means barbarity, greed, violence, brutality, savagery, and the "flicker" means the temporary prevalence of civilized values. Yet if there is no real difference between the conquering Romans and the colonizing Europeans what grounds are there for us to believe that "we", Marlow and his listeners, have overcome the human proclivity to evil? The pessimism and despair of this question pervade the prologue, which is the product of Marlow's long reflection on his journey to the Congo.

Moreover, Marlow's phrase "an unselfish belief in the idea" occurs in an ambiguous context: "An idea at the back of it; not a sentimental pretence but an idea; and an unselfish belief in the idea—something you can set up, and bow down before and offer a sacrifice to . . ." (51). The ellipsis is Marlow's, making us wonder about his judgment of the "idea". His words provide no clarification, though we may adumbrate it in terms of the ideal of efficiency, as it is understood by a developed civilization; and since his words occur amid the forebodings of the prologue the "idea" cannot have resoundingly moral implications. There is no real possibility of clarification, even on the basis of a reflective reading of the entire story; the idea is part of a strictly formal gesture of reassurance, and the remarks made in the course of the gesture disrupt any serenity the gesture would seem to offer. Yet the idea is not without substance; the meaning one may ascribe to it, however, is not normally associated with deliberate belief or high principle or moral tenacity. Thus the gesture is finally a corrosive and ironic caricature of the idea's supposed positive force. One only need think for a moment of "an unselfish belief in the idea" in terms of an attitude that makes one "set up, and bow down before, and offer a sacrifice to . . ." and ask if this suggests much difference between prehistoric man in the wilderness and the civilized European. The power of Marlow's expression derives from the evocation of a sincere feeling reaching a moment of corrosive parody; his words break off because of his pained consciousness that the parody reveals the desecration of the idea. And his words perhaps explain his posture of a meditative Buddha with which he both opens and closes his narrative.

The prologue thus frames and provides interpretive clues for Marlow's story, though it does not determine how we will understand the events he describes. It has, however, a recursive interest which will become important when we ponder, for instance, Marlow's conversation with Kurtz's Intended.

The detached tone of the prologue, its amalgam of assertion and ambivalence, of bluff confidence and evasive vagueness, and its striations of contradictory meanings possess a significance hard to grasp without effort.

II

It is not surprising that Marlow doesn't find the experience he is about to relate "very clear", though, as he says, "the experience seemed to throw a kind of light" (51). Almost from the beginning of his journey Marlow speaks of gradually losing his hold on reality. As he and his companions penetrate "deeper and deeper into the heart of darkness", Marlow invests the journey with peculiar power:

> We were wanderers on a prehistoric earth, on an earth that wore the aspect of an unknown planet . . . The prehistoric man was cursing us, praying to us, welcoming us—who could tell? We were cut off from the comprehension of our surroundings; we glided past like phantoms, wondering and secretly apalled; as sane men would be before an enthusiastic outbreak in a madhouse. We could not understand because we were too far and could not remember, because we were travelling in the night of first ages, of those ages that are gone, leaving hardly a sign—and no memories. (95—96)

Marlow here feels befuddled because he confronts a moment of experience which allows for no decipherable meaning. Understanding requires a cultural context in which "praying" might be "welcoming" or "cursing". But here the slippage of response from "cursing" to "praying" to "welcoming" leaves the mind utterly bewildered. Memory, too, is helpless when confronted with things it cannot interpret. And hence Marlow's feeling that the past as well as the future are there in the mind of man:

> The earth seemed unearthly. We are accustomed to look upon the shackled form of a conquered monster, but there—there you could look at a thing monstrous and free. It was unearthly, and the men were— No, they were not inhuman. Well, you know, that was the worst of it—this suspicion of their not being inhuman. It would come slowly to one. They howled and leaped, and spun, and made horrid faces; but what thrilled you was just the thought of their humanity—like yours—the thought of your remote kinship with this wild and passionate uproar. Ugly. Yes, it was ugly enough; but if you were man enough you

would admit to yourself that there was in you just the faintest trace of a response to the terrible frankness of that noise, a dim suspicion of there being a meaning in it which you—you so remote from the night of the first ages—could comprehend. And why not? The mind of man is capable of anything—because everything is in it, all the past as well as all the future. What was there after all? Joy, fear, sorrow, devotion, valour, rage—who can tell?—but truth—truth stripped of its cloak of time. (96—97)

In this celebrated passage Marlow, while remaining in the present, plunges into a psychic-genealogical past, a past which offers hints about that which he has a moment before considered indecipherable. The behavior of the natives, for all its ostensible savagery, seems human to Marlow, and awakens him to his bond with them, which his civilization cannot conceal. His conjectural history of savage life in prehistoric England now seems to be derived from an ironic perception which has sprung from that sudden wrenching of his self from its culture into a wilderness fraught with unidentifiable passions.

The emergence of meaning in the wilderness is a moral recognition of one's essential identity with that which seems to Marlow savage and alienating. But his sense of kinship with the natives cannot help him decipher the passions let loose in the wilderness. Understanding at this level would be possible only for someone who already belongs to the community which Marlow rightly considers alien. Marlow sees the natives in their otherness but also in their humanity, which he identifies with his own. To the pilgrims, though, Marlow's response would be as alien as the natives'. But Marlow's perceptual acuity here does not amount to cultural relativism, since relativism, while professing both respect for cultural diversity and hostility to dogmatic absolutes, underlines the essential truthfulness of all or at least many perspectives. Marlow's narrative thus questions cultural relativism, moving from demystification to an ironic characterization which allows for both despair and morality. His ironic mode of perception resists any strictly existentialist perspective, just as it resists any strictly ethical, historical, or Marxist perspective.[2]

Despite his sense of kinship with the natives, Marlow is aware that he is separate from them. This awareness allows him his gesture of moral self-assertion even after his profession of kinship: "For good or evil mine is the speech that cannot be silenced" (97). Marlow seems here to hold out the possibility of moral certitude. His contemporary European culture appears to him to have engendered sepulchral cities characterized by exalted idealism and moral indifference; his moral certitude does not derive from the values of the sepulchral cities, but from the stability and strength gained from his own fidelity to the tradition of work. The necessity of work, says Marlow, prevented him from joining the natives "for a howl and a dance" (97). It is work that helped him to keep his "hold on the redeeming facts of life" (75) in the Congo, and for Marlow it appears to afford the only possibility of finding oneself (85).

Thus Marlow does, for a moment, seem to idealize work; he is thrilled to discover, for instance, Towson's manual of navigation *An Inquiry into Some Points of Seamanship*. Yet he fails to see, for all the book's alleged practicality and its accounts of navigational errors and altered courses, that it is in fact an instrument in the service of colonization. His blindness must be construed as the result of his pleasure when he learns about Kurtz's dedication to work. And it underlies his remark, after discovering the truth about Kurtz: "I am not prepared to affirm that Kurtz was exactly worth the life we lost in getting to him . . . [the helmsman] had done something, he had steered" (119).

Marlow's insistence on the value of work, however, is not unqualified. He realizes that, while work can be liberating, it may also conceal one's real relation to one's surroundings. The chief accountant, whom Marlow meets after his unexpected entry upon the scene of disease and death, values his work in a disconcerting and degenerate fashion. He appears to Marlow "a sort of vision" (67) as he comes out "to get a breath of fresh air" (68). In this landscape of man-made destitution and misery, the accountant is a distorted form of humanity, meticulously busy keeping his books, coming out for a breath of fresh air when his work has driven him into a stupor. The accountant hates the natives because their tumult distracts him in making correct entries; his unreflective devotion to work has dehumanized him. Similarly, the manager, another votary for work, "originated nothing" but "could keep the routine going" (74). Marlow wonders what sustains such a man and surmises, "Perhaps there was nothing within him" (74).

Work, then, does not provide the moral coordinates that give life stability and definition beyond the immediate moment. Indeed, work may be redeeming precisely in so far as it conceals reality: "When you have to attend . . . to the mere incidents of the surface, the reality—the reality, I tell you—fades. The inner truth is hidden—luckily, luckily. But I felt it all the same; I felt often its mysterious stillness watching me at my monkey tricks" (93–94). But the refusal to look beneath the surface, as in the case of Winnie Verloc in *The Secret Agent*, has its own terrible consequences. Work has not prevented Marlow from probing and evaluating his environment; he privileges work because, in part, it casts an illusory and self-deceiving veil over the horror of reality. He retains his fidelity to the tradition of work, but he sees no such fidelity in the conduct of the pilgrims, though they take themselves as the guardians of morality.

He thus comes to a deeper understanding of both the external and internal restraints that sustain the tradition of work: external checks are made possible by the social organization and are represented here by the policeman and the butcher (116). They inspire and quell fear and anxiety, and are at the basis of whatever restraint and stability may exist in society. What is problematical, however, are internal checks when the custodians of the law are absent. For man, as Marlow says in a moment of expansiveness, is in principle "capable of anything" and his mind encompasses "everything" (96). The savage and the civilized are separated only by the cloak of time, and their apparent distance does not imply moral progress.

Yet Marlow, as he travels farther into the Congo and experiences a remote kinship with the howling and dancing natives, makes a plea for internal restraint. "[Civilized man] must meet that truth [of his kinship with the primitive] with his own true stuff—with his own inborn strength. Principles won't do. Acquisitions, clothes, pretty rags—rags that would fly off at the first good shake. No; you want a deliberate belief. An appeal to me in this fiendish row—is there? Very well; I hear; I admit, but I have a voice, too, and for good or evil mine is the speech that cannot be silenced" (97). In distinguishing principles from "deliberate belief" Marlow seems to identify belief with internal restraint, and relates the moral impulse behind his story to this form of restraint: "And there . . . your strength comes in, the faith in your ability for the digging of unostentatious holes . . . your power of devotion, not to yourself, but to an obscure, back-breaking business" (117). If Marlow has reason for hope, he has not discovered it in the behavior of civilized man, but in the cannibals' extraordinary restraint, though they are on the verge of starvation. Marlow's outburst on restraint deserves close scrutiny: "Restraint? What possible restraint? Was it superstition, disgust, patience, fear—or some kind of primitive honour? No fear can stand up to hunger, no patience can wear it out, disgust simply does not exist where hunger is; and as to superstition, belief and what you may call principles they are less than chaff in a breeze" (106). The cannibals could not feel disgust or fear at the prospect of eating their greatly outnumbered white employers. They have shown a profoundly human capacity for restraint. Marlow's statement of utter negation is brilliantly and bitterly paradoxical: it applauds the cannibals' inner restraint in adhering to a contract, even if that contract is an unspeakably exploitative instrument devised by the colonists. The pilgrims, on the contrary, seem to Marlow mere tools of an imperialism which adopts and discards values as its rapacious interests require.

26

III

Heart of Darkness is not a tragic narrative in the sense in which *Lord Jim* is. Nor is Jim a younger version of Kurtz, since Jim is quintessentially innocent, though deeply marred by a flaw he can neither admit nor overcome. Kurtz is a man of experience. In the wilderness, he has unconsciously taken a wager on experience, a wager which makes it impossible for him to escape from the atavistic regression he has undergone. He is unlike the cannibals, who restrain themselves through a spontaneously human respect for a social contract; he is, from the beginning, driven by a destructive combination of uninhibited aspiration and eloquent idealism, and in this he is truly a representative as well as an instrument of imperialism.

Long before Marlow meets him, Kurtz has had an extravagant reputation in Europe, where he was thought capable of doing anything, heading any party, as long as it was extremist. This capacity for role-changing has not made anyone question Kurtz's lack of moral commitment; it is connected to his eloquence, which is the source of his ontological self-sufficiency and moral self-confidence. Why should such a man be forced to question the implications of his discourse, or the power of his eloquence, or the relation of his words to his actions, especially if he gets the work done? Given his belief in the boundlessness of self, Kurtz cannot raise this question, until his narcissism is cataclysmically intruded upon by a moral will—an intrusion which allows him a momentary dignity. The critique of Kurtz, as we shall see, is the critique of imperialism. Imperialism disguises itself in self-contradictory moral fictions such as those surrounding the International Society for the Suppression of Savage Customs (117). To the blinkered rationality of this society, savage customs require savage treatment for their elimination; one may say its efforts are simply another episode in the history of primitive tribes fighting one another. This notion forces itself on us because Marlow recognizes the pilgrims as the real savages while he is struck with the humanity of the natives.

It is a striking irony of Marlow's narrative that this society has requested Kurtz to write a report for its own future guidance—a testimony to the status of Kurtz in Europe. As Marlow says, "All Europe contributed to the making of Kurtz" (117). Marlow responds to Kurtz's report with uneasy evasiveness and acute criticism:

> And he had written it too. I've seen it. I've read it. It was eloquent, vibrating with eloquence, but too high strung, I think. Seventeen pages of close writing he had found time for! But this must have been

before his—let us say—nerves, went wrong, and caused him to preside at certain midnight dances ending with unspeakable rites, which—as far as I reluctantly gathered from what I heard at various times—were offered up to him—do you understand?—to Mr. Kurtz himself. But it was a beautiful piece of writing. (117–18)

This suspicion of eloquence is an element in the critique of language and writing, one that we will examine shortly. For now let me say that this passage reflects on Marlow's mode of storytelling as a whole. Marlow indulges here the polite fiction that Kurtz is a man who disintegrated in the jungle, though beforehand he had been eminently suited to write his eloquent pamphlet on savage customs. The manager, who condemns Kurtz's method as "unsound", would have believed in Marlow's fiction, but the crucial sentence is a mixture of polite irony and unsparing moral criticism: "But this must have been before his—let us say—nerves, went wrong, and caused him to preside at certain midnight dances ending with unspeakable rites, which—as far as I reluctantly gathered from what I heard at various times— were offered up to him—do you understand?—to Mr. Kurtz himself." Marlow begins with the intention of saving Kurtz from moral opprobrium; as the process of qualification and disclosure continues—ending with the parenthetical question, "do you understand?"—Marlow's own incredulity at Kurtz confounds the attempt to spare him. And the last sentence—"But it was a beautiful piece of writing"—while seeming to retrieve something for Kurtz's eloquence, retrieves nothing.

As Marlow says of Kurtz's eloquence: "There were no practical hints to interrupt the magic current of phrases, unless a kind of note at the foot of the last page, scrawled evidently much later, in an unsteady hand, may be regarded as the exposition of a method." The note, continues Marlow, says: "Exterminate all the brutes!" (118). Marlow's mildly exculpatory conjecture that Kurtz wrote the document before his degeneration and the note afterwards suggests more questions than answers. Why, for instance, may the marginal note not represent a change in Kurtz's mood rather than a disintegration? For if Kurtz could write an eloquent document for the suppression of savage customs and at the same time brutalize a whole village in his craze for ivory he could certainly feel the urge to write the marginal note. If his discourse remained eloquent even in the final stages of his life when he became a god in native ceremonies—the Russian harlequin attests to all of this—the violent revulsion of his disintegration may have underlain his eloquence from the start. Marlow has not interrogated Kurtz about the matter; and the testimony of others toward the end of *Heart of Darkness* suggests that Kurtz was always a hollow man, capable of assuming role upon role, the eloquent not precluding the savage.

Thus it is not as if Kurtz possessed any moral clarity before his alleged disintegration; his whole purpose had been to gain quick fame and wealth. We need only recall the picture Kurtz had painted, more than a year before Marlow met him, of the goddess of justice, "draped and blind-folded, carrying a lighted torch". Marlow's description and comment are revealing: "The background was sombre—almost black. The movement of the woman was stately, and the effect of the torch-light on the face was sinister" (79). The irony of the figure of justice carrying a lighted torch, symbolizing power (instead of carrying a pair of scales), deepens when we realize that what the torch illuminates is not the so-called pervasive darkness of Africa, but the sinister expression on the goddess's face.[3] If this peculiarly allegorical painting renders questionable Kurtz's status as an emissary of light and hope, it also discloses the problematical nature of the very idea of enlightenment. The document, whenever it was written, already contains the seeds of perversion; the marginal note only encapsulates the brutishness of Kurtz's recent activities.

There is a profound irony in Marlow's remark that he imagined Kurtz discoursing, but never doing. The image of a European discoursing to African natives is emblematic of the imperialistic attitude toward those it dominates. Kurtz separates his ruthless action from his discourse, a separation that allows for the manipulation of political, economic, and ethical concepts. Kurtz could not have discoursed to the natives; his purpose was not to educate them but to collect ivory. The only person who testifies to the power of Kurtz's discourse was the Russian, who did not himself escape Kurtz's threats. The passion in Kurtz's discourse, then, had nothing "moral" about it; it simply legitimized European expansion and domination. This is most dramatically revealed when Kurtz mutters to the wilderness, "I'll wring your heart yet" (148). And he has visions of returning to Europe where kings would come to meet him at railway stations.

It is Kurtz's conviction that every station should be "a centre for trade of course, but also for humanizing, improving, instructing" (91). The symbiosis of trade and idealism does not make Kurtz suspicious of the value of idealism which so easily cohabits with commerce and profit. It is logical that Kurtz should be a spokesman for this symbiosis, for the era of great industrial development and imperialist success was also the era of idealism in philosophy and politics. This idealism was profoundly sanguine, and profoundly blind to the social-economic forces operating in the West and, through the agency of the West, in the rest of the world. And it is Marlow's residual idealism which attracts him to the man who is "equipped with moral ideas of some sort" (88). Marlow's interest in Kurtz, though accompanied by a strain of doubt, derives from his desperation: surrounded by barbarism on all sides, he clutches at the only hope presented in the remote figure of Kurtz, being powerless, in himself, to grasp the meaning of his experience.

Imperialism, then, operates in this novel as a machine conscious of its own power, since those who created it and keep it in motion have little control over it. Imperialism distorts the relations between words and acts, marking the language with its own inhuman stamp. The French man-of-war shelling the coast conjures up the most concentrated image of this absurdity: "In the empty immensity of earth, sky and water, there she was, incomprehensible, firing into the continent" (61—62). She fires at random, without reason or target, yet filled with blind self-confidence in this act of reckless brutality. The absence of a conventional target is really the absence of legitimacy in the imperialist incursion into an alien land.

The image of the pilgrims as gun-carrying traders is an apt emblem for the tactics of an imperialism which uses commerce to justify its ventures into remote regions of Africa, and self-defense to justify violent usurpation of whole native populations. Yet self-defense has become indistinguishable from uncalled-for aggression; the colonists go to Africa with tools of war because they know the natives will not welcome them, and must be brutalized into submission. Marlow's systematic exhuming of the facts reveals that the colonial venture was neither efficient nor moral. The natives were treated first as enemies, and Marlow perceives that they will soon be treated as criminals:

> Another report from the cliff made me think suddenly of that ship of war I had seen firing into a continent. It was the same kind of ominous voice; but these men could by no stretch of imagination be called enemies. They were called criminals, and the outraged law, like the bursting shells, had come to them, an insoluble mystery from the sea. (64)

Thus the law of imperialism is without justice; it is as implacable as "the bursting shells" which pronounce judgment on their victims at the moment of killing them. The bursting shells and the words of judgment—"enemies", "criminals"—are sustained by the assumption of insuperable authority, and they authorize Kurtz, an agent of this imperialism, to write his marginal note.

In pursuing imperialistic exploitation to its logical extreme, Kurtz shows the absurdity of the restraints which imperialism adopts as a matter of policy;

he differs from the manager, for whom brutality and exploitation, pursued with caution and restraint, make for a sound method, which he rejects as "unsound" (137). But for Kurtz a sound method is extraneous to the goal of imperialism, which is rapacious plunder. As the manager's uncle says, with no one to watch and condemn one's conduct, any action carries its own legitimization. And those emissaries of imperialism removed from the plunder, who wish to civilize the Africans, are wealthy old ladies and self-appointed moralists who have no real knowledge of either the culture they want civilized or the people they employ in order to realize their goal. Imperialism puts them in the service of goals they might have refused had they known the real nature of these goals. A characteristic Conradian insight here is that imperialism blinds those who serve its purpose to the real implications of their actions, so that ideals, seemingly altruistic, bring into being the practical realities of colonial exploitation.

The pilgrims are different from Kurtz only because their cowardice prevents them from taking the last plunge into atavistic passions. Kurtz's regression into atavism is connected to both his capacity for role-changing and his boundless egotism. His egotism is that of imperialism itself, which inspires his idealism and his self-confidence. Without the imperialist conviction of his essential supremacy and without the means afforded by the colonial venture, Kurtz could not have become a ritual god. Still Kurtz bears resemblance to the manager and the pilgrims, though he combines the most grotesque and frightening qualities of both culture and atavism. The culture which gave rise to imperialism in practical politics and to idealism in philosophy and political thought loses its bearings when it discovers its basis in the passions, when it sees its best emissary crawl on all fours to join primitive rites ending in human sacrifice. As we shall see, Marlow, who remains an authentic representative of this culture because he is also its most relentless critic, experiences this loss of self-confidence, a loss necessary to his moral insight into the workings of the imperialist idealist nexus.

IV

Marlow's interest in meeting Kurtz is mediated through the meeting with the Russian harlequin who gives Marlow his first inkling of the power of Kurtz's personality. He tells Marlow that Kurtz has made the whole tribe adore him, that he presides at certain midnight dances which end with unspeakable rites offered up to him. The Russian asserts that he, too, adores Kurtz: "I'll never, never meet such a man again . . . he enlarged my mind"

(140); his adoration is blind, innocent, pitiable. He conveys the truth about Kurtz to Marlow, but does not himself understand it. He is in possession of all the external features of a shattering experience, but the meaning of the experience remains sealed off from him. He is an embodiment of the idealism and innocence of youth whose most tragic expressions will be Razumov, before his confession, and Lord Jim. The Russian is the product of a society which shelters its youth by idealizing its brutal ventures in primitive societies: "Glamour", Marlow says, "urged him on, glamour kept him unscathed" (126). Yet in *Heart of Darkness* innocence remains bound to the very essence of savagery, for it has no insight into evil. To Marlow's mind, the Russian "crawled" before Kurtz "as much as the veriest savage of them all" (132). The Russian, a creature of civilization, adores Kurtz for his power to discourse on everything; but this youthful adoration of discourse, unqualified by regard for the implications of Kurtz's actions, entails a fatal incomprehension of both culture and youth.

Like the Russian, the Intended reveals the difficulties inherent in culture and innocence. Of course, the drama of Marlow's meeting with the Intended derives not from her tragic helplessness but from Marlow's response, which culminates in his lie to her. Conrad himself was not happy with his treatment, and Conrad criticism has noted a radical shift in the narrative.[4] It seems to me that the narrative shift is integral to Marlow's experience because it captures his relation to the culture about which he has become so disillusioned. Early in his narrative when Marlow nearly lies to the brickmaker he has this outburst of conviction: "You know I hate, detest, and can't bear a lie, not because I am straighter than the rest of us, but simply because it appalls me. There is a taint of death, a flavour of mortality in lies—which is exactly what I hate and detest in the world—what I want to forget" (82). So why, then, does he lie to the Intended? Could his reasons be morally compelling, and could they represent an ethic which may become a bulwark of a life which, in Marlow's experience, is devoid of values? To answer these questions, we need to understand Marlow's despair and its implications for human existence.

Marlow's lie to the Intended is not a moral compromise, nor is it a failure to live with realities of his experience. He recognizes, with his characteristic gift for insight into the human personality, that the Intended possesses "a mature capacity for fidelity, for belief, for suffering" (157). However utterly she is deceived about Kurtz, it is her capacity to live with her grief, born of a faith in the man she loved and has lost, which is the mark of her culture. Marlow, the great ironist, is moved to bow his head "before the faith that was in her, before that great and saving illusion that shone with an unearthly glow in the darkness, in the triumphant darkness from which I could not have defended her—from which I could not even defend myself" (159). How could he tell the truth with any redeeming intention? What would be the point of removing those last supports which make possible such sincere feelings? Before the sincerity of the Intended, consolation, even involving deception, seems morally superior to honest disillusionment. Marlow's response contradicts the truth of his own experience, which affords him no satisfaction.

Consolation founded on morally useful deception, however, does not imply an absolute communal ethic. For, as I shall suggest in my reading of *Lord Jim*, a community cannot maintain itself without construing its ideals, however contradicted by the pragmatic constraints of human life, in terms of their transcendental status. Nor does Marlow's consoling lie imply that her capacity for grief protects the Intended from a taint of pathetic emotion. Her situation is best captured in the following exchange with Marlow:

"His words will remain," I said.

"And his example," she whispered to herself. "Men looked up to him—his goodness shone in every act. His example—"

"True," I said; "his example too. Yes his example. I forgot that."

"But I do not. I cannot—I cannot believe—not yet. I cannot believe that I shall never see him again, that nobody will see him again, never, never, never." (160)

The knowledge we share with Marlow that his Congo experience verges on nihilistic despair complicates our response to the Intended's last words: they are refined and sincere, yet they have something atavistic about them. Marlow is suddenly shocked as he sees in her tragic figure an image of the magnificent native woman inconsolable in her sorrow at losing Kurtz.

Marlow's refusal to tell the truth to the Intended has its own moral force; to tell the truth would be to misunderstand the meaning of Kurtz's struggle and final judgment. Given a summary account of the truth, the Intended might have disintegrated with horror, though she might have refused to believe it. For she is utterly committed to her idealized image of Kurtz, and in this state of mind she receives Marlow's lie as truth. One cannot assume, however, that Marlow could have told her the truth without recounting his entire Congo experience, culminating in Kurtz's final judgment; mere mention of Kurtz's immersion in savage passions would have been, for Marlow, a grievous slander. The lie to the Intended is not in any sense an affirmation of Europe's values, though in telling it Marlow is unable to free himself from some idealizing of European civilization, one that had prompted his initial interest in Kurtz. What we need to pay attention to, however, is Marlow's manner of telling the lie, since it is this manner which ironizes his words to the Intended and thus separates him from its implied affirmation. Marlow's remarks on his own hesitations and gestures reveal the parodic side of the lie, and they reveal as well his own sense of difficulties in extricating himself completely from the conflicting relations between Europe's ideals and practices.

Marlow's encounter with the Intended reenacts what Frank Kermode has called, in another context, "the familiar dialogue between credulity and scepticism". In telling the lie, Marlow "respects our sense of reality".⁵ His relentless exposure of brutalities in the Congo establishes him as a truth-teller; we are jolted when he lies. His lie, however, keeps faith with the fidelity of the Intended, and his mode of storytelling also converts the lie into a judgment of a society unable to receive the scalding truth of experience. Not only his society but also its conventional modes of storytelling were inadequate to deal with the experience that he can only recount with great difficulty and uncertainty. The Intended represents, for Marlow, an aspect of the community which dictates the nature of "the truth" from a perspective of innocence, generating unresolvable problems in narrative discourse. Marlow's lie, with its many implications, is not an act of deception in the ordinary sense. It is all that enables Marlow to honor the only form of integrity and sincerity he has known in the sepulchral city. Marlow, the man who wanted to see Kurtz's moral ideas in action, now finds his moral response entangled in deception; this is the predicament *Heart of Darkness* creates for the man of experience. Conrad diverges here from traditional accounts which allegorize experience, emphasizing the quester's purification through suffering and moral self-discovery.

V

We come now to Kurtz's famous deathbed judgment. Here is Marlow's description of the moment:

> It was as though a veil had been rent. I saw on that ivory face the expression of sombre pride, of ruthless power, of craven terror—of an intense and hopeless despair. Did he live his life again in every detail of desire, temptation, and surrender during that supreme moment of complete knowledge? He cried in a whisper at some image, at some vision—he cried out twice, a cry that was no more than a breath—
> "The horror! The horror!" (149)

34

The ordinarily resonant voice of Kurtz becomes, at the moment of uttering this judgment, a mere whisper, and dissociates his words for the first time from the mode of discourse whose real function is "to hide in the magnificent folds of eloquence the barren darkness of his heart" (147).

Lionel Trilling has said that Marlow may have misrepresented the significance of Kurtz's last words: "To me it is still ambiguous whether Kurtz's famous death-bed cry 'The horror! The horror!' refers to the approach of death or to his experience of savage life."[6] It seems to me that the last words could refer to death only in implying the frustration of an egomaniac aware of his impending death. There is, of course, ample evidence of Kurtz's egotistic preoccupations: his pursuit of "lying fame, of sham distinction, of all the appearances of success and power" (147—48), and the recurrence of "images of wealth and fame revolving obsequiously round his unextinguishable gift of noble and lofty expression" (147). He once threatened to shoot the young Russian for his small lot of ivory "because he could do so, and had a fancy for it, and there was nothing on earth to prevent him killing whom he jolly well pleased" (128). In this context Kurtz's final judgment could have nothing extraordinary about it which could transform him into a hero of the spirit. The other alternative, relating Kurtz's judgment to his experience of savage life, seems to me more compelling. He is horrified not just by his own appalling behavior, but by his knowledge that his eloquence and idealism are only masks which hide the truth. This may appear to be an overly metaphysical account, unconnected to the complexities of either Marlow's or Kurtz's experience. But Kurtz is associated, from the beginning of his Congo venture, with moral norms which invest human life with meaning; Marlow has hoped Kurtz's conduct would dispel his bitter disillusionment with the pilgrim's corruption and self-deception. Kurtz's judgment, however verbally or emotionally heroic, can have no real effect on one who has experienced the primal nature of reality. His stark phrase expresses horror at his entrapment in gross passions, and at the thought that humanity, in venturing as far as he did, risks all its saving illusions. Thus Kurtz's final words refer not merely to his own condition, but to culture as well. In judging himself at this level, Kurtz is rendering judgment on the ideal of the self and on the culture that projects and sustains that ideal. His final words disclose, with desperate certitude, the impotence of that ideal.

Kurtz's judgment is a moral gesture in which he transcends his own egotism; he struggles without faith, restraint, or fear, without hope of any consoling certitude. Kurtz's struggle involves what Marlow calls "the inconceivable mystery of a soul" (145). This is perhaps the reason Marlow thinks Kurtz was "a remarkable man" (151). His "remarkable" nature is best suggested in the distance Marlow puts, somewhat offensively, between Kurtz and ordinary humanity:

> You can't understand. How could you?—with solid pavement under your feet, surrounded by kind neighbours ready to cheer you or to fall on you, stepping delicately between the butcher and the policeman, in the holy terror of scandal and gallows and lunatic asylums—how can you imagine what particular region of the first ages a man's untrammelled feet may take him into by the way of solitude—utter solitude without a policeman—by the way of silence—utter silence, where no warning voice of a kind neighbour can be heard whispering of public opinion? These little things make all the great difference. When they are gone you must fall back upon your own innate strength, upon your own capacity for faithfulness. Of course you may be too much of a fool to go wrong—too dull even to know you are being assaulted by the powers of darkness. (116—17)

The one positive norm which is suggested here and rendered problematical at the same time is one's "own innate strength". Thus Kurtz's cry of "affirmation" (151) is a hope which springs from, and remains bound to, utter hopelessness. This is why Kurtz's final judgment is delivered in a voice divested of its usual sonority; it is the stark expression of an insight which is beyond self-deception.

This interpretation is, I think, at the basis of Trilling's view of Kurtz as a hero of the spirit; and it is at the basis of the liberal-romantic redefinition of art which values art for its exposure of the destructive contradictions that underlie both self and community. There is much to be said for this liberal-romantic reading of Kurtz's judgment but, despite its demystifying nature, neither this reading nor the conception of art that sanctions it is able to check its idealizing quest for heroes of the spirit. An explanation of this would require analysis of Marlow's final stance toward the Congo experience, a stance I will discuss after clarifying certain features of Marlow's mode of storytelling.

VI

The first narrator aptly describes Marlow's mode of storytelling in saying:"to him the meaning of an episode was not inside like a kernel but outside, enveloping the tale which brought it out only as a glow brings out a haze, in the likeness of one of these misty haloes that sometimes are made visible by the spectral illumination of moonshine" (48). The first narrator's remarks may reflect his own and his companions' feeling about how Marlow's stories have often left them without a clear definition of things, or a clear set of values in terms of which to comprehend and judge human experience. The peculiarity and originality of Marlow's storytelling are here appreciated as well as criticized. By contrasting his storytelling with yarns of seamen and their direct simplicity, the first narrator injects a skeptical attitude toward Marlow's subtlety as sometimes being so elusive as to be meaningless or illusory. Yet it is Conrad's characteristic act to value subtlety in the act of narrating human experiences. It is inevitable that Marlow himself should say that the experience is not clear to him. For what Marlow relates is not a series of completed and coherent episodes, but a knot of experiences which remains tantalizing and enigmatic. The experience of *Heart of Darkness* does not necessarily invalidate notions of coherence and completeness, but it questions them, and questions the coherence and completeness which fiction traditionally has conveyed. Marlow likens his attempt to convey the reality of Kurtz to a dream: "He was just a word for me. I did not see the man in the name any more than you do. Do you see him? Do you see the story? Do you see anything? It seems to me I am trying to tell you a dream—making a vain attempt, because no relation of a dream can convey the dream-sensation" (82). Marlow seems for a moment overpowered by doubts: What was Kurtz? Could he be deciphered by Marlow or, through Marlow, by others? These questions cut across his own deeply divided feelings about the telling of his story; the strength of the story would be in making his listeners "see" Kurtz, "see" the story. Yet he cannot believe that they can see the story, for he himself sees a knot of issues and responses impossible to unravel. Marlow's remarks, then, result from an anxiety that perhaps his narrative has no moral center, that events cannot crystallize and become a story. One may say he is, at this point, protesting too much, for he hasn't yet described Kurtz in the context which gives him a meaning; nevertheless, his anxiety reveals his apprehension that his story transgresses all bounds of ordinary life, that he is without confidence, that Kurtz and his experience will escape his most sincere endeavor in the telling.

Marlow's narrative, however, recaptures his own experience of profound disorientation. This necessarily indirect narration transcends the traditional goal of storytelling, which may be to recount an event, to pose a puzzle or dilemma, or to dispense wisdom. Marlow's storytelling is not cut off from these traditional goals but, rather, complicates its relation to them; it does recount events, and it poses dilemmas conceivable only in terms of the Congo experience, and it is, finally, a demystifying wisdom tale. But it is a wisdom tale devoid of consolation; it critiques and discredits any consolation one may seek in wisdom tales.

Though his narrative is retrospective, Marlow's final experience of Kurtz does not determine the narration of events. Instead the story veers away from the anticipation of Kurtz's disintegration, toward an unfolding of puzzling events which juxtaposes the historical praxis against an idealizing metaphysics with its comforting moral imperatives. This disconcerting narrative turn forces Marlow into a self-reflexive and despairing state of mind. As he says:

"No, it is impossible, it is impossible to convey the life-sensation of any given epoch of one's existence—that which makes its truth, its meaning—its subtle and penetrating essence. It is impossible. We live as we dream—alone. . . ."

He paused again, as if reflecting, then added—

"Of course, in this you fellows see more than I could then. You see me, whom you know. . . ." (83)

This seems to be a statement of radical solipsism, and there is, of course, a certain trite sense in which all experience is impossible to communicate: one cannot duplicate an experience for an audience, nor can one be certain of capturing its essential truth and meaning in language. Marlow's last statement, however, introduces an important qualification. In his telling the story now, his listeners understand what Marlow, as the novitiate in his venture, could not. Thus Marlow's misgivings do not diminish his passion to shatter his listeners' self-confidence, as his has been shattered. His self-reflexivity and his ruminations about his narrative dilemmas are genuine gropings for an adequate language; his is not the self-conscious and self-indulgent posturing of much post-modern fiction. It is not only the inadequacy of language which distresses Marlow: he also knows language is the instrument of deception and manipulation.

The treacherous relation of language and experience that so unsettles Marlow casts a shadow on his own discourse, for the act of storytelling contains the same potential for unreality that underlies the speech of Kurtz. Marlow suspects "eloquence" because there is no guarantee that its possessor will act in terms of the values he espouses, or that his eloquence has any connection to his lived experience. Language and discourse, like work and action, are exposed to malignancies which pervert them.

The objection that Henry James among others raised to Conrad's mode of storytelling in *Heart of Darkness* was that Kurtz is never fully dramatized.[7] James's interest was always in capturing the psychological fullness of a character, though theoretically he was skeptical that such fullness was possible. But Marlow only speaks abstractly about Kurtz's struggle: neither

Marlow nor Conrad can give a full psychological portrayal of a man who has entered into monstrous and forgotten passions. For traditional allegory, the portrayal of evil was possible because evil is controlled by an affirmative teleology; but the violently antithetical passions in Kurtz allow no resolution in terms of an affirmative teleology. Kurtz's experience reveals a bleak dimension of life that Marlow can hope, without confidence, to communicate. There is a real difference between Isabel's anguished reflections on her fatal misjudgment of Gilbert Osmond in *Portrait of a Lady* and Kurtz's inner struggle only inferentially grasped by Marlow in *Heart of Darkness*. The problem for Marlow is that the very act of telling the story must take into account a skepticism that one can ever come to terms with the experience of another human being.

It is clear by now that the dramatic import of Kurtz resides in the entire complex of experiences that fuels Marlow's increasing obsession. Conrad is dealing with moments of experience for which there can be no adequate expression; thus his impressionistic technique differs from the impressionists' own purposes. Marlow's "telling" is an anguished clarification of his own Congo experience, and the Kurtz who was in the beginning just a word generates hopes that become their own grotesque parody, leaving Marlow with a paralyzing metaphysical insight into the condition of humanity. A straightforward account of Kurtz's eloquence, of his acts of nameless ritualized barbarity, would result in uncontrolled melodrama and sensationalism which could not disclose the turning of Marlow's hope into negation and despair.

VII

Kurtz's regression into atavism is connected to both his capacity for role-changing and his boundless egotism. None the less, Conrad criticism has often romanticized and simplified the complicated knot of implications which holds together Marlow's narrative of Kurtz. To romanticize Kurtz because he has experienced the abyss, to call him a hero of the spirit,[8] is to ignore both the reality of his degeneration and its ties with the imperialist venture that has made his transformation possible; the abyss is privileged and idealized, made into an oracle of modern art. It is here that Nietzsche's warning "when you look long into an abyss, the abyss also looks back at you", provides a necessary caution.[9] Just as Freud's uncovering of fierce passions in the family does not result in a celebration of the repressed, so the disclosure of the demonic passions in *Heart of Darkness* does not culminate in a celebration of darkness. The narrative ends in skeptical despair and silence; it is finally an act of remembrance that grasps at meaning. .

Benita Parry has recently argued that the final words of *Heart of Darkness* do not repudiate "the West's colonialist ambitions", and "with the superven- tion of themes registering ethical standards as fixed by ethnic sentiments and severing acts of personal honour from a wider conception of moral responsi- bility, the political protest is crucially muffled and the grace of visionary aspirations invested in imperialism triumphs over representations of the disgrace attending its historical practice".[10] Parry's reading of *Heart of Darkness* in particular and Conrad in general restores a certain balance to Conrad criticism which has hitherto focused, rather exclusively, on ethical and existential themes. Her response is reductive, however, in seeing the novel's ending as in some ways muffling the political protest. For to bring to critical consciousness the very fact of a culture's impasse on the question of what constitutes appropriate ethical conduct in both private and public life is to disclose the inextricable entanglement of political and ethical questions. It is not an escapist attitude for Marlow to have taken recourse to the act of storytelling to disclose this impasse. What is his own personal responsibility? Should he have told Kurtz's Intended the truth, and would even truth have been countenanced as truth? And how would he have explained Kurtz's conduct in the Congo and his final judgment? Answer to these questions is not easily decidable.

Conrad's attitude here seems to be determined in part by a feeling that under all circumstances individual integrity, in response to others as indi- viduals, has primacy over all other obligations. But he does not reduce this response to a pietist stance by refusing to recognize its problematic status in the context of larger social and political questions. Hence the strain of parody throughout Marlow's brief meeting with the Intended. His response is far from a triumph of imperialism's visionary aspirations, and it does not give the narrative a closure conceivable as a triumph of imperialism's visionary aspirations. What would be the point of denouncing imperialism if that meant leaving unexposed the tragic reality of those whose faith is kept alive by imperialism's visionary aspirations? Marlow's meeting with the Intended seems to me a consummate Conradian invention disclosing the separation of theory, conceived here as imperialism's visionary aspirations, from its violent manifestations in practice. There can be no honest political community, however, without some implicit norms of ethical conduct. Marlow here has no answer in terms of theoretical or practical certainties; the only answer he can provide in his current impasse is to lead us to experience the moment of this impasse through the act of storytelling. For the moment, then, storytelling becomes the means by which imperialism's problems—which are also the problems of the society which engendered imperialism—are shown in all their stark forms, at home and in the colonies.

Marlow's speech challenges the reader to participate directly in the deciphering of his Congo experience. If, as Trilling says, Kurtz is a hero of the spirit, it is because his moral will asserts itself when all is beyond hope. Despite its derisory irony, Marlow's statement that "Kurtz was a remarkable man" still contains an element of admiration. Marlow's duplicitous response to the Intended, on the other hand, suggests he has reached the point where moral protest or self-assertion, despite its abiding intention, must end in silence. This perhaps explains Marlow's posture of a Buddha with which he begins and ends his story. We might draw back with horror from Marlow's tale but discover no unquestionable values in either self or community. This is Conrad's modernist version of tragedy, fully consonant with Nietzsche's statement in *The Birth of Tragedy* that "tragedy denies ethics".[11] For how could the moral triumph of Kurtz's cry, if we grant that it is a triumph, provide a communal ethic? And what are the implications of a story that does not restore the self-confidence of a community in its cherished ideals?

Through Marlow, Conrad has posed and explored certain serious questions concerning the nature of European civilization, specifically the nature of the community and the relations among its people fostered by that civilization. Before he left for the Congo, Marlow had already felt disillusioned about the so-called civilized life of the European city, and had found its rhetoric of values to be dishonest and hollow. The representatives of Europe he encounters during his journey show a passion for wealth and power over which they can exercise no restraint during the colonial ventures. The values evolved in their own community lie at the basis of their self-description as civilized people, but their values have no efficacy whatever outside the community. Marlow, however, is not only not sanguine about that community, he is downright skeptical about its ability to make possible relations that would make its members politically and ethically honorable. The middle and lower classes in that community lived under conditions barely distinguishable from those under which any colonized poor people lived. Consequently, those in the middle and lower classes in Europe sought to improve their lot by seeking fortune abroad. The colonial venture whose foundations were laid in the seventeenth and eighteenth centuries became the common dream of the economically lower classes.

For Marlow, then, Europe never possessed the ideals it professed, though he hopes to see them realized in the practice of representative Europeans such as Kurtz. His disillusionment with Kurtz leads him to the deeper insight that a community can provide no guarantee for the realization of the values it professes. Indeed, the community at best inspires fear in its members, and thus impels them to allegiance. So when he tells the lie to the Intended, Marlow has already come to the skeptical conclusion about civilization's false rhetoric of morality and values; and he has despaired of civilization's ability to create a form of life free from hypocrisy and distortion. In the Intended he sees a tragic individual sustained by the community's values, irrevocably cut off from any knowledge of the community's moral fragmentation. The tragedy implied by the figure of the Intended is that her purity of sentiment can exist only in the presence of ignorance and inexperience. She exemplifies an innocent consciousness impossible for the larger community; and, as Marlow has seen in the innocence of the Russian harlequin, innocence cannot sustain our confidence in civilization and its values, nor can it help us to reconstitute the community through some deeper grasp of the individual.

Nevertheless, Marlow's skepticism is not nihilism; it does not entail a rejection of values as such. It despairs over the possibility of founding the community on values that might sustain its social institutions. Marlow's lie to the Intended is an act of integrity, one that enables him to know that in certain contexts telling the truth is itself a failure of restraint, that the doubts about community and self he has felt become destructive if they are not informed by a capacity to know how to talk and thus to live. The irony in his lie to the Intended is not that of corrosive laughter, but of a paradoxical insight into the possibility of moral phenomena—such as the Intended's fidelity—in the context of a fragmented, incoherent communal life.

Marlow, in his seemingly reposeful posture of a Buddha, is not an exemplary figure of detachment and moral calm that the image of the Buddha may suggest. His inner turmoil sharply differentiates him from the Buddha of ancient India whose reposeful calm is the result of his renunciation of this world of ceaseless toil and acquisition, suffering and death. Marlow's turmoil marks him as a representative of Western culture; he has not renounced the world, but has believed in the redeeming possibility of values, and is shattered by their absence. Hence his words: "It was not my strength that wanted nursing, it was my imagination that wanted soothing" (73). If morality originates in the fear of violence, if the police and the butcher must restrain the self that cannot autonomously restrain itself, there can be no absolute redemptive value in morality, self, or work. After such disillusionment one cannot seek foundations for morality. Marlow's moral will can claim to alter nothing, though it can narrate the events that form the basis of his experience.

Thus a reading of *Heart of Darkness* which places Marlow close to Socrates and distant, say, from Sartre ignores those elements in Socrates which lead to an unmasking of actual life.[12] Moreover, as Nietzsche argued, Socrates undermined the foundations of practical life in classical Athens.[13] Marlow's narrative takes on neither a Socratic nor a Sartrean configuration; it is composed of dramatic moments that complicate Socratic or Sartrean perspectives. The Socratic view, in any case, would be that Kurtz is foolhardy rather than courageous, belligerent and unreliable rather than wise and good. For Socrates insisted the brave man considers only the good life worth living. Kurtz has, in this view, capitulated to base impulses which render his courage reckless and self-destructive.

Marlow, on the other hand, knows that the Socratic desire to provide a foundation for moral values is illusory. In Conrad, as in Nietzsche and Freud, the critique of moral foundations is a profoundly moral endeavor, though in Conrad, as in Nietzsche, it produces no ethical principles.[14] It takes the form of moral criticism of social-political institutions and their impact on our private lives. In this sense Marlow exhibits what one might call Sartrean anguish and despair. This does not mean that Marlow implicitly embodies Sartrean philosophy, or that Conrad anticipated Sartrean thought, or that Sartre's philosophy will help us understand Marlow and his experience in the Congo. Indeed, an interesting complication arises when we realize that *Heart of Darkness* reflects upon the limits of language and human understanding unavailable to Sartrean thought. It is also possible to argue that Socrates would be critical of Marlow because Marlow appears to renounce joy. But Marlow's vision questions the Socratic assumption that moderation and reason can ever prevail in human affairs. Thus Marlow's narrative engenders a complex skepticism which cannot be reduced to metaphysical certitudes about reality and human consciousness.

Marlow's act of storytelling, however, does involve a commitment to preserve the truth of experience, though it is a commitment devoid of conventional piety or hope. In this sense Marlow may be said to have evolved a self beyond culture, a self that knows the awesome terrors held at bay by its awesome will to be human. It is here that Lionel Trilling's idea that the highest value of a culture is in its capacity to create the possibility of a self that exists apart from and beyond culture seems relevant.[15] But there is in a sense no such thing as "self" beyond culture. Culture here means the context of historically developed social practices which helps create the possibility of a self. This self, in so far as it is founded on ideals, is impossible to realize in practice; thus it generates restraints which protect against transgressions that damage the social well-being. Having known Kurtz in his extremity, Marlow has come to see the self as an arbitrary construct, rather than one created by transcendental values. Thus Marlow is a representative of Western culture who is distanced from that culture's grandest claims about itself; he is utterly devoid of confidence. This is why he says: "life is a greater riddle than some of us think it to be. I was within a hair's breadth of the last opportunity for pronouncement, and I found with humiliation that probably I would have nothing to say" (150–51). His speech culminates in silence.

Marlow's "self", however, cannot be institutionalized, for to believe that it can be would be to ascribe to human beings unlimited capacity to bear the truth. One cannot forget the moral force of the lie to the Intended or her tragic sanity. One cannot imagine the Russian harlequin learning from experience, or the manager and the pilgrims living lives of moral pessimism that comprehends and endures the nihilism pervasive in our social-political institutions. Neither can one hope to redeem the idealism whose moral complicity with imperialism *Heart of Darkness* delineates with such brilliance.[16]

CHAPTER TWO
Narrative and Authority:
Lord Jim

Toward the end of *Heart of Darkness* Marlow sums up his experience of Kurtz in these words: "I was within a hair's breadth of the last opportunity for pronouncement, and I found with humiliation that probably I would have nothing to say. This is the reason why I affirm that Kurtz was a remarkable man. He had something to say" (151). In a sense, Marlow's meeting with the Intended and his lie confirm his remark that he had "nothing to say". With our discussion of the ending of *Heart of Darkness* in mind, I want to begin this chapter with an interpretation of Marlow's final remarks about Jim. Marlow's experience, in *Heart of Darkness*, of the complicity of idealism with imperialism opens a reflection on the nature of the self and its foundation in the community. This is the reflection Marlow probes, more directly, in *Lord Jim*. If Kurtz has surrendered himself to archetypal passions, Jim has surrendered himself to an impossible ideal of the self. Marlow's narrative of Jim is, as we shall see, a tragedy of innocence, made all the more poignant by the fact that in its background lies Marlow's Congo experience.[1] In *Lord Jim* the tragedy of innocence works at a level where the narrative becomes neither a mere celebration of Jim nor a recounting of his failure, but a critique of the values underlying a community's vision of itself. For through a treatment of the nature and implications of individual psychology as revealed in different characters Conrad explores issues that are simultaneously ethical and political. The apparently existentialist treatment contains layers of questioning that constantly put the individual back into the community and thus investigate the problematic status of the community's relation to its own ideals. The more self-reflexive turn the narrative takes, the more inescapable the larger ethical and political questions become. My discussion attempts to explore how, in *Lord Jim*, the moral, political and epistemological issues are deeply intertwined, generating Marlow's paradoxical responses to Jim and forcing him to raise questions concerning the status of his own narrative and authority as

45

the story's narrator and as a member of the community of which Jim is the enigmatic figure of transgression and affirmation.

I

And that's the end. He passes away under a cloud, inscrutable at heart, forgotten, unforgiven, and excessively romantic. Not in the wildest days of his boyish visions could he have seen the alluring shape of such an extraordinary success . . . we can see him, an obscure conqueror of fame, tearing himself out of the arms of a jealous love at the sign, at the call of his exalted egoism. He goes away from a living woman to celebrate his pitiless wedding with a shadowy ideal of conduct. Is he satisfied— quite, now, I wonder? We ought to know. He is one of us—and have I not stood up once, like an evoked ghost, to answer for his eternal constancy? Was I so very wrong after all? Now he is no more, there are days when the reality of his existence comes to me with an immense, with an overwhelming force; and yet upon my honour there are moments, too, when he passes from my eyes like a disembodied spirit astray amongst the passions of this earth, ready to surrender himself faithfully to the claim of his own world of shades.

Who knows? He is gone, inscrutable at heart, and the poor girl is leading a sort of soundless, inert life in Stein's house. Stein has aged greatly of late. He feels it himself, and says often that he is "preparing to leave all this; preparing to leave . . . " while he waves his hand sadly at his butterflies. (416—17)

These are Marlow's concluding words to the story of Jim's life, of his own response to Jim; they also end *Lord Jim*. But they do not signal for Marlow a conclusive response to Jim, nor do they signal for the reader the possibility of a reading that would decipher both the meaning of Jim's life and the meaning of *Lord Jim*. The ending is a compound of poignancy, confidence, and uncertainty, perhaps best characterized as a profoundly disturbed and disturbing ambivalence, an ambivalence that seems to show the inadequacy of language, yet one that we cannot know or feel as ambivalence without language. The statement "we ought to know" deepens into the rhetorical question "Was I so very wrong after all", a response that seemingly implies a positive answer. Yet, by referring us back to his narrative of Jim, it implies further questions about Marlow's response to Jim. The ambiguity of the end of *Lord Jim* culminates in Marlow's final question, a question that puts

Marlow's own interpretation of Jim into question and, more significantly, invites the reader to engage in the process of interpreting Jim again.[2] Marlow thus speaks in a double epistemological mode: one emphasizes the inscrutable nature of Jim, whereas the other insists on Jim as "one of us". His narrative is therefore inconclusive, since he admits that he cannot declare the truth about Jim, that Jim remains an enigma to him, that his being "one of us" remains in a peculiar way indistinguishable from his compelling but enigmatic power over us.

What, then, is the nature of authority that Marlow can claim for his narrative? What is the nature of Marlow's knowledge of Jim, and what does his memorial reconstruction of Jim seek to achieve?[3] These questions are crucial to an understanding of *Lord Jim* because they are implicit in Marlow's narrative as well as in the structure of the novel. For almost from the beginning Marlow suggests that he cannot claim real knowledge of Jim: "I wanted to know—and to this day I don't know, I can only guess" (79). Marlow thus speaks, not from a vantage-point of knowledge and certainty, but with an awareness that understanding does not possess a spontaneous clarity in the mind which can be articulated in words. Language itself poses problems, since, as he says, "the power of sentences has nothing to do with their sense or the logic of their construction" (75). Consequently, Marlow's narrative proceeds in a self-questioning mode: "I don't pretend I understood him. The views he let me have of himself were like those glimpses through the shifting rents in a thick fog—bits of vivid and vanishing detail, giving no connected idea of the general aspect of a country . . . Upon the whole he was misleading" (76).

Marlow's narrative, then, is an expression of a knot of complications: language is problematical, his own understanding of Jim is not clear, and Jim himself is misleading. No doubt each one of these features is sufficient for complicating Marlow's as well as our own response to Jim; yet in *Lord Jim* all three features are meshed together in such a manner that for Marlow the success of his narrative is closely interwoven with his admission of its failure clearly to grasp Jim. It is not as if Marlow's self-deprecatory remarks, or his uncertainty, or his narrative duplicity is merely the product of a gentle irony, an irony that has matured through the prior shattering experience of Kurtz in *Heart of Darkness*. For just as Kurtz's experience "is posited outside Marlow's discourse",[4] so, too, is Jim's experience exterior to Marlow's narrative, though by claiming Jim as "one of us" Marlow seeks to appropriate that experience. Marlow is therefore aware that in a strict sense his authority is a sham, but he remains committed to his project of bringing Jim within the empirical bounds of human understanding, even at the cost of duplicity. For example, Marlow sees that if the unexpected erupted in Jim's life it could occur in anyone else's life, too, as it does in Razumov's in *Under Western Eyes*. Given the inscrutable nature of Jim's experience, real failure would consist in making no attempt to record and articulate it for us. It is therefore inevitable that Marlow should perceive Brierly's suicide as a refusal to confront and grasp the implications for human existence of Jim's fatal jump from *Patna*.

Marlow's perception of the duplicity and inauthenticity of human life as it is ordinarily lived constitutes a central urge behind his interest in Jim. He recognizes in Jim's facing of the trial "a redeeming feature in his abominable case" (68). In an important sense, then, Marlow has, despite the pervasive ambiguity in his narrative, made a judgment of Jim, and the judgment is a positive one. It consists in his feeling, reinforced by Brierly's suicide, that Jim's is an exemplary case: "I hadn't been so sure of it before" (68–9). It is, however, not a question of mere confirmation of this certainty, but a question of not being able to ground this certainty in any finality of response which constitutes the center of Marlow's narrative. For Marlow cannot sum up Jim's life, or his response to it, in some irreducible and essential meaning: "End. Finis. The potent word that exorcises from the house of life the haunting shadow of fate. This is what—notwithstanding the testimony of my eyes and his own earnest assurances—I miss when I look back upon Jim's success . . . He was not—if I may say so—clear to me. He was not clear. And there is a suspicion he was not clear to himself either" (176–7). Clarity, self-understanding—the goals of an epistemology of the self—are thus put beyond the possibility of attainment, though, paradoxically, these goals are among the motivating factors that put in motion Marlow's narrative and the reader's interest.

There is thus a contradiction at the heart of Marlow's narrative, though it is not a straightforward logical contradiction. Rather, it operates in the form of a sliding, so that, if at one point Marlow seems to assert one thing, soon he asserts another. This sliding suggests a shifting of the ground of his interest in Jim. It can be construed as involving a logical contradiction if we translate Marlow's responses at different junctures into specific propositions. Take, for instance, Marlow's explanation of his initial interest in Jim: "I wanted to see him overwhelmed, confounded, pierced through and through, squirming like an impaled beetle" (42). This is a moral response stemming from his feeling that Jim "stood there for all the parentage of his kind . . . whose very existence is based upon honest faith, and upon the instinct of courage" (42). If Jim is thus a representative of humanity, Marlow needs no other grounds for his interest in Jim. Yet Marlow has another, more compelling ground for that interest: "I have a distinct notion I wished to find something. Perhaps unconsciously, I hoped I would find that something, some merciful explanation, some convincing shadow of an excuse. I see well now that I hoped for the impossible—for the laying of what is the most obstinate ghost of man's creation . . . the doubt of the sovereign power enthroned in a fixed standard of conduct" (50). If Marlow's first response was to see Jim experience moral agony, the second shares with it its moral drive in a contradictory fashion. It shows that along with a desire to see Jim morally "squirming" there existed in Marlow the desire to find some excuse for Jim. At another level, however, from the perspective of Marlow's many encounters with Jim that he describes until the end of chapter 35, Marlow recognizes that his interest in Jim stemmed from a prior skeptical feeling that the code of conduct had no absolute authority over human life.

Marlow's desire to seek an explanation, and to provide a justification, for Jim's history is necessarily a drive to seek objective content, to discover objective significance, and to communicate it to his listeners. Its foremost task is that of comprehending a human being whose transgression does not minimize his human significance. That is why Marlow insists, "You must understand he did not try to minimize its importance . . . therein lies his distinction" (82). Marlow, however, doubts his narrative ability because he doubts his capacity for seeing innocently or with the epistemological certainty which is presumed to make him a representative of his profession. Consequently, his narrative, though about Jim, also turns into one about himself, about his own potential transgressions, about the impossibility of pure allegiance to one's values, the impossibility of fulfilling the dream which Jim himself never abandons.

As I will try to show in this chapter, Marlow's narrative is more profound than his explicit interpretive remarks suggest, for these remarks also indicate his moments of failure to understand. His narrative contains implicitly and through distortions interpretive signposts which disclose Marlow's failure and exceed his intention partly by contradicting it. Yet this contradiction cannot sustain itself without showing at the same time in Marlow's interpretation a quality of response that will signal his listeners' willingness to entertain Marlow's apprehension of Jim. The reader consequently is implicated in a movement of contradiction and is at the same time forced to carry on an activity of decipherment that Marlow must, caught in his own contradiction, leave unarticulated. Moreover, the transgressor, Jim, seeks a mode of being that, in his effort to realize it, not only brings to light the fundamental inadequacies of all modes of (human) being, but also succeeds in a way that is not separable from failure. The narrative of *Lord Jim* therefore pulls and strains in ways that reveal contradictions as conjunctions, success as failure, and ideals as perversion. It discloses the necessity of ideals for the effective functioning of the community, but it at the same time discloses the ideals as possessing an inhuman and absolute status in human life. If they seem human and necessary for life in one context, they seem inhuman and destructive in another context. Each context implicitly leads to the other, and neither is unquestionable.

II

Marlow's encounters with the French lieutenant, the German merchant and entomologist, Stein, and Jewel are among the most important moments in his narrative, moments when he seeks to invest his narrative with authority. Each provides Marlow with a different vantage-point on Jim, and each complicates his understanding of Jim. The immediate perspective that each offers on Jim at once opens up the gulf between them on the one hand and Jim on the other. For instance, the French lieutenant has stood the test of experience, whereas Jim has failed it; Stein has proved himself in the past by combining practical action with romantic idealism, whereas Jim, driven by the same longing, has not; Jewel has initially made an unromantic acceptance of failure as the basis of her life, whereas Jim, defiantly self-assertive, has lured her into the circle of his illusion.

The French lieutenant represents the authority of practical reason and experience, an authority that derives its power, not from an unqualified assertion of the self, but from a recognition of the self's liabilities.[5] For instance, he says: "Each of them . . . if he were an honest man . . . would confess . . . that there is somewhere a point when you let go everything. . . . Given a certain combination of circumstances, fear is sure to come" (146). He thus does not present himself in the light of an exalted ideal of self. Instead, he admits: "Man is born a coward. . . . It is a difficulty—*parbleu*. It would be too easy otherwise. But habit—habit—necessity—do you see?—the eye of others—*voilà*. One puts up with it. And then the example of others who are no better than yourself, and yet make good countenance" (147). This is the clearest, because the most unpretentious, statement of the code of conduct. It defines and delimits the question of personal authority, and it perceives a relation between fear and courage. The strength of the lieutenant's perception resides in his refusal to allow this relation to undermine the authority of the code of conduct. For he says "one may get on knowing very well that one's courage does not come of itself (*ne vient pas tout seul*). There's nothing much in that to get upset about. One truth the more ought not to make life imposs-

ible. . . . But the honour. . . . The honour . . . that is real—that is. And what
life may be worth when . . . the honour is gone . . . I can offer no opinion—
because. . . . I know nothing of it" (148). The French lieutenant here recognizes
the possibility of failure of courage or, rather, the possibility of being overcome by fear; but he does not allow it to open any skeptical reflection on
life.

Courage, as the French lieutenant says, is grounded in habit, a practice
learned in the community of other men. It is not the result of either conscious
reflection or deliberate preparedness, but is manifested in obedient and
decisive action. It does not imply elimination of the instinct of fear; rather, it
implies a restraint on fear by practical exercises of daily living. Courage, in
other words, is the result of an action grounded in moral dictates of the
community; it brings one honor, and contributes to the stability and health
of the community. Nevertheless, the code, as held by the members of a
community, tends to possess a transcendental ontological status. For, as the
French lieutenant explains, honor depends on the fulfillment of the code of
one's craft, and this honor is real since it grants moral sanction to one's life.
Consequently, for the lieutenant, despite his recognition of the overwhelming
nature of the instinct of fear, the code, ostensibly a matter of habitual
obedience, is inflexible. If honor is gone, one's life can have no meaning or
justification.

Though sprung from the pragmatic context of human transactions, the
code thus demands an unswerving allegiance and possesses a status not justified
by either the instinct or the possibility of experience. To the extent, then,
that the French lieutenant acknowledges the power of fear and the possibility
of failure, his thirty-hour watch in *Patna* can claim to be not an exemplary act
but simply a performance of duty. The helmsman at the inquiry, we remember,
gives a list of names that puts the French lieutenant's action in a longstanding tradition of seamanship. The lieutenant admits that he wouldn't
know what to do or say when honor is gone—an admission that recognizes
one's helplessness before failure. It is, moreover, an admission that refuses to
engage in reflective thought about transgression and its implications for
human action and intention. From the pragmatic perspective, however, that
is as it should be. Yet the refusal to ponder further discloses the code's
inhuman, transcendental status, for it concedes the authority of the court to
conduct its inquiry on the assumption that a transgression of the code under
any circumstances is an immitigable offense.

Contrary to the view of some critics, then, the French lieutenant's conduct
does not necessarily undermine Jim's. Similarly, the elitist perspective that
finds the lieutenant repudiated by Marlow's privileging of the quality of

one's feeling or consciousness is not correct, either. Both perspectives are, of course, allowed a play, but neither is dominant. They coexist with others in a movement that constitutes the ambiguity of *Lord Jim*, not reducible to the certitudes of any perspective. For if the quality of feeling alone mattered it would do so only by a denial of the pragmatic context of simple virtues disclosed in the fulfillment of daily obligations. Brierly's suicide, to take a concrete example, does not simply confirm the impossibility of an unqualified assertion of the self. By a contradictory movement it also confirms the necessity and importance of the French lieutenant's action. If, to take another example, the helmsman and the French lieutenant seem heroically to mock Jim, Jim seems to mock them by a heroic gesture of self-assertion. Neither response by itself is adequate, and each requires the other to comprehend *Lord Jim*. The oscillation of response that occurs in the novel is extremely complex, and functions at the level of a fundamental questioning of the nature of authority and its relation to Marlow's narration of Jim's story.

If the French lieutenant is antithetical to Jim, Stein is closer to Jim by an affinity for adventure which in itself had little value for the lieutenant. Stein possesses, in addition, a reflective bent, and presents a sharp contrast to the French lieutenant. Marlow comes to Stein for advice in the matter of Jim. And the advice is stated in what are perhaps Stein's most notoriously ambiguous remarks:

> A man that is born falls into a dream like a man who falls into the sea. If he tries to climb out into the air as inexperienced people endeavour to do, he drowns—*nicht wahr?* . . . The way is to the destructive element submit yourself, and with the exertions of your hands and feet in the water make the deep, deep sea keep you up. (214)[6]

In this credo of a romantic idealist, existence is conceived as "the destructive element", as a medium irrevocably hostile to humanity, which can keep itself alive only through a constant struggle. The idea of struggle is invoked here for the human capacity for generating ideals and aspirations which enable human beings to transform the very hostility of natural existence into a means for realization of their own goals. Stein's conception combines toil and vision, reality and dream to underscore the extraordinary nature of the vigilance and commitment required by the ideal. This entanglement of visionary aspirations with unremitting toil avers an imperative of endurance because, while these aspirations constitute what is fulfilling about human existence, they must end in failure. Stein's imperative, then, embodies a romantic exhortation: make your ideals and aspirations help you to live. But why, one may ask, such an irrevocably tragic imperative from a romantic idealist? Stein's answer is unequivocal: "Man is come where he is not wanted, where there is no room for him" (208). There is, in other words, no natural necessity for our (human) existence, none at any rate for us to exist as anything other than mere creatures of nature; there is indeed an antithetical relation between us and the natural world. Because we have the burden of living in the hostile natural world, we must create ideals and aspirations which, however illusory in the final reckoning, make it possible for us to live.

This situation is further complicated by the fact human beings are also driven by antithetical desires. "We want in so many different ways to be" (213). These self-divisive aspirations make it impossible for us to live in harmony either with the natural world which is not our proper habitat since we cannot ever live without engaging in various constructive projects, or with our aspirations which are opposed to the world since they are the product of our imagination. Thus our visionary aspirations themselves also constitute the "destructive element" because we can neither live without them nor make them natural to the world in which we must live. Consequently, if the natural world is immitigably hostile to us, and our ideals are self-divisive and finally destructive, Stein's advice takes the form of tragic-romantic imperative: forge a possibility of meaningful life out of that which will sooner or later enclose and defeat you. This vision of human existence, with its marks of the German romantic tradition of which Stein is a progeny, embodies a theory of consciousness as well as that of the meaning and necessity of human action. As a romantic visionary he prefigures certain radical political tendencies that are important precisely because his relation to them is practical and experimental rather than abstract and theoretical.

Stein, however, has already insisted on the inevitability of failure of all our aspirations in the final sense, and his explanation of this inevitability only deepens the tragic-romantic conception underlying his vision of human endeavor and its outcome: "because you not always can keep your eyes shut there comes the real trouble—the heart pain—the world pain. . . . It is not good for you to find you cannot make your dream come true, for the reason that you not strong enough are, or not clever enough" (213). Stein here adds elements which specify the relation between consciousness and action. It is better for us, Stein suggests, to remain blind to the inevitability of failure, for neither our strength nor our cleverness is adequate to the visions our imagination conjures and drives us to realize. In other words, under no circumstances can we subdue the natural world whose contingencies invade and destroy our fondest hopes. Nor can we control and manipulate our own aspirations and ideals *vis-à-vis* those of our fellow beings; it is indeed the inexorable logic of our ideals to subvert our best intentions. Innocence is nevertheless the protective shield which helps us to pursue with passion and commitment our particular visions. But innocence must come to an end somewhere, and the wisdom of experience brings the "heart pain", the "world pain" which shrouds all our visionary hopes. It is therefore inevitable that Stein should not find it easy to answer his question: "So if you ask me—how to be" (214). "His lips uttered no word, and the austere exaltation of a certitude seen in the dusk vanished from his face" (214).

But the question remains whether Stein's meditation on action and failure is to be construed as an admission of his own failure and despair, whether his "heart pain" results from the problematical nature of his own effort in the "destructive element". For long before Jim's ideal reveals its destructive power, even as it also reveals the hostile contingencies that erupt around his life with the arrival of Gentleman Brown, Stein has been living a rather ghostlier version of his own ideal aspirations. He now collects dead butter-flies and meditates on their magnificence. Yet Stein does go on to answer the question he has posed: "In the destructive element immerse. . . . That was the way. To follow the dream, and again to follow the dream—and so—*ewig—usque ad finem*. . . ." (214–15). The use of the past tense—"That was the way"—describes Stein's sense of pain for his abandonment of the dream, and it gets its full meaning when he confesses to his own failures before the close of his conversation with Marlow:

> "And do you know how many opportunities I let escape; how many dreams I had lost that had come in my way?" He shook his head regret-fully. "It seemed to me that some would have been very fine—if I had made them come true. Do you know how many? Perhaps I myself don't know." "Whether his were fine or not," I said, "he knows of one which he certainly did not catch." "Everybody knows of one or two like that," said Stein; "and that is the trouble—the great trouble. . . ." (217).

The interesting point to observe here is that Stein's experience of his own defeat does not deter him from his commitment, at the level of thought, to visionary aspirations. Hence his hope that Jim may yet accomplish in Patusan what he himself had failed to accomplish. Marlow's response undermines Stein's Utopian romanticism: "One had not the courage to decide; but it was a charming and deceptive light, throwing the impalpable poesy of its dimness over pitfalls—over graves" (215). This response questions Stein's conviction very much as Marlow's response had earlier questioned the French lieutenant's confidence in the norms of professional conduct. But we cannot argue that the undermining of Stein's visionary attitude amounts to a repudiation of the politics implicit in the attitude, or that without a fore-grounding of the dimension authorizing the legitimacy of Utopian aspirations the novel degenerates into a celebration of dark metaphysics and pessimistic existential ethics. These arguments simplify and distort the issues at stake, for Conrad's moral critique is inexorably political as well, though without resolving itself into any didactically expressible moral and political formulas.

From Stein and the French lieutenant Marlow sought advice, some moral grounds for excusing Jim's lapse, just as Jim himself seeks from Marlow a means of "absolution" (97). From his encounter with Jewel, however, Marlow does not seek advice or help for Jim. For if the French lieutenant has sympathized with Jim, and if Stein has seen his own younger romantic self in Jim, they both at least believe in his transgression committed in the grip of fear. Jewel, on the contrary, refuses to believe that (320).⁷ Yet she has an unfailing intuition that he is haunted by some private demon and will one day leave her to follow it. She, too, like Jim, seeks some sort of release from a painful knowledge of the past. Unlike Jim, however, she is not responsible for it. It is this difference that guides her at first in wishing that Jim leave Patusan before she feels his love for her and therefore knows happiness in life. Prior to Jim's arrival in Patusan, and for some time after, she has been viciously abused by Cornelius, Stein's agent, who married her mother when Jewel's father abandoned both mother and child. She has no other knowledge of the world from which Jim has come to Patusan: "all that she knew of its inhabitants were a betrayed woman [her mother] and a sinister pantaloon [Cornelius]" (307). Inevitably, Marlow's encounter with Jewel leaves him feeling that her life is unalterably tragic, that she is the very "spectre of fear" (327).

Almost from the beginning Marlow realizes that love has not brought Jewel happiness, "as if fear and incertitude had been the safeguards of her love" (313). On her insistent questioning as to why Jim would not return to his own society, Marlow replies, "Because he is not good enough" (318). Jewel, of course, rejects the answer as a lie. Marlow softens the remark by telling her, "Nobody, nobody is good enough" (319). For Jewel, however, Jim's character is unassailable. The conversation, then, does not bring any relief to Jewel, but it is shattering to Marlow. He loses his normal sense of composure and experiences an "utter defeat" (324) before Jewel's inconsolable questioning. "The very ground on which I stood seemed to melt under my feet" (315). And he acutely experiences the impossibility of communication with her: "It was impossible to make her understand. I chafed silently at my impotence" (316).

The skeptical consequence of Marlow's encounter with Jewel is a remarkable moment in *Lord Jim*, because neither the French lieutenant nor Stein had shattered the authoritative consciousness that characterizes Marlow's response to them. Marlow's description, for instance, of the parting between himself and the French lieutenant stands in sharp contrast to his sense of "utter defeat" with Jewel. If the first occasion ends in a grotesque posturing of civilized amenity (149), a comedy at the heart of ordinary life, the second ends with a wrenching sense of failure, a tragic knowledge that Jewel's life is wrought in tragedy and that she is as inaccessible as Jim. Marlow's meeting with Stein also ended with a melancholy reflection, yet had a positive aspect to it. Stein seemed to Marlow an older version of Jim, and evoked a hope that Jim might yet master his fate on Patusan. But, with Jewel, Marlow seems to lose all conviction. Marlow's characterization of Jim and Jewel is very apt: "They had mastered their fates. They were tragic" (316). Thus Jim has mastered his fate by mastering its very source, fear, by becoming fearless, whereas Jewel has mastered her fate by becoming the very "spectre of fear". Jim's fearlessness and Jewel's fear together constitute a powerful contradiction, one that is rendered ironic by their conjunction. I want to discuss, in the next section, the implications of such contradictions and conjunctions for Marlow's narrative.

Lord Jim, then, dramatizes the vectors of the mind's relationship to its desires. The French lieutenant insists on both the necessity of subservience of desire to duty and the mutual implication of fear and courage. For Brierly, on the other hand, the principle of authority is invested in the code, and the self derives its authority and power from his absolute confidence in the code's sovereign power. The self's self-confidence, in other words, Brierly's egotism, has its basis in *trust* in the code, but this trust has, until Jim comes along, never been tested. It hasn't been tested in the form of a contingency that can bring about failure or defeat. Brierly's egotism, naïve as it is, is too fragile to sustain itself in the face of any evidence against the code's sovereignty. For him to have sustained his confidence in the code, he would have had to internalize it as thoroughly as Jim has. Unlike Jim, he is no romantic idealist. Consequently, when Jim's case compels him to see the code's fragility, life becomes unacceptable to him. In contrast to the French lieutenant and Brierly, Stein had once lived a life that combined visionary idealism and practical action. Yet, despite his initial success, he admits to Marlow that many times he had let the dream pass (217). His confident moralizing tone, intent on explaining "how to be", thus changes into an admission of failure. Even Stein cannot provide a principle of authority. Neither can Jewel. Indeed, she brings Marlow to the very brink of epistemological uncertainty.

And it is from the vantage-point of this uncertainty that Marlow's narrative seeks to interpret Jim.

Since there is no true or absolute authority, Marlow must from time to time put his narrative into question, and claim for it only contingent authority, for even the act of putting into question is an act claiming some sort of authority. Without such a claim, Marlow could not characterize Jim as an enigma. Jim would then be left as an object of contempt or embarrassment as he is to Brierly, good only for exploitation by the Australian desperado Chester. Marlow's perspective thus differs from the perspectives of both the French lieutenant and Stein, though it cannot traverse the distance between itself and Jim's own experience. This distance, interpreted, reflected, puzzled over, and at times repudiated by Marlow, constitutes the nub of the enigmatic nature of *Lord Jim*, of Jim himself, and of Marlow's narrative. The novel, then, functions as a critique of various assumptions of authority and self and their relation to communal or transcendental values, and cannot arrive at a structure of values that can be conceived as unquestionable. And it raises questions that undermine our normal assumptions concerning self, self-knowledge, and knowledge itself. The novel's structure is labyrinthine, with perspectives within perspectives which do not converge upon any unquestionable single understanding but, rather, disclose the problematic status of what we know and value. Jim remains an other, a tantalizing figure of the imagination that is not fully known, but only caught in a web of words that remain sincere yet duplicitous, disturbingly true in their impact, yet contingent and inauthentic, proximate to our knowledge of ourselves and our uncertainty about that knowledge yet distant by virtue of their disclosure that Jim is a fictional character. The compelling power of Jim as a fictional character therefore resides in the complicated mediation between fact and fiction that he represents.

III

The first and anonymous narrator, for all his cynicism about the clergy, takes Jim to be morally flawed precisely because of Jim's wandering imagination and his infatuation with the ideal—tendencies which make it impossible for him to comply with his community's established norms of conduct. This characterization, however confidently evoked, is quickly put aside as soon as Marlow resumes his narrative and brings in view the perspectives that complicate Jim's relation to Marlow and his society. Marlow's characterization of Jim as "one of us", then, springs from considerations of ethnic solidarity: "I liked his appearance; I knew his appearance; he came from the right place; he was one of us" (43). Though he is "one of us", by his transgressions Jim has released certain responses in Marlow's mind that make it crucial for him to explore Jim's attempts to come to terms with the transgression. These responses concern the truth and falsity of the ideals cherished by the community, and the implications of one's success or failure in adhering to them.

The narrative of *Lord Jim* constitutes a search for an explanation of the meaning of Jim, not simply as a solitary individual, but as an individual whose enigmatic solidarity with his community Marlow unequivocally asserts. For Marlow this solidarity is defined by a capacity to feel: "The thing is that in virtue of his feeling he mattered" (222). At the moment, then, of telling the story, Marlow's interest in Jim cannot be ascribed to an illusory hope that through Jim he may overcome "that doubt which is the inseparable part of our knowledge" (221).[8] If the code of conduct has no absolute basis, if its truth is not separable from its illusory nature, then what matters is the relation that obtains between one's consciousness and the code of conduct; the relation, in other words, that one's intentions have to one's actions and their ramifications in the private and public spheres of life. The narrative of *Lord Jim* seeks to capture this relation by explicating, deciphering, and translating the signs that make up the complex and elusive context of Jim's life.

Lord Jim thus comprises a system of signs which exceed any stated intention of either Marlow or the impersonal narrator. Any deciphering of these signs must therefore require many criteria, and the criteria must themselves be established by two contradictory viewpoints. First, there is the inescapable fact of Jim's fatal jump from *Patna*. On an obvious level, this weakness is not something finally overcome and transcended, but is, rather, repeated and renewed in another crucial failing which must remain forever concealed from Jim. Second, there is Jim's attempt to purchase his innocence, or to expiate his guilt—an attempt which completely entraps him within his desired conception of self. The logic of this contradiction requires that guilt and innocence must not remain opposites or contraries but must, rather, coexist as mutually interdependent sources that make up the fractured modality of the human self.

Marlow's narrative discloses a conception of his own identity which participates in this consciousness of the fissure in the self. For example, Marlow says: "I at least had no illusions; but it was I, too, who a moment ago had been so sure of the power of words, and now was afraid to speak" (179). His effort to understand Jim and to make him accessible to others is already beset with insuperable difficulties—first, because he finds language inadequate to the task which he must undertake and, second, because Marlow has an acute consciousness of having been left "strangely unenlightened" (185) by his experience of Jim. Marlow's fragmented narrative, however, is not a deliberate mystification on his part, but is the necessity lying at the heart of his response to Jim. For, though Jim remains an enigma, he is, paradoxically, a form of revelation. Jim, for instance, surrounds and protects the ideal he has conceived of himself, and at the same time remains imprisoned within that very ideal.

Marlow's avowals therefore do not undermine his own response to Jim and mystify him; instead, his avowals confirm that response in a disturbing manner. The enigmatic Jim is "one of us", he is a necessity lying in our own selves. For Jim constitutes for Marlow a profoundly complex reality of human aspirations, a reality upon which Marlow attempts to confer the stability and solidity of a perceived object. Hence the impressionist technique in Marlow's narrative, a technique which has important consequences for the structure of *Lord Jim*. Consider, for instance, the task of language in presenting Jim as an enigma. The task is a highly complex one, since an enigma is by definition intractable to the representational powers of language. Nevertheless, because it is an enigma, it has to be presented in a language that discloses the inadequacy of language. Consequently, that which is intractable to language must be re-presented in language in order to repudiate the latter. Such a repudiation itself, however, must occur in language and thus empower language with self-reflexivity initially shown to be lacking in it. If, as Marlow puts it, "words . . . belong to the sheltering conception of light and order which is our refuge" (313), Marlow's problem is to strain language against itself. The triumph of language, which is the same as the triumph of consciousness (since neither is conceivable without the other), is therefore announced at the very moment when its inadequacy is admitted and confirmed.

Given the ambiguity of his response to Jim, Marlow must attempt a technique of evasion and fragmentation, a technique of seemingly alternative views which are sometimes offered as opposed but which sometimes turn out to be simplified versions of the ideal represented by Jim. The Conradian universe is thus fragmented. There is no Logos which can bring together and unite its fragmented stories into a totality; there is no Logos which comprehends them and refers them to the finality of a truth which makes for the meaning and possibility of confident moral action. For instance, Marlow, admitting the impossibility of saying the last words about Jim, says: "Are not our lives too short for that full utterance which through all our stammerings is of course our only and abiding intention" (225). For the link between self and the world on the one hand and on the other the truths that are presumed to give a solidity and wholeness to self and the world is absent. Jim's steadfast holding to an egoistic (moral) conception of self thus conceals a more profound, fragmentary, and self-destructive human reality. This is brilliantly captured in the innumerable shifts in Marlow's response from confidence and certainty to doubt and uncertainty. His confidence in "a few simple notions you must cling to if you want to live decently and would like to die easy" (43) is short-lived; it is plagued by doubts and hesitations which open him to problems that cannot be resolved by a recourse to received opinions and conventional pieties:

> I felt the risk I ran of being circumvented, blinded, decoyed, bullied, perhaps, into taking a definite part in a dispute impossible of decision if one had to be fair to all the phantoms in possession—to the reputable that had its claims and to the disreputable that had its exigencies. I can't explain to you who haven't seen him and who hear his words only at second hand the mixed nature of my feelings. It seemed to me that I was being made to comprehend the Inconceivable—and I know of nothing to compare with the discomfort of such a sensation. I was made to look at the convention that lurks in all truth and on the essential sincerity of falsehood. (93)

Marlow's response to Jim, in so far as it is admiring, turns the community around from its position of judgmental authority to that of self-defence, and the novel as a whole, which meant to be an inquiry into Jim's conduct, turns into an inquiry into the community's relation to the ideals it claims to cherish.

But the entanglements of Marlow's narrative do not allow for a unity which would coalesce the different and conflicting parts, a unity which would totalize the fragments. The narrative, straining toward an aesthetic of idealism, causes ruptures in that aesthetic and introduces movements that put into question the nostalgia for a reconciliation of opposites. The principle of reconciliation sees art as a drama of opposite or contradictory forces emerging in formal harmony variously defined as tragedy, as comedy, or as tragi-comedy. The modernist strain in fiction, however, of which *Lord Jim* is a supreme exemplar, brings about fundamental generic distortions in our expectations from literary experience. Marlow's narrative is thus in search of a form that would comprehend his uncertainty caused and complicated by Jim's own response to his actions. As Marlow says, "What I could never make up my mind about was whether his line of conduct amounted to shirking his ghost or to facing him out . . . as with the complexion of all our actions, the shade of difference was so delicate that it was impossible to say. It might have been flight and it might have been a mode of combat" (197). By characterizing Jim in terms of "the complexion of all our actions" Marlow refuses to define Jim as a mere idealist aberration. Jim, in other words, embodies the unconscious story of all human life brought to the level of awareness in Marlow's narrative.

Hidden from Jim's knowledge of himself and foreshadowed in Marlow's narrative is a self that we may identify as a form of desire, narcissistic desire, which self-destructively turns in upon itself. Marlow's puzzled, though critical, fascination with Jim, as our own with him, is an attempt to look this desire in the face, and to explore this desire as the community's own inner drive. This drive always functions at the idealistic level at which it manifests itself in terms of norms. For all his endeavor Marlow cannot quite look this narcissistic desire in the face, except in the form of Jim as an enigma. For Jim has so completely internalized the norms that the very attempt to keep faith with his community keeps him strangely removed from it, even when he most resoundingly appears to affirm his connection to it. The community itself remains protected from this self-destructive consequence of Jim's attitude because it is always particular individuals who may fail and who therefore may be brought to the bar of judgment, while the community as a collectivity continues to retain its prerogative to affirm certain ideals. It is by bringing to our critical attention this aspect of the community's relation to the individual that Marlow interrogates the community and thus distances himself from it.

It is important to keep in mind that Jim's concept of self is rooted in both his community, from which he learned his ideals, and his reading of books of romantic adventure, from which he learned to give fictional shape to his ideals.[9] In this respect he is, like Don Quixote, a novelistic character. Don Quixote, everyone would agree, reads the world in order to prove the books he has read. Jim, too, would like to read the world in order to prove his ideal of conduct. He would like adventure to offer itself to him in a moment he can predict and control. He therefore cannot conceive of adventure as the naïve fictional form of the contingent or the accidental. He cannot see that the contingent is not subject to a supervening will; otherwise, it could not be conceived as contingent. For Jim, however, the contingent is synonymous with the expected. In thus not recognizing the power of the contingent to subvert human intentions Jim has assimilated it within the boundaries of the rational or the predictable. The assimilation is a dangerous one, for he has reduced the inhuman to the level of the human. It is of course the consequence of the mind's desire to establish its dominion over every condition of life.

Yet the mind that desires the reduction of the inhuman to the human cannot realize that it is already itself contaminated by the inhuman. Jim's failure to realize this is illustrated in the second half of *Lord Jim*, which is concerned with Jim's attempt to realize his dream in Patusan. His failure is given a trenchant ironic force by his admission to Marlow of both his love for Jewel and his triumphant conviction that the people of Patusan trust him with their safety. Talking of his love for Jewel, Jim says, "You take a different view of your actions when you come to understand, when you are *made* to understand every day that your existence is necessary . . . to another person. I am made to feel that" (304). And, talking of the people of Patusan, Jim says, "I must go on, go on for ever holding up my end, to feel sure that nothing can touch me. I must stick to their belief in me to feel safe and to . . . keep in touch . . . with those whom, perhaps, I shall never see any more" (334). Jim has thus put his relationship with both Jewel and the people of Patusan, love and public role, in a context which is defined for him by the ideal and by a consciousness of his transgression in *Patna*. However, the larger context of his ideal by which he seeks to invest his self with authority already contains the seeds of its own destruction, and leads Jim once again on the path to failure.

Jim's entrapment within his ideal is so thorough that he continues to defend it even when it has become severed from the context in which it possessed its significance. This entrapment is at the basis of Jim's failure to understand Gentleman Brown. And it is at the basis of his failure in self-understanding. There is, of course, a compelling reason behind Jim's response: he refuses to make arbitrary judgments of good and bad. The inquiry into the *Patna* affair by the court has left Jim convinced that no amount of factual data could explain the psychological forces that made him jump. Moreover, to Jim his jump meant an act of unconscious identification with the other transgressors. Yet he saw himself as apart from them, separated by a morality of feeling that he has no grounds for attributing to his partners in the act. With Brown, however, Jim's response is more complex than that of unconscious identification. For, though no direct incriminating evidence against Brown is available to him, his experience in *Patna* has taught him to be wary of any such evidence. For example, after he has promised a clear road to Brown, Jim tells Jewel, "Men act badly sometimes without being much worse than others" (394).

The tragic paradox of Jim's treatment of Brown, however, is that his failure in *Patna* generates a moral insight that cannot provide him with discriminating powers to separate good from bad. Jim's predicament, then, resides in his being an exemplary moral agent whose insight does not just cause but, rather, reveals his moral blindness: it prevents him from using moral concepts. More precisely, Jim so thoroughly equates morality with his conception of the self that he cannot perceive that moral action is helped as well as hindered by others. Intentions, in other words, even if they are motivated by moral impulse, do not necessarily lead to commensurate moral consequences. Gentleman Brown, for instance, takes his frustrated revenge on Jim by killing Dain Waris and his party. Jim, on the contrary, seeks to redeem his honor by letting Dain's father, Doramin, take his life. The result of Jim's conflation of the code of conduct with his egotistical ideal of self is that he cannot understand the propriety of his act of martyrdom with regard either to Jewel or to the people of Patusan. Instead of giving him moral stability, the ideal has now lost its intersubjective value and become detached and inhuman. It is put in the service of death rather than of life. Jim's statement to Marlow that his life was necessary to Jewel, or that the people of Patusan trusted their safety to him, reveals a contradictory relation to his final moral posture. Jewel loses her love, and Patusan is once again open to desperadoes like Brown.

By a peculiar and inexorable logic of thought, however, Jim's final action is unavoidable. When, for instance, Jewel urges Jim to defend himself against Doramin because he had promised her that he would never leave her, Jim says, "I should not be worth having" (412). From the vantage-point of his ideal of self Jim's response is unanswerable. Nevertheless, the moral predicament of Jim's ideal is that it must remain detached from its consequences. Though sprung from the moral practices of his community, it has lost its vital relation to those practices. Patusan is merely a dream-world where the ideal has its full sway for Jim. Enclosed in this solipsistic understanding of his ideal, Jim cannot see that martyrdom and courage have little significance since they are no longer distinguishable from suicide. The meanings of words—"trust," "honor," "courage," and "love"—central to Jim's action have lost their contextual stability or usefulness because the contexts have become merged, because ideal and perversion have become one. The tragic paradox of this sequence of events is that, where Jim had found his own self reflected in Gentleman Brown, Doramin now finds Brown in Jim. The result of this inversion for Jim is that, while Jim says "Nothing can touch me" (413), he is also cut down by the most ruthless principle of revenge. At one level of response a preparedness to accept punishment for his mistake certainly frees Jim from any potential ignominy others may seek to attach to his character. Yet the narrative calls into play that response only in order to complicate and contradict it. For the other, and more compelling, response is that he has purchased his ideal at a spiritual price that involves nothing less than a dehumanization of that self.

Jim does not have a choice because in order for him to think of choice he will have to see himself confronting alternatives. The context of moral choice, in other words, involves a sense of the strength of each available alternative, a sense that helps one determine a choice. Moreover, to experience the tension of alternatives is to make a judgment as to the importance and validity of a choice. Entrapped within his idea, however, Jim cannot make a choice; he is chosen by the ideal he has lived for; the ideal has become his surrogate for living. He therefore cannot even think of his situation in terms of alternatives. To Jewel's plea to fight or escape, Jim replies: "There is nothing to fight for . . . nothing is lost. . . . There is no escape" (412). Jim has thus made a radical choice. And it is inevitable that he should not think of his choice as the result of a reflection on his moral predicament. Jim's radical choice does not allow him to experience his situation as a moral dilemma, nor does it allow him reflection on its consequences. For the Sartrean man radical choice springs from a dilemma but also entails no looking back or remorse on the part of the moral agent.[10] Conrad's treatment of Jim's radical choice, it seems to me, opens up a serious questioning of the very concept of radical choice. Radical choice, from the perspective of *Lord Jim*, is always already infected by the element of chance or contingency. The moral agent (in this case Jim) can escape it only by a romantic idealization of self. The escape, however, is no more than a failure of the consciousness to look upon one's capacity for causing ruin in a moment and through a conjunction of forces over neither of which it has control. Marlow's description of Jim's state of mind clearly illustrates this point. After the news of Dain Waris's death, Jim tries to write a letter—to his father, to Marlow, or to those with whom he is trying to regain his solidarity. But he couldn't write. "The pen had spluttered, and that time he gave it up. There's nothing more; he had seen a broad gulf that neither eye nor voice could span. . . . He was overwhelmed by his own personality—the gift of that destiny which he had done his best to master" (341). Thus the ideal that enabled Jim to invest his life with a semblance of order and hope has now brought him to a point when his choice reveals its radical incoherence.

Thus contrary to the French lieutenant, who recognized that there is a gulf between fear and courage bridged only by an unromantic exercise of duty, Jim takes a radical step. He does not connect the two, he squelches fear. He becomes fearless. Yet the code, we remember, is the result of a recognition of the instinct of fear, a recognition that requires courage for the functioning of the community. Jim's fearlessness, then, is a distortion of the human self, since the community perceives the self as a compound of fear and courage. Jim has therefore assumed an identity which has no connection with the community within which the code of conduct has its meaning and value. It is inevitable that Jim should not only allow himself to be shot by Doramin but also ignore Jewel's desperate but all too human plea to defend himself. For when courage separates itself from the context of other human instincts and relations it has no place for love or responsibility. And it does not recognize the obstacles generated in one's conception of public identity by personal relations.

Nevertheless, to define Jim's last action as a revelation of the failure of his ideal and as a repetition of his jump from *Patna* is to simplify both Marlow's response to Jim and the structure of *Lord Jim*. Indeed, Marlow, in telling the story of Jim's life and in seeking an articulation of his own responses to it, ventures on a forbidden territory for the context of practical life, for a reflection on Jim reveals a fundamental contradiction between the community's concept of moral life and the hidden possibilities within the self—a contradiction that Jim seeks to overcome through his refusal to conceive of human life as a compound of fear and courage. Jim cannot accept the self in its mundane role as entailing small victories and defeats incurred in the performance of one's duty. Yet it is not as if the community views its ideals as pragmatic, having no transcendental ontological status; for, if it did, the door to radical skepticism would be opened. The French lieutenant, for instance, refuses to ponder the consequences of a possible loss of honor because he cannot conceive them apart from a denial of life itself. The community therefore cannot do without ascribing an absolute status to its ideals. Such a status, however, introduces a fundamental duplicity in the life of the community, since it pretends to bring skepticism under control, though at a deeper level it recognizes lying as a necessity in order that intersubjective action and responsibility become meaningful in human life.

This contradiction in the community's conception of its ideals is enabling rather than destructive, since its predication of life on the fulfillment of ideals is compatible with the possibility of failure. For Jim, however, fulfillment of the ideal fully depends on a denial of failure. Consequently, its fulfillment becomes synonymous with death. Yet, if Jim is the product of the contradiction inherent in the community's life between practice and ideal, he is its exemplary representative for having sought to overcome the contradiction. It is, I believe, on this insight that both the force of Marlow's narrative and his interest in Jim depend.

If Kurtz, in *Heart of Darkness*, defines himself by relinquishing his ideals and by rejecting the surface reality that sustained those ideals, Jim defines himself by an opposite response. He relinquishes the truth of experience, the contingency that threatened his confidence in himself in *Patna*, and molds and defines his reality by an unswerving commitment to the ideal. Moreover, while Kurtz remains essentially anonymous and is inaccessible through his potential capacity for multiple roles,[11] Jim is enigmatic and compelling for Marlow through his steadfast grip on his ideal. Jim may even be characterized as arbitrary and artificial, as a character in a book. Yet he remains closer to Marlow's interest because Jim's reality, though heartrending, is a moral reality deriving from the code's inflexibility, a reality for which the community has its own share of responsibility.

Marlow is therefore intended by Conrad to provide a principle of authority by which to view Jim as well as the world within which and out of which Jim moves. The structure and narrative of *Lord Jim*, however, do not sustain this principle but, rather, let it face a confusing reality by which its various constructions begin to lose their solidity. As a consequence, the impressionistic technique that Conrad employs in *Lord Jim* enables him to create and dissolve alternative perspectives. Marlow, for instance, reflects on Jim in order to appropriate the quality of Jim's experience which must remain forever within the area of the inaccessible. For Jim, like Don Quixote, is overdetermined, incapable of conceiving reality realistically. That, however, is precisely the purpose of *Lord Jim*: to question realistic constructions of reality and thereby to bring into view perspectives that would dissolve the boundaries of the familiar. Paradoxically, then, Jim disconnects the link between romantic adventures and books about them on the one hand and his community on the other hand; and he shows the disconnection as a possibility inherent in the very logic of the community's ideals. It is by this paradox that Jim can be comprehended. His initial failure of will ultimately becomes his will to personal authority; failure and success, life and death, become synonymous in Jim's final act in Patusan. This act is martyrdom only from the perspective of his exalted ideal of conduct, for that perspective enfolds within it a commonsense perspective that would recognize that act as suicide. The novel thus does not present the two perspectives as alternatives, but rather as mutually implicated views generating an unresolvable textual ambiguity.

IV

Jim's life, then, takes the shape of real tragedy, though it is important to realize that Marlow's narrative of Jim isn't intended to develop a tragic response. It is only in a superficial sense that Jim's fall is the consequence of historical causality, the intrusion of Gentleman Brown in Jim's idyllic kingdom where the intruder succeeds in manipulating and finally destroying Jim. The deeper reason for Jim's fall, however, lies within Jim himself, in the essence of his identity. It is neither mere malice of others nor their ignorance of Jim but, rather, Jim's ignorance of both himself and the world in which as a human being he must live that has put in motion, almost from the very beginning, the process of his self-destruction. Marlow's narrative, then, tries to decipher the intricacies of this process of self-destruction; and, to the extent that he, too, is an idealist, his narrative celebrates, even as it reveals, the corrosive element underlying Jim's personality. The situation of Jim is a reworking of Greek tragedy in that it is no longer the limited and partial nature of each antagonist's insight, as in *Antigone*, that leads to the conflict and subsequent fall of both. Jim is so completely enclosed within the luminosity of his ideal of self that other considerations do not matter to him.

To Marlow, Jim is a remarkable man because of his refusal to deny his cowardice during the *Patna* incident: "He did not try to minimise its importance. Of that I am sure; and therein lies his distinction" (82). Yet Jim's activities carry, as Marlow suggests, deeply unsettling and contradictory implications; they are imbued with "a sort of sublimated, idealised selfishness" (177). Intensely aware of having leaped, Jim nevertheless blames the other fugitives for his own fatal act: "Oh, yes, I know very well—I jumped . . . but I tell you they were too much for any man. It was their doing as plainly as if they had reached up with a boat-hook and pulled me over" (123). Such remarks make us ask what conception Jim really had of his crime, and what exoneration or atonement he sought. Does he—could he—recognize the true criminality of his act, or does he instead see it primarily as a "chance missed" (83)? Such questions underlie Marlow's remark that Jim "made so much of his disgrace while it is his guilt alone that matters" (177). Consequently, a balanced view of Jim must examine and even question the propriety of his actions following the *Patna* incident. We would need to determine whether Jim has in fact found his redemption, or has only become further mired in the destructive illusions of his "exalted egoism" (416).

Thus Marlow's ironic remark, after Jim's exuberant assertion to him that he has made a "clean slate", reveals the problematic nature of Jim's conduct and perception: "A clean slate, did he say? As though the initial word of each of our destiny were not graven in imperishable characters upon the face of a rock" (186). Jim is quite unaware that he lacks that fundamental restraint essential to human existence.[12] Upon his first direct encounter with Marlow, a single word strips him of "that discretion which is more necessary to the decencies of our inner being than clothing is to the decorum of our body" (74). It would then appear that, from the very beginning, Jim's quest for self-vindication is fundamentally flawed. His actions are prompted by a fatal intermingling of dream and reality. And his egoism marks all of his actions, driving an ineradicable wedge between himself and others, sealing thereby the loneliness in which he pursues his dream as the very substance of reality.

In Patusan, Jim reenacts his fatal leap from *Patna* when he lands deep in the mud, an experience that one may describe as a symbolic reenactment and escape from an earlier crisis. Critics have described Jim's triumphant experience when he successfully overpowers the four assailants, shooting the first one dead and forcing the others to jump off the cliff into the water. With the man dead at his feet, Jim feels himself "calm, appeased, without rancour, without uneasiness, as if the death of that man had atoned for everything" (302). This whole incident, in its context, is Jim's first significant act of courage; he has faced danger, acted with discretion, consummated a symbolic reenactment of his worst visions, and feels for the first time free of his characteristic fierce egoism.[13] And this moment culminates in his recognition and acceptance of Jewel's love. The Patusan phase thus seems to show that Jim has vindicated and fulfilled the sovereignty of his code of conduct by winning the trust of the "old mankind" and gaining peace within.

In fact, however, even before Brown's arrival, Jim remains tragically immersed in isolation and egoism. As my discussion above of Marlow's talk with Jewel suggested, Jim remains completely blind to the anxiety that attends Jewel's love, just as Jewel remains completely ignorant about the invisible fight Jim has been waging against his own past. Their love is defined by a lack of reciprocity in communication engendered primarily by Jim's failure, or, rather, refusal to connect his past with the present. Hence what some critics have characterized as Conrad's descent into the paradigm of romance and consequent weakening of the novel misinterprets the implications of Jim's Patusan phase for the entire narrative of his life.[14] Marlow sees Jim among the people of Patusan as "a creature not only of another kind but of another essence", in "total and utter isolation" (229) from them. The Patusan phase certainly perpetuates the Kiplingesque myth of the white man's nobility, power, and ingenuity, and shows Jim as still a nostalgic figure invented by Conrad's interest in the tradition of colonial adventure romance. For all Conrad's demythologizing critique of imperialism, Jim brings peace and prosperity to a beleaguered island and is an exemplary figure of the colonial myth. And the myth acquires a certain melancholy nobility, since for "all his conquests, the trust, the fame, the friendships, the love—all these things that made him master had made him a captive, too" (247). Yet Jim's utter isolation from Jewel and the people of Patusan keeps him "imprisoned within the very freedom of his power" (283). His relations with Jewel and the people of Patusan are indeed formed by an abstract link which keeps Jim invisibly tied to a different people and different aspirations. The Patusan phase, then, not only contains the essence of Jim's personality, it also dramatizes the problematic that attends both that personality and the ideals it represents. This dramatization occurs, moreover, in a context in which Jim's deeply cherished values, of fidelity to the code of conduct and love, do not simply come into opposition but, rather, reveal their inner alienation from each other in his conduct.

It is Marlow's fate to discover, from the very beginning of his narrative, the forces as it were of negation within the luminous hope that Jim projects. And it is his fate to be unable to intervene in Jim's affairs in a way decisive enough to alter the course of his life. For it is not just the desperadoes such as Brown and Chester who are homeless in this world; men of character and insight such as Stein and Marlow are also homeless. Jim's fate would seem to indicate that he must perish by his own twisted moral drive at the hands of those who have the power or cunning to destroy others. And yet the peculiar power of Jim is that homelessness is rendered implacable by his tenacious pursuit, in the innocence and inexperience of his youth, of the ideals that alone may signal, though not assure, the possibility of overcoming one's homelessness.

Jim's final posture, then, embodies his insistence on affirming his own self, affirming the truth and justice of his essential self. It does not assert the truth and justice of his behavior to Brown, though any critical response to Brown himself must recognize the decency of Jim's attitude to him. Jim's self-affirmation, however, cannot be separated from self-glorification, and it is in the identity of these two that Jim's final posture is morally unsettling in the way that Socrates' decision to meet his death rather than escape for life is not. The tragedy of Jim's stance inheres in his attempt to prove to the world the essential wholeness and integrity of his self. Jim is so completely entrapped within his vision of things, within his affirmation of the abstract ideals of honor and self, that he is alienated from those in relation to whom his values make relative and human sense. His act of imaginative sympathy with Brown, by granting him innocence where he cannot yet prove Brown's guilt, puts in motion forces that will make it impossible for him to engage in morally more crucial acts of sympathy. It is here that Jim's egoism is born, not out of the practical ideal of self-sacrifice made supple and necessary by the context of lived communal interchanges and relations. His egoism contains the germ of a corrosive solipsism which continues to grow until Jim becomes completely separated from his relations and is shown encircled, in the luminosity of his ideal of self, by that peculiar element of darkness captured so trenchantly by Marlow.[15]

Jim was thus put in an implacably paradoxical position by Brown's dastardly act. And the tragedy of Jim's life, which is the fate of a certain species of idealism, of values conceived in a solipsistic and egoistic fashion, is that he could have saved his life only by doing that which would destroy his self-respect. Jim's is an utterly logical choice, a consequence of the implications of the way he has conceived his self and its relation to the world. Jim inhabits the world he himself has created. Jim the romantic idealist lives beyond irony, in the world of metaphor and myth, where heroic action and romantic idealism help constitute his identity and its relation to the community. Love is, for Jim, a contingent aspect of his current situation. To have forged a form of life, as he believes he has, is to have escaped the realm of contingency and accident, uncertainty and anxiety. When the external world intervenes and cannot harmonize with that form of life, it first drives him to his idyllic island and from there into the innermost recesses of his egoism where there cannot be any distinction between life and death, suicide and self-affirmation.

V

Jim's attempt to coincide with himself, which is to say with his ideal, cannot be realized. Jim thinks his integrity derives from some pristine source within his own being, rather than from the community with its pragmatic restraints and its tacit acknowledgment of the difficulties that attend its ideals. Jim indeed takes himself to be larger and more important than the community whose ideal he seeks to represent. This relation to the community blinds Jim to the power and limits of the self. His alienation is simply a more refined and idealized version of his initial separation from his companions in *Patna*, before and after his jump. Thus the self's preoccupation with purity and integrity makes it blind to the sources of the self's power and value. The self, of course, has its basis in the community, but there is no guarantee that either self or community will always be able to meet situations without self-contradiction or moral failure.

It seems to me a characteristic feature of Marlow's narratives in both *Heart of Darkness* and *Lord Jim* that their critiques of life do not culminate in any positive alternatives. Their unmasking, in other words, does not disclose a luminous hope which may render life more valuable. One might be tempted to say that, just as Socratic interlocutors were led by Socratic dialogue to experience the mask-like worthlessness of their lives, Marlow's twin narratives expose his listeners/readers to similar disenchantment. It was a condition, however, of the Socratic interlocutors' disillusionment that they at the same time were reminded of the potentially divine core within themselves, waiting for actualization. This is where Marlow cannot claim to be Socrates, nor his listeners Socratic interlocutors. We might claim to arrive at the understanding and disillusionment experienced by Marlow, though perhaps only at the level of reflective response, yet Marlow's own enlightenment, or ours, can spell no defense of civilization or morality, though it might ask for one. There is a logic to Socratic teaching, and it is the logic of self-improvement leading men to live the good and examined life which alone is worth living. For Marlow, on the other hand, the experience grasped in its full complexity is both bewildering and paralyzing. It provides no logic of self-improvement or the good life. The more deeply life is examined through the abyssal depths of experience, the more shattering are its implications for a logic or ethic that might hope to provide man with order and values.

Trying to be more than what is permitted by the pragmatic conception of life, Jim must finally take his place as a character in a book, as a fantastic figure of romance, though at the same time for Marlow and for us he also destroys the realistic constructions of reality. Jim consequently construes life itself as a book. Personal authority, however, is something for which there will always be contention between life and book although a clear answer will be possible only if a clear separation between them is made, and reality separated from illusion. But that cannot be done. Jim is therefore "one of us" through his tragic endeavor to put life and book together. His self-mystification, though inseparable from his tragic failure, is nevertheless the source of his personal authority, whereas Marlow's experience is one of gradual demystification whereby the depth of reality is seen to lie embedded in illusion. *Lord Jim* is thus a story of the transfer of the principle of authority from Marlow, in whom it is first invested, to Jim, but in traversing the difference between them the real principle of authority that emerges is a questioning of both language and self. For the difference, though it can be imaginatively apprehended, cannot be overcome. Nevertheless, *Lord Jim* would not have its compelling interest for us if Jim did not represent a powerful drive of the human self already implicit in the very tendency of language to invest its concepts with a special ontological status. It is to this tendency that the fundamental tensions which the narrative of *Lord Jim* creates between language and self, ideal and experience can be traced.

The fact, however, that Marlow discloses and questions the tendency of language to invest its concepts with a special ontological status shows the extent to which he refuses to admit that language is absolutely arbitrary. For Marlow language, like the self, is forged within the community, and is inextricably tied to the context of human action and social life. Jim is a product of his community and therefore of the ideals provided by that community. Cut off from his own community, Jim has nevertheless organized his life in order to represent its cherished ideals. In Patusan, though he works as a servant rather than as a colonialist adventure hero who might set himself up as a ruler, Jim has nevertheless made the community dependent on himself and thus contributed to its internal weakness. Thus, though the community is instinctively distrustful of Gentleman Brown and considers Jim's decision to let him go erroneous, its very dependence on Jim makes it incapable of exercising any influence on Jim's decision. This dependence is at the basis of its revenge on Jim, an act that opens its people to external threat and to internal conflict and uncertainty. Jim has in effect worked in a way that prevents this community from evolving its own social-political process for its eventual stability and growth. The narrative of *Lord Jim* explores this aspect of the problems arising from Jim's ideal of self, an ideal whose cultural meaning derives from an entirely different context of lived relations. It is this juxtaposition of the novel's different elements which places its self-referential elements within the perspective of moral and political questions and their relation to human action. In *Nostromo*, which we will discuss next, these questions constitute the heart of Conrad's dramatic interest.

CHAPTER THREE

The Politics of History:
Nostromo

In a letter to his American literary agent, J. B. Pinker, Conrad put aside his characteristic self-lacerating tone and struck a rather positive note about the writing of *Nostromo*, then under way: "It is a very genuine Conrad. At the same time it is more of a Novel pure and simple than anything I've done since *Almayer's Folly*."[1] More than all his earlier novels, *Nostromo* is no doubt a novel "pure and simple"; for all its exotic strangeness, its breadth and scope have antecedents in George Eliot's *Middlemarch*. But there are also things about *Nostromo* which Conrad's remarks do not capture. His later reminiscence about the strain he experienced during the writing of *Nostromo* gives some hints about the nature of his undertaking. There he talks about "the intimacy and the strain of a creative effort in which mind and will and conscience are engaged to the full, hour after hour, day after day, away from the world, and to the exclusion of all that makes life really lovable and gentle—something for which a material parallel can only be found in the everlasting sombre stress of the westward winter passage round Cape Horn".[2] The strain might be attributed not merely to the greater scope of *Nostromo*, but to the bleakness of Conrad's vision of political and material forces operating in history.

Heart of Darkness and *Lord Jim* deal with the relation between man and ideals, as well as the sustenance these ideals provide to the community from which they have sprung. *Nostromo* deals with these same preoccupations, but at a level which is technically and thematically much deeper; they possess a political significance never as fully examined in the earlier tales. *Nostromo* is the first and most compelling of Conrad's political novels overtly to dramatize the unavoidably political nature of human life; yet the dramatization of this Hegelian insight calls into question the confident propositions of both Hegel and Marx about the workings of history.

Conrad's portrayal of *Nostromo*'s major protagonists reveals his explicit preoccupation with the operation of political forces in society. If in the beginning Nostromo stands for unimpeachable fidelity, Charles Gould signifies pragmatic steadfastness coupled with tenacity of moral purpose and clarity, and Decoud represents a skeptical intelligence free from the illusions of all idealizing aspiration. But the novel goes on to dramatize the remorselessness with which history brings about a fundamental reversal of the governing attitudes of these protagonists. Nostromo becomes a thief, Gould a moral and personal failure, and Decoud a sentimental romantic unable, in his loneliness, to withstand the power of his skepticism. *Nostromo* is thus a novel which at first appears diffuse and chaotic, moving in multiple directions; but it gathers a peculiar force from the interweaving and intersecting of its narrative strands. The protagonists, though differing in attitude and perception, are brought into the same arena of historical action. And events culminate in failure or, at best, in a specious form of success which is inseparable from failure. The structure of *Nostromo*, then, reveals a curious logic operating through history in such a way that events initially disparate proceed seemingly in accord with the hopes of men, only in the end to proceed with profound indifference to those hopes. Thus the interweaving of the protagonists' actions and attitudes is not a celebration of the organic unity of art conceived as a matter of detached aesthetic contemplation, nor is it a celebration of history conceived as a Hegelian unfolding of historical progress.

In *Nostromo* Conrad reinvents the story of *Lord Jim* in the arena of socioeconomic historical forces. He seeks to measure the individual in the modern world, especially as the individual aspires to heroic behavior. My reading of *Nostromo* is done partly in terms of character-analysis which shows how the actions of most of the major protagonists contradict their aspirations and reveal the protagonists as far from being in control of either their intentions or their projects. Conrad's portrayal of particular characters in *Nostromo* is attempted, as so often in his other novels, in terms of a phenomenology of behavior and response, a phenomenology that seems to result in a sustained ethical critique of the meaning and implications of their roles as social beings in particular historical and political contexts. The focus on their roles as social beings enables Conrad to raise what appears as an essentially narrow ethical critique to the level of serious political scrutiny of the power and limits of the protagonists' politics.

I

Though on a first reading it is Charles Gould's father who appears to have had a likeness to Lord Jim because, like Jim, he, too, was "well read in light literature" (55—56), in reality it is Charles himself who is closer to Jim. Both Charles and Jim are versions of the self refusing to accept potential or real failure. Conrad's portrayal here of Charles becomes doubled in that, as Albert Guerard has remarked, Gould's dream of empire is a reenactment of Stein's dream—on a vaster and more self-consciously historical scale.[3] Conrad's treatment of Gould struggling to overcome his father's failure with the mine functions, at a different level, as an intertextual endeavor to reconstitute and realize the essential qualities of Stein's vision.

The parallel here between genealogy and intertextuality is not an accidental one, but is inherent in the relation between the generations within a family and the characters in Conrad's novelistic career.[4] In *Lord Jim* Stein's vision and adventure are one until they fall apart and reduce Stein to the status of a helpless romantic sentimentalist. In *Nostromo* Gould's vision and action are motivated by the desire to forge liberty, justice, and progress, until they fall apart and undermine his initial commitment. The nature of Gould's failure, and his failure to comprehend fully the consequences of his unswerving commitment to the mine, are matters I shall discuss shortly, but first I want to clarify Gould's relation to his earlier literary avatar, Lord Jim.

Gould wants to make the mine "a serious and moral success" (65). He wants to replace "the unnatural error of weariness and despair" of his father by "a vigorous view of life" (74). He wants not only to reconstitute the family history, but also to put it at the center of his adopted country's moral and economic success in the future. This venture is as profoundly idealistic as Jim's, since in Gould's case private desire and parental failure prompt him to take a stance aimed at transforming the destiny of a nation. The paradigm of the narrative strand that elaborates Gould's project is derived, like that of *Lord Jim*, from the genre of romance, and its strongly allegorical feature is revealed in the implications Gould supposes the mine's reopening to have for himself as well as for his country. Thus Gould's quest is as comprehensive as Jim's: while seeking to overcome a blight on his past, it is intended to turn "the cause of an absurd moral disaster" (66), the mine, into the very fount of moral good. In this, like Jim, Gould, as Decoud aptly characterizes him, "cannot act or exist without idealizing every simple feeling, desire, or achievement" (214—15).

Gould, however, is a practical idealist, and puts no trust in words as such. There is some justification for his attitude to words, since in the arena of political interests in Costaguana words idealize and even conceal the real motives of politicians and military generals. Yet the picture is more complicated than Gould realizes. Holroyd, the American financier, and many Costaguana politicians put their trust in words as well as in silver, and it is generally the case that they put their trust in words because they believe that their words are connected, in a political-economic sense, with silver. If silver corrupts the judgments of politicians, it also corrupts the judgment of Gould inasmuch as he refuses to consider the impact of silver on Costaguanan politics. And he withholds his judgment in avoiding a critical view of his own posture. For Gould silver carries the authority of words. He can therefore take refuge in "taciturnity" (364); silence represents his mode of communication, and signifies his obstinate and unswerving determination to stay on his chosen course. He of course has a deeply personal reason for his distrust of words and their eloquence. His father "could be eloquent, too" (83), though his eloquence hadn't helped him wrestle successfully with the mine. Parsimonious with words, Gould, like Jim, has little reflective relation to language, and he would like his action to embody what tenacity of purpose words might convey. In that sense, Gould is a transformation and continuation of Jim. His determination is itself the content of the communication he allows. Consequently, Gould, though he may occasionally seem to justify or explain his attitude, considers his stance inherently unquestionable. Conrad's portrayal of Gould thus depends on the considerable logical and moral force he attributes to Gould, but its strength derives from the relentless exposure of its destructive nature—one that Gould can neither grasp nor remedy. Possessed of the vision of liberty, justice, and progress, Gould remains unaware that his vision is already doomed, partly by his own practice. And it is a tragic irony of Gould's life that his avoidance of eloquence, his suspicion of words, will result in his total defeat by the mine.

Though, as Gould tells his wife, "we Goulds are no adventurers" (64), his decision to reopen the mine is a form of adventure. He clothes his adventure, in Decoud's words, "in the fair robes of an idea" (239). Nevertheless, Gould's uncritical commitment to his idea was as inevitable for the functioning of the mine as were the mixed blessings the mine bestowed on Sulaco and the republic. But Gould does not understand that the mine could not remain a neutral repository of material interests in the Costaguanan political process. Gould's feeling, however, that the mine must be prevented from becoming the locus of political corruption has its own moral justification. In fact, as the progression of events in the novel shows, political neutrality, when it is not moral cowardice, is often tantamount to moral compromise. For the desire to ensure neutrality takes on or reveals an imperialist aspect, one that becomes increasingly clear and stark as Gould ties his personal safety to the mine's safety. Gould's action finds its initial trajectory in his desire to succeed where his father had failed; and it takes its course through the arena of political interests in which Gould becomes cut off not only from any redeeming relation with his wife but also from the moral values by which he has seemed to justify the mine. Gould had thought of his father's death as "an absurd moral disaster" wrought by the mine. The course of his own life, however, makes Emilia (and us) feel that his life repeats that disaster in ways that leave him completely self-alienated. Emilia has effectively lost a husband, Gould has lost his moral sanity, and paradoxically Sulaco has made material gains which corrupt its political and social life.

A sense of these losses is evoked many times in *Nostromo*. At one point Gould says to his wife: "I thought we had said all there was to say a long time ago. There is nothing to say now. There were things to be done. We have done them; we have gone on doing them. There is no going back now. I don't suppose that even from the first there was really any possible way back. And what's more, we can't even afford to stand still" (207). The note of detached sadness breaks through Gould's stocktaking attitude to the past and the present, and shows his resolute pragmatic stance caught in a fatalism he would have resisted in the fervor of his youth when he first decided to operate the mine. Now, from the perspective of experience, he realizes the necessity that underlay his seemingly autonomous decision. What is more tragic, of course, is his admission to his wife that there can be no other reflection on the mine, that what could be said was said long ago. This sense of his irrevocable ties to the mine accounts for all his later actions. When the political storm begins to threaten his own safety and his ownership of the mine, the logic of Gould's position forces him into the classic imperialist posture which considers total control of material interests as the sole guarantor of power and success. The power and success, however, are purchased at a cost too great for the moral imperative that initially seemed to justify Gould's interest in the mine.

Gould's intention is to respond to a threat to his life by destroying the mine, if necessary, and this intention reveals the fundamentally perverse nature of his mode of realizing his ideals. Gould's difficulty, however, is deeper still. It stems from his failure to understand his father's outcry over the oppression brought upon the Gould family by the mining concession. The son takes the difficulties of working the mine as primarily having to do with his father's technical incompetence. While this was certainly a factor, it completely obscures from the son's view the crucial factors which brought about the Gould Concession. He ignores the politico-economic ground which created the Concession as a political expedient to extort money from his father. Rather, the son sees the mine as a potential harbinger of moral order in his country. To the extent that he cuts the mine off from its social nexus, he cuts himself off from any effective, morally examined relation to

77

his family as well as to his adopted country. And that, along with his decision to operate the mine, marks the beginning of his inner separation from his wife, and of his isolation from his society.

Nevertheless, Conrad's portrayal of Gould is not that of a capitalist administrator as utter simpleton. Rather, it undermines the assumption that the destiny of a nation or society can be controlled and guided by a single family; it questions the dream of capitalism at a particular stage in its history. The Gould family, seeking to supervise the destiny of Costaguana, does not realize that it is at best an element in the complex and bewildering forces in the country's history. Instead Gould dreams of history as an unfolding of events shaped by an individual's intelligent handling of material resources. Yet Gould has a penetrating insight into the nature of material interests, one that distinguishes him clearly from the arch-capitalist Holroyd. Take, for instance, Gould's observation to his wife: "[Holroyd] may have to give in, or he may have to die tomorrow, but the great silver and iron interests will survive, and some day will get hold of Costaguana along with the rest of the world" (82). In this statement of uncanny lucidity where he sees through the ephemerality of Holroyd and hence of specific individuals Gould himself remains naïvely idealistic about the mine's capacity to be a permanent source of social well-being. He fails to comprehend the irony implicit in his statement, for the statement characterizes historical progress as a deterministic force before which specific individual wills are doomed to remain blind and inefficacious. On this view matter unfolds its own history, and the whole world is inexorably and helplessly, though for its own eventual benefit, entangled in that history; this view of material interests idealizes them as a moral agency.

Gould's glorification of material interests is heightened by his glorification of the weakness of human beings as individuals. Though he considers Holroyd only an instrument in the inexorable process of history, he seems to think he is immune to the destruction and defeat that time and history were to bring upon Holroyd. Because of his total commitment to the mine Gould must conceive of himself as necessary to the proper functioning of material interests. This is why he has to come to identify himself so intimately with the mine that "he promised himself to see it shattered into small bits before he let himself be wrenched from its grasp" (294). He is utterly blind to the mine's power over him; feeling himself at one with the great silver and iron interests, he cannot comprehend his inhuman bondage to them.

Gould's remark about Holroyd is rendered even more uncanny by the description that follows: "They had stopped near the cage. The parrot, catching the sound of a word [Costaguana] belonging to his vocabulary, was moved to interfere. Parrots are very human" (82). The parrot incident is related here in order to expose "the unthinking use of words".⁵ Gould's words, quoted earlier, are mechanical inasmuch as they do not bear a reflective relation to his own life. He is, in other words, human in the sense that the parrot is: his language does not illuminate for him the meaning of his own actions. For Gould, however, words are instruments to be used strictly for practical purposes, rather than means of self-criticism. Consequently, understanding in Gould becomes treacherous, allowing him to criticize others, but not allowing him to comprehend the relation of that criticism to himself. Understanding thus becomes fissured from within in order, perhaps, to protect the human agent who claims it, and historical reflection becomes problematical because it remains cut off from one's own history. The clearest development of this insight occurs in the treatment of Decoud's skepticism.

II

Martin Decoud is a complete skeptic. He has devised what he calls the principles of "a sane materialism" according to which desires alone justify the actions one undertakes. Consequently, he takes Gould's idealism for a sham that shields him from the knowledge of his exploitation of Costaguana's natural resources. It is Decoud's conviction that the concept of disinterested acts operates as a screen to conceal one's real relation to one's actions. True to his conviction, Decoud's initial concern is free from any interest in forcing or determining the course of events in Costaguanan history. Decoud, the ironic journalist, remains ruthlessly detached from the events, disclosing the covert motives and interests that underlie the other protagonists' actions. His accounts—subtle mixtures of verbal elegance and superficial psychological depth—tend to draw his readers into complicity with his detachment. The historical picture that has emerged before Decoud's appearance in *Nostromo* is already bewildering, though Decoud, with his daring observations, renders the entire clouded history suddenly intelligible. This intelligibility justifies, for Decoud, his stance as an ironist. He thus succeeds in doing what Mitchell could not do. Captain Mitchell's history, even where it may appear true, remains naïvely simple. His record provides facts, but they are provided in a fashion that both calls his reading of them into doubt and makes them appear as real features of Costaguana's bewildering history.

The presence of Decoud, on the other hand, is more than just a rhetorical necessity for the structure of *Nostromo*. A personality of his sort is necessary to the internal dynamics of the history being unfolded; without the presence of an ironic personality such as Decoud's, which serves the purposes of both analytical observation and dramatic participation, the impersonal narrator, like the Marlow of both *Heart of Darkness* and *Lord Jim*, would have to enter the arena of action.

"No one is a patriot for nothing" (189). This is the political axiom which enables Decoud to expose others. Nevertheless, he is irresistibly drawn to resist the Montero revolt, even before he is aware of his love for Antonia. When he realizes the intensity of his love, then his participation in events is logical in terms of his skepticism; the principal axiom of this logic is captured in Decoud's remark: "What is a conviction? A particular view of our personal advantage either practical or emotional" (189). But, as he admits, "I suppose I am more of a Costaguanero than I would have believed possible" (176). This complicates his political cynicism, and presents problems for his analysis of Costaguanan politics and for the stance underlying that analysis. These problems concern the role of the skeptic in society, specifically in the context of human actions, and the nature of his relations to others; the complexity of Conrad's portrayal of Decoud derives from his subtle fictional meditation on these problems.

The conjunction of elements in Decoud's growing involvement with the fate of his country and with Antonia represents no simple picture of the skeptic's problematic relation to his world. It is here that the impersonal narrator undermines the self-confidence and clarity which Decoud believes characterize his intentions and acts. For it is a strange form of patriotism which impels Decoud to seek the division of his own country for the sake of realizing his love for Antonia. But it is also inevitable that patriotism should take on such an impure form in a man "with no faith in anything except the truth of his own sensations" (229). Neither love nor patriotism, then, guarantees moral responsibility. This problem becomes all the more acute for Decoud, since his skeptical stance hasn't emerged from the rigors of active life, but from the playfulness of a Parisian boulevardier. Removed from the nexus of patriotism and love, Decoud loses the perspective which has repressed the deeper and darker skepticism that will drive him to suicide.

His patriotism and love, however, are already tinged with the corrosive irony of his playful indifference: "She won't leave Sulaco for my sake. There-fore Sulaco must leave the rest of the Republic to its fate" (215). Thus the skeptic who has discovered an unsuspected element of patriotism in his own self must destroy it in order to free himself from an idealizing attitude (that of patriotism), and opt for what he most desires. As skeptic, then, Decoud ascribes no value to patriotism. Conrad thus reveals the paradox of a political process by which an essentially alien and hostile being—alien and hostile because of his deep-seated skepticism—should author the constitution of Sulaco and persuade others to a secession of Sulaco from Costaguana. Decoud's rootlessness is emblematic of the rootlessness of several major participants in Sulaco's politics. Yet as long as Decoud remains an ironic observer he provides valuable insights into the events he describes and judges, for his insights are not contaminated by personal gains or losses that may follow the turn of events in Costaguana. But this, of course, does not free the ironist from a moral obligation as a member of his society. It only frees him from the urge to idealize the people, or their values, who find themselves embattled. Decoud's political involvement, then, leads him to idealize the state he would like to found, though his idealization is grounded in his love for Antonia and frees him, at least in his own mind, from any charge that he, too, is an idealist like Gould or Holroyd. As Decoud says, "No man of ordinary intelligence can take part in the intrigues of *une farce macabre*" (135). Ironically, this applies to himself as much as to others, though he does not realize the extent of his own complicity. Thus Decoud's mode of being is constituted by a rhetoric of ironic criticism, but as soon as he becomes serious and participates in action he is out of his element. The logic that informs his action is not so much false as it is unrelated to his identity as a human being. This identity, constituted by ironic playfulness and moral indifference, reveals its great fragility as he begins to take an interest in Antonia.

Decoud's skepticism prevents him from seeing human beings as bearers of meaning. What he does or refrains from doing, what he values or subjects to his scrutiny, necessarily implicates his own self in the socio-historical world permeated with meaning and value created by human beings. Such meaning and value, however devoid of transcendental substance, are at the basis of all human action. Love for Antonia drives him to participate in events that otherwise were only occasions for his ironic judgment. His interest in the destiny of Sulaco is now tied to his private desire, and thus he feels he is right in proposing the secession of Sulaco from Costaguana. From his skeptical perspective others are not merely ignorant of their desires, but even devoid of them, since their desires have become sublimated by aspirations and ideas. Consequently, what clarity of perception and sense of action Gould, Don José, Nostromo, and others might possess are really abstract and false because as ideas they are unconnected to their sentient being.

Decoud, in other words, romanticizes himself as a human agent in claiming a knowledge of the passions that underlie his actions and ideas. He believes he is connected to the deepest sources of his being which, on his account, would seem to be founded on the sensations of his physical and psychological self. This is an interesting complication of the skeptic's relation to history and to his own self; he denies to others that knowledge which enables him to participate in the events of history. He thus takes himself for a privileged participant in Sulaco's history, whereas others are victims of their illusions. He does not realize that the skeptic cannot write a record of history that would necessarily be better than the one produced by Don José, and his initial feeling that his detachment assures him accuracy in reading history is a pre-critical prima-facie conviction that he understands events better than others. Decoud, however, can claim no justification for his feeling that his stance grants him some form of objectivity that others may be constrained to accept. Once he decides to enter the arena of political action, he is, in principle, no more detached than Don José. Driven by love, Decoud has forsaken the detachment of his ironic perspective; the story of his life is one about the difficulties of the skeptic in his relation to the world. Love makes it impossible for him to maintain his skepticism, and his philosophical stance makes it impossible to sustain the hope without which love is an empty abstraction. Thus the relation between love and skepticism is not just problematical but antithetical. This, as we shall see later, is the relation Conrad would thematize more directly, almost schematically, in *Victory*. Though love reveals Decoud in his human response, Conrad does not treat him in a simple manner. Decoud, for instance, is not shown as having lost the capacity for skeptical criticism of others; instead, love and skepticism generate contradictions that become fatal in his life.

As the narrator observes, Decoud has "pushed the habit of universal raillery to a point where it blinded him to the true impulses of his own nature" (153). This undercuts Decoud's conception about his own self, about the nature and source of his response to the world. His words to his sister suggest his undistorted relation to his own desire when he castigates "the sentimentalism of the people that will not do anything for the sake of their passionate desire, unless it comes to them clothed in the fair robes of an idea" (239). His presumed skeptical sanity succumbs, however, to a more disabling skeptical response when his love for Antonia presents itself to him in the guise of an illusion: "I have only the supreme illusion of a lover" (189). This is an unsettling consequence of the skeptic's power of introspection, though Decoud is disturbed by this reflection. "That can lead one very far, though," he inaudibly mutters (189). Yet skepticism gives him no respite, so that he experiences love only in the negating context of skepticism. How can he experience love without perceiving it as illusory, without being alienated within? And how can he sustain his supreme illusion of a lover when, in the solitude of his island, he is so completely removed from the presence of Antonia?

Consistent with the skeptical stance which now takes its revenge on him, Decoud can feel his sensations only in the form of a conviction of his utter futility before nature's immense indifference. The history that he treated with witty playfulness is not there to deflect his attention from his own self which is no longer distinguishable from non-being. The felt logic of his experience now finds consonance with the island solitude of nature which embodies the total context of that logic. In committing suicide Decoud is, as it were, subsuming himself under that force whose real impact he had escaped in the play of a demystifying intelligence engrossed in the absurd historical spectacle in Sulaco; he is swallowed up by that which he had imperfectly apprehended. Decoud's failure is the failure to grasp that his skepticism was sustained by the historical events he exposes to irony and ridicule. His metaphysics is useful precisely to the extent that it allows him a limited perspective on history; when he is removed from the context of actual history, his metaphysics leads to inner alienation and suicide. Decoud remains cut off from his own nature and from grasping the consequences of the stance he has taken to the world.

III

If the most important structural elements of *Nostromo* are the complex parallels, on the one hand, between Gould and Nostromo and, on the other, between Decoud and Doctor Monygham, the novel's most compelling thematic element is the subtlety with which the change in Nostromo's personality is dramatized. His personality bears within it the contradictions and confusions of his own society; this is clarified for us by Decoud and Teresa Viola, who provide perhaps the most crucial insight into Nostromo's behavior.

In his journal Decoud makes a remark that goes to the heart of Nostromo's character: "The only thing he seems to care for . . . is to be well spoken of. . . . He does not seem to make any difference between speaking and thinking" (246). Like Gould and Jim, Nostromo is parsimonious with words, and has little reflective relation to language, but unlike them Nostromo values words of adulation from others. Before the journey with Decoud to the island Nostromo is, in an egotistical way, sustained by the praise he receives for his courage and fidelity. His words to the dying Teresa Viola capture the essential superficiality of his moral character: "It concerns me to keep on being what I am: every day alike" (256). In the midst of changing and embattled historical forces Nostromo seems stable and trustworthy, as the natives do not. He views himself as others do, and is thus relieved from a reflective relation to the welter of events in Costaguana.

Teresa Viola's accusations reveal a dimension of Nostromo's character not immediately apparent, although it is a constitutive feature of his being: "You never change, indeed. . . . Always thinking of yourself and taking your payment out in fine words from those who care nothing for you" (253). He is characterized here as being utterly selfish and naïve, though both features are hidden from Nostromo by the apparently sustaining nature of his public identity. For Teresa the people who praise him have little real interest in him, and Nostromo, dupe that he is, is blind to the real nature of his relation to others, which is that of serving the European interests in Sulaco. Consequently, the protection he provides for the Viola family remains within the domain of his public identity, since it only confirms his reputation for courage and fidelity. It is only fitting that Nostromo does not ponder Teresa Viola's accusations or fulfill her deathbed wishes. For Nostromo, his rejection of her purely private wishes cannot diminish his achieved identity; indeed, to fulfill those wishes would undermine his unthinking allegiance to the public responsibilities, which is at the basis of his personality.

The unreflecting naïveté of Nostromo's consciousness, the consequences of which he cannot possibly understand or control, may be illuminated by placing some of his statements in the contexts of his actions. Take, for instance, the moment when Nostromo explains to Decoud why he had not killed Hirsch upon discovering him in the boat: "I could not do it. Not after I had seen you holding up the can to his lips as though he were your own brother" (284). Moments before this Nostromo had been fretting about not having fulfilled the dying Teresa Viola's final wishes, and feeling what would be later described as a "burden of sacrilegious guilt" (420). Later, with Doctor Monygham, Nostromo would see Hirsch's corpse hanging by a rope, and experience a pity utterly unconnected to the fate of Decoud, whom he had seen as Hirsch's savior-brother. The point of these juxtapositions is that Nostromo's compassion for Hirsch, both in life and in death, has no real depth of feeling. Moreover, his compassion, rather than being simply an implicit ironic commentary on his eventual betrayals of Decoud and the Viola family, is a corrosive element in a self which is not founded in community and hence in relations of reciprocity; his public identity is the product of forces that render it unthinking and hollow. Teresa Viola's characterization of him is therefore apt. Nostromo does not understand the forces that sustain his public identity. When he begins to understand them, he becomes self-divided, duplicitous, and corrupt. This is not just an ethical observation about Nostromo's disintegration; it is also a genealogical analysis of the foundations of his ethics in relation to the material and political interests prevailing in his society.

Prior to his disintegration Nostromo's ethic is simply a moralistic appearance buoyed up by the network of political-economic interests he serves. The power of this network is in its ability to create a man of the people, for the people, and to make him serve values and interests neither the people nor he, their idealized representative, would support. Nostromo thus is a hollow man; his being so is the price of his heroism in his society at its particular moment in history. And when Nostromo does acquire a self-consciously founded identity that identity is cut off from any effective relation to the public domain which guided his former sense of self. During the fateful journey to the island, in the absence of others to applaud and sustain him, Nostromo discovers the truth about others' exploitation of him; but in his morally schizoid way he remains blind to its psychological implications for his own nature. And it is here that Conrad's treatment of Nostromo becomes subtle and compelling, for given the nature of his relation to the public domain Nostromo cannot have any insight into either the forces that have constituted his ego or the transformation that is beginning to take place in him.

Before his journey to the island, we are never given a glimpse of what Nostromo might be apart from his public identity, because up to that point he has had no private self—none, that is, that differs from the public self which acts to draw praise from others. Nostromo is "our man" precisely because he is "no man". The magic of his incorruptible public self begins to dissipate when he undertakes the journey to save the treasure of silver. The danger of the task awakens a self-consciousness that questions his assumption of confidence and authority. The idea of a heroic adventure, in the solitude of the Golfo Placido, with no one but a skeptical politician and journalist to watch and admire, is utterly alien to him. The sheer privacy of the task intensifies both the sense of the danger involved and the fear of public disgrace should he fail. He loses his composure, for the usual support of his identity has vanished, and now the man of courageous action becomes voluble and unnerved. His words to Decoud about Hirsch thus convey meanings he could not have intended. For us these words take their full resonance in the context of his earlier refusal to grant Teresa's deathbed request and his later betrayal of both Decoud and the Viola family.

On his return from the island Nostromo is shown awakening from a long sleep. The awakening, as several critics have remarked, reveals a landscape of death and decay.[6] Nostromo has entered a new symbolic order within which he is no longer incorruptible; shortly thereafter, coming upon Doctor

Monygham, Nostromo tells lies. When he finally agrees to take the train ride to bring Barrio's army, it is not because he has made a critical decision about his own obligation in the context of events in Sulaco; it is only that he has been flattered by Monygham. This heroic and public act will be undertaken in complete disregard for the safety of Decoud, whose meager supply of food will not save him, for more than a few days, from starvation. His heroism thus becomes tainted with the egotism denounced by Teresa Viola. Having developed a private self, and left to his own devices, Nostromo will now have no one to reproach him for his betrayal of Decoud.

At this stage Conrad's depiction of Nostromo's contradictions and confusions is consummate art. When Nostromo returns with Barrio's army, he jumps into the dinghy because he wants to find out if he is the sole possessor of the buried treasure, not because he is remorseful for deserting Decoud. Once he has discovered Decoud's disappearance and possible death, Nostromo resolves to live with his double identity, maintaining the semblance of his former public self while nurturing his new greed and corruption. The double identity, as I have suggested, is not as antithetical as it might at first appear, since his public identity, essentially hollow and naïve, contains in a concealed form the foreshadowings of the self that will be revealed in the end. The Conradian paradox in Sulaco's newly won independence is that Nostromo, perhaps the crucial actor in the drama of events, has lost his own independence; he has become a slave to the silver hidden on the island. And the paradox grows. Nostromo by now has come to recognize his former public identity as a sham, and now literalizes the sham in order to hide the truth from others. What Nostromo does in private will have consequences for what he might do in the public arena—an arena filled with self-motivated and self-destructive interests, ostensibly devoted to transpersonal goals.

Nostromo's enslavement to the silver is so binding that he is forced to echo and obscure his theft for the rest of his life. It affects especially his relations with the Viola family. Afraid that Linda, with her father's austerity and her mother's reproachful sternness, will condemn his theft and betrayal, Nostromo develops an illicit passion for Giselle, who he thinks will approve of his plan to become "rich slowly" (544). Thus Nostromo's thieving and illicit passion dramatize the helplessness of a man whose consciousness of his own former exploitation by others has no liberating consequences for him and for his community. This, I think, is the essence of *ressentiment* conceived in tragic historical terms, which will become clearer as we discuss Nostromo's confession to Emilia Gould. In the beginning his actions and attitudes had a specious unity, a unity which was really the absence of reflective thought on his part; toward the end the unity has broken apart, and his private self has no connection to the public identity he still wishes to preserve. But now that public identity is in the service of a private and corrupt end there can be no connection between his past incorruptible self, however naïve and unreflective, and the current false semblance of that self:

> A transgression, a crime entering a man's existence, eats it up like a malignant growth, consumes it like a fever. Nostromo had lost all his peace; the genuineness of all his qualities was destroyed. He felt it himself, and often cursed the silver of San Tomé. His courage, his magnificence, his work, everything was as before, only everything was a sham. (523—24)

Bereft of his self-confidence, Nostromo's is an "unhappy consciousness", one that is tied to his corruption and self-division. I borrow the notion of "Unhappy Consciousness" from Hegel, though I do not employ it here in the strictly Hegelian sense. In Hegel, Unhappy Consciousness, an enormously complicated concept, is a stage in the process of self-consciousness. It is a state of the alienated soul; it seeks to overcome the contradiction and split that characterize the self but is unable to at this stage.[7] Nostromo's is an unhappy consciousness in that he has moved from a simple self-certainty, founded in his public identity, to a state which is characterized by a split within himself. This split is at least partly the result of genuine insight into his relation to society. He now feels that "What he heard Georgio Viola say was very true. Kings, ministers, aristocrats, the rich in general, kept the poor in poverty and subjection; they kept them as they kept dogs, to fight and hunt for their service" (415). Though he has gained an insight into his real relations with those he serves, his insight is bound up with his corruption; it is a rationalization which brings him no closer to the people who, like him, are exploited by the powerful.

This insight, in its distorted form, is at the basis of his confession to Emilia Gould before his death. Nostromo says:

> And Decoud took four. Four ingots. Why? *Picardia!* To betray me? How could I give back the treasure with four ingots missing? They would have said I had purloined them. The doctor would have said that. Alas! it holds me yet! (559)

Thus Nostromo begins his confession with the rationalizing of a thief, though he has a certain logic on his side (for we know that four ingots were missing and Decoud was the only person privy to the treasure's site). Yet as readers we have a fuller perspective on Nostromo. He had carefully inspected the dinghy with its bloody spot which had given him some idea of Decoud's fate. He had, in fact, abandoned Decoud to die, since he had told no one about Decoud's scant provision of food. And now he construes Decoud's disappearance as an act of betrayal, a construal that entraps him in telling and living a lie. When Emilia asks Nostromo about Decoud's fate he replies:

> Who knows? I wondered what would become of me. Now I know. Death was to come upon me unawares. He went away. He betrayed me. And you think I killed him. You are all alike, you fine people. The silver has killed me. It holds me yet. Nobody knows where it is. (559)

Nostromo's accusation here that Decoud betrayed him is a blatant avoidance of his own betrayal of Decoud. But he rightly senses the accusation in the minds of others that he killed Decoud. The terrible truth that Nostromo does acknowledge is that the silver has taken him into bondage, but he cannot see that this bondage deprives him of any redeeming sense of remorse over his betrayal of Decoud. He can now offer to disclose the location of the hidden silver, but he knows that it will change nothing. Emilia's sympathetic statement that "No one misses it now" (560) reflects her feeling that in view of a life lost the silver has no value. It is not that Emilia does not want the truth to become known; it is that such a truth would make no real amends either in Antonia's life or in her own.

Nostromo's confession thus is dramatically compelling because it is the effort of his ambivalent and resentful imagination, which seems to confess guilt and wrongdoing, yet seeks to justify the betrayal. However, it could be dismissed as rationalization only by a moralistic attitude that fails to take into account the complex interplay of historical and personal elements in Nostromo's situation. By confessing to the only person he considers pure and above politics, Nostromo puts his faith in confession as an act of moral value. By his confession he may not only regain the sense of his incorruptibility, but also put the burden of guilt on those who gave him the most dangerous of tasks; it is as if betrayal were part of the task of escorting the silver treasure. He had assumed the magical fidelity of his public self would protect him from the corrupting force of the silver, only to find he was a simple man of the people, unequal to a challenge that lay so far outside his lived experience.

Before he is accidentally shot there are no lengths to which Nostromo would not go in order to avoid being detected, to keep the treasure to himself. He thus has Georgio take charge of the lighthouse, so he may visit the island without giving rise to suspicion. Nostromo has always viewed personal relations as trifling in comparison to public and potentially spectacular occasions for action; it is inevitable that his betrayal of Teresa Viola should repeat itself, in a far more complicated manner, in his treacherous disregard for Decoud. And it is also inevitable that his confession be an act of duplicity, bitterness, and confusion rather than a distilled essence of his real intentions and motives in relation to his deeds; he cannot truly be said to possess a capacity to confess. Confession as a concept is totally alien to his mode of living, to his public identity as the incorruptible captain of the Cargadores. Given all of this it is not possible, even at the moment of his confession, that Nostromo should know and mean what he needs to say if his confession is to have any efficacy.

From the very beginning of his career Nostromo's authority was without moral sanction because it was not tied to the aspirations of his community. This is not a criticism of Nostromo's personality so much as a disclosure of the conditions that confront a person like Nostromo in a society in pervasive economic and political disarray. Nostromo might be considered a type produced by the nature and history of his society, and his career the unfolding of a trial staged by capitalism. When he becomes self-conscious, he also becomes confusedly aware of the deeply entrenched contradictions within him. Though he seeks to retain his reputation he cannot look back upon his past in a nostalgic manner. Nor can he find consolation in his present condition; he is truly entrapped. Each of his major actions—his letting Teresa die without the priest she requested, his stealing the silver treasure, his abandoning Decoud to his tragic fate, his illicit love for Giselle while engaged to Linda, and even his confession—has an inexorable and awesome logic to it. Strictly speaking, these were not choices made by Nostromo but, rather, choices dictated by the whole context of his circumstances. The tragedy of Nostromo is that, given his identity, formed by historical conditions, he did not have the freedom necessary for making his actions consonant with deliberate choices. Nostromo, like Gould, is an individual fundamentally determined by the nature and history of his society.

Nostromo, of course, makes specific choices, but he eventually realizes how misplaced his allegiances were, though he does not quite understand why they were misplaced. Given his public identity, Nostromo is not afforded the occasion to discover what he is, or what the implications of his actions are, or the extent of his responsibility for the turn of events in Costaguana. He can neither raise these questions nor answer them, yet he cannot escape responsibility for his share of the blame. In this respect he is like Charles Gould, and both are utterly unlike Kurtz, who was privileged to consort with evil, to denounce himself for having made a pact with it, or to denounce life itself for its inability to resist the evil and blankness he has discovered in all existence. Like Nostromo, the society which has formed him is itself embroiled in the conflicts and contradictions partly native to it and partly introduced by foreign interests. His helplessness is emblematic of the helplessness of his society, especially of his own people, before the ideological and technical resources of an imperialism which exploits them.

IV

The only person who retains his detachment and refuses to idealize his action is Doctor Monygham. He puts no faith in economic interests, and is skeptical toward all political action. This stance, far from contributing to the perverse political process, grants Dr Monygham strikingly true insights into Sulaco's economic-political history. He tells Emilia Gould:

> There is no peace and no rest in the development of material interests. They have their laws, and their justice. But it is founded on expediency, and is inhuman; it is without rectitude, without the continuity and the force that can be found only in a moral principle. Mrs. Gould, the time approaches when all that the Gould Concession stands for shall weigh as heavily upon the people as the barbarism, cruelty, and misrule of a few years back. (511)

But this insight breeds no false sense of personal triumph or historical mission; to Monygham the historical process is devoid of logic and mercy.

Like Jim, Doctor Monygham is acutely conscious of his failure, a transgression committed in youth, under torture. Unlike Jim, however, he does not idealize himself or the values which blind him to the nature of events around him. Jim acts with a self-blinding conviction in his values, but Monygham never loses his stoic detachment, even in moments of arduous hope, as when he attempts saving Charles for Emilia's sake. Jim's idealism makes him flee his past and his transgression; to maintain his confidence he must even deny that a transgression really occurred, except in the form of a contingency that caught him unawares. Monygham, on the other hand, is a skeptical idealist who countenances no excuses. Jim's endeavor to deny his past is a product of his romantic idealism which Monygham would castigate as self-adulatory and self-destructive. It is an appropriate irony of the narrative that Monygham saves Gould through a fraudulent scheme invented to thwart Sotillo through his own greed. Unlike Monygham, the way Jim deals with the desperado Gentleman Brown is the result of his own self-deception. Jim has placed trust in Brown because he uncritically trusts himself, and sees in Brown a mirror-image of himself. Brown's deception of Jim is, in a manner of speaking, an objectification or externalization of Jim's self-deception. Being self-deceived, Jim cannot see that Brown is deceiving him for his own reasons; the fragility of Jim's self-confidence requires that he grant Brown a purity of motives he must grant himself and expect others to acknowledge as well. Monygham's own terrible betrayal hasn't cut him off from his past so much as it has complicated his present. During the many years since his betrayal, he has kept himself on the margins of Sulaco society, serving as usefully as he can as a doctor. And he moves toward the center of the action because he thinks his old betrayal will inspire confidence in the rapacious Sotillo. Sotillo is another version of Gentleman Brown, and Sotillo's behavior, almost like Brown's, is bound up with greed and viciousness. Monygham's self-denigrating skepticism, his refusal to deceive himself, on the other hand, enable him to wrest a certain moral victory even through an act of deception, whereas Jim's entrapment within his idealism produces moral heroism inseparable from tragic self-deception. Through Monygham, Conrad seems to reclaim an element of the romance paradigm, though in a radically altered fashion from its use in *Lord Jim*, since in *Nostromo* a moral victory involves the use of deception, reprehensible to a romantic idealist.

Monygham is a practical moralist who maintains a skeptical stance toward the maddening historical reality around him. His is an unhappy consciousness, but, unlike Nostromo's, his is ethically directed, and links irony with morality; in this, it resembles the consciousness of Marlow in *Heart of Darkness* and *Lord Jim*. I will discuss this further in the last section, but for now let me say that Conrad is more indulgent to Dr Monygham than to anyone else, except perhaps Emilia Gould. Though maimed, Monygham is the true moral hero—he accomplishes what Jim, with his youthful strength and essential decency, fails to accomplish. Monygham's form of moral heroism repudiates the romantic paradigm which Marlow's narrative of Jim tries to depict and question; still, Monygham's success reenergizes this paradigm, infusing it with sobriety and skeptical realism so alien to romance in its traditional form. *Nostromo* is part of Conrad's rethinking of the genre of romance; it continues the questioning of the genre and its values, a task begun in *Almayer's Folly* and *An Outcast of the Islands* which realizes considerable success in *Heart of Darkness* and *Lord Jim*.

The price Monygham pays for genuine self-realization is the dislike others feel toward him; he is not a hero in their eyes. Yet he has been astoundingly heroic—in a way people could not have foreseen. Monygham's action is inspired by the sincere selfless love that he feels for the sincere selfless Emilia Gould. His betrayal, we remember, was betrayal of friendship; and now, in his maturity, what matters is fidelity to his emotional bond with another human being. By the cunning exploitation of Sotillo he brings about circumstances that resemble the events that had led him to his betrayal; but now he empties them of their terrible content. This resolute confrontation with the past puts an impassable distance between his present and his tragic past. Jim, on the contrary, sought to deny the past and was thus enslaved by it. Monygham takes up and completes the task Jim could neither understand nor hope to finish. Thus the careers of Jim, Decoud, Nostromo, and Charles Gould trace heroism as it is bound up in varieties of inner failure, but Monygham's career ends in an act of moral heroism that undermines the heroism of his more self-conscious counterparts. He had not decided upon heroic action, for he never entertained a heroic or idealizing conception of himself; it was only that an opportunity suddenly presented itself enabling him to affirm his tender feelings for Emilia Gould. His personal heroism was a mere byproduct of his sentiment for Emilia, a sentiment that would have remained unchanged, though it might have remained hidden had the occasion for his act not arisen.

V

The major protagonists of *Nostromo* are driven to act by a romanticization of their roles in history. Each has an idealizing life-project which he hopes to realize but which the actual unfolding of his life complicates; for the life-project does not remain under his control for long, but takes on its own power that determines the limits of what he can and cannot do. The novel thus dramatizes the conditions that define the limits of autonomy that the characters seem to assume for themselves. It is a dramatized discourse on freedom, autonomy, and history, showing the blindness of many of the protagonists to the implications of their ideas and actions. The narrative of *Nostromo*, however, is not confined to this level of exploration. It recognizes the need for technological and scientific advance, but recognizes as well that social-historical forces do not harmonize with such advance. In their contingency, these forces, however recurrent in man's history, are catastrophic. Thus the vision of hope puts into motion forces that tend to subvert that vision.

Gould, for instance, is a materialist for whom matter has primacy over mind, and material-scientific advance is unavoidable for a complex and populous civilization; the mind, for Gould, could not entirely achieve its own forms of freedom. Conrad explores many ways in which human beings unthinkingly pursue autonomy from the forces of history which are at least partly those generated by matter; and the nineteenth-century myth of progress, in spite of our disillusionment, is of supreme importance in *Nostromo*. Conrad's questioning of the myth implies the same for the myth of our own epoch when the myth has become a monstrous fact in its own right. We cannot do without technology, or without the pursuit of science that leads to technology: we are materialists, as Gould was. Thus Conrad's exploration of the dynamics of failure, of the subversion of hope, is very much that of contemporary society and its politics.

Economic and political activity in Costaguana is the very cause of violence and disorder. Complete detachment leads to Decoud's dilettantism and irony, Nostromo's naïveté, and Gould's political and moral degradation. Moreover, Costaguanan political regimes change with harrowing rapidity, politicians and generals scrambling from one alliance to another, all in the name of liberty and democracy, though in fact to gain personal power and wealth. As Fredric Jameson puts it, *Nostromo* is about the coming of capitalism in a world which is not prepared for it.[8] The native culture has had no time to develop a mature political sense, or a sense of national problems around which conflict and debate might take place. Thus, for instance, General Montero abandons the Riberist cause at the first sign of a popular uprising; he leads the opposition to the very regime that had entrusted him with its highest military power. Gamacho's demagogic rhetoric is a parody of political discourse, and Sotillo panics over General Montero's imminent arrival in Sulaco, which would make his own position politically precarious. The ideal of parliamentary democracy finds its degraded form in Lopez; Pedro Montero hopes to play the enlightened statesman, a duc de Morny, to General Montero, his Louis-Napoleon.

Costaguana's frenzied politics is a parody of the political process; it lacks the enabling fictions of logic and legality, underscoring the absurdity of those Europeans, including Gould, who wanted to export their political institutions to a society neither prepared for them, nor flexible enough in its own tradition to assimilate them. Events in Costaguana, then, reenact Kurtz's imperialist dream and its brutal parody, but on a scale larger and more elaborate than that of *Heart of Darkness*. The imperialist dream begins as reason's self-conscious entry into the arena of political-economic forces, an entry reason hopes will overcome the chaos of passions which pervade these forces. Hegel's celebrated concept of the Cunning of Reason holds that, though men follow their passions, they in fact end by serving some world-historical purpose of which they are unconscious. Similarly, Adam Smith, Hume, and others before Hegel praised capitalism because they believed that it would bring about greater good and justice in society, while at the same time repressing, perhaps eliminating, destructive tendencies of our human nature. In *The Wealth of Nations*, for instance, Adam Smith proposed a strong economic justification for the unchecked pursuit of individual self-interest; but he also felt that increase in wealth and retrenchment of political power go together, which leaves his attitude toward material progress ambivalent. For he insisted that political progress is neither a consequence of, nor a prerequisite for, economic advance. Nevertheless, the idea that dominated nineteenth-century political thought—conceived variously as Adam Smith's notion of the Invisible Hand or Hegel's Cunning of Reason or Marx's dialectical materialism—was that destructive passions could be transformed by economic progress. But neither Adam Smith nor Hegel nor yet Bernard Mandeville, who dramatized the idea in *The Fable of the Bees*, shows how a financier tycoon like Holroyd or an administrative wizard like Gould might accomplish this transformation.[9]

The point of my small excursus in the history of ideas is that in *Nostromo* Conrad undermines the idealism which aligns capitalism with morality, justice, and order. It is an alignment with a long history in Western thought, beginning in the seventeenth century and acquiring rich and systematic expression in Adam Smith, Hume, Hegel, and others. The American financier Holroyd seems both to exemplify and to reject Adam Smith's view of the relation between economic strength and political power. He exemplifies it in that he would like to give laws for everything, and rejects it in that political power does not interest him unless it yields large profits. The irony of Costaguana's history is that self-interests, far from being a countervailing force against the passions, contribute to arbitrary despotic folly in governments; Montero's argument to Gould, his wanting total possession of the mine, is a most dramatic illustration.

One of the major themes of the novel is that the main characters learn little from the past; they reinscribe the problems of the past in the present. This is, of course, the genealogical distortion of history, whereby the present is viewed in an unproblematical relation with the past. Gould's naïve notion that the past is just an obstacle to get rid of leads him to idealize the mine, which in fact belongs in the network of historical and economic forces; the mine exists apart from the allegorizations that Gould and others construct around it. Decoud and Nostromo, in their turn, allegorize the mine and its silver, attempting to reorder unmanageable forces of history; they also see their historical present as a detached reality amenable to their manipulations. Thus Charles Gould, Decoud, Nostromo, and the other participants in Costaguanan politics do not stand over and above historical forces, but are, as Michel Foucault would suggest, functional elements in the vectors of power relations in history.[10] Their choices may spring from their desires, but the choices cannot find unproblematical manifestations in actual practice. Gould, for instance, chooses to safeguard material interests; but his choice perverts the very meaning of progress for Costaguana, since the progress he envisions has little relation to the happiness which human beings seek.

Gould had of course taken up the challenge of the mine, wishing to succeed where his father had failed. To announce his potential failure from the very beginning is to assume a complacent sense of superiority, for his commitment to the mine was as necessary as the aspiration of Costaguanans for material progress and political stability. That neither can be realized as an imagined project of men is a dominant theme in *Nostromo*; it reveals the relentlessness of the historical process, while denying that historical processes are logically predictable or (as Marxists would put it) that a form of necessity operates in history. Though events seem deeply interconnected, they defy the expectations and aspirations of men. The conflicts of men are compounded by the historical process itself, which generates contingencies that wrench apart any dialectical process of history which men may hope will transform the present.

Conrad himself no doubt remains committed to an ethical stance which underlies the denunciations by Monygham and Emilia Gould. Nevertheless, the novel itself is more complex, and does not reduce its complex evaluations to the moral certitudes and pessimism of either Monygham or Mrs Gould. Consider, for instance, Monygham's ethical assertion:"There is no peace and no rest in the development of material interests. They have their law, and their justice. But it is founded on expediency, and is inhuman; it is without rectitude, without the continuity and the force that can be found only in a moral principle" (511). Monygham here sunders morality from politics, from the context of struggles between those who possess property and power and those who are dispossessed and strive for equality and justice. As long as morality is placed above embattled forces in material and political contexts, one can, like Monygham, maintain moral detachment and castigate all who are engaged in struggle. But this morality which makes its negative judgment while assuring itself of its own truthfulness is in fact alienated and abstract. No amount of personal good deeds performed by Monygham and Emilia Gould can help minimize the fact of their essential helplessness in the larger historical drama unfolding before them. It is not a matter, however, of the helplessness of morality as such but, rather, a matter of the helplessness of a morality that remains cut off from the nexus of economic and political forces.

Monygham's remark that the development of material interests is "founded on expediency, and is inhuman" represents a firm metaphysical view of history and reality, one that is characteristic of Conrad's own attitude. Monygham holds his ethical stance in the teeth of his dark metaphysics, very much as Conrad himself often appears to balance his metaphysical pessimism with a commitment to moral values. The tendency to see the arena of social and political action as irremediably caught up in moral evil is made explicit in Mrs Gould's attitude: "There was something inherent in the necessities of successful action which carried with it the moral degradation of the idea" (521). The metaphysical pathos underlying Mrs Gould's attitude is similar to that underlying Monygham's remark, but it does not generate in her the cynicism characteristic of Monygham or the pessimism characteristic of Conrad. She remains committed to her idealism founded on daily good deeds for the poor and the sick.

The ethical stances of Monygham and Emilia Gould are idealistic. The novel, however, radically challenges them by placing the activities of the bandit Hernandez in opposition to the oppressive landlords and corrupt government. The bandit is not marked as a thief but, rather, presented as a figure that interrogates the institution of private property. It is this interrogation which alters the very meaning of Nostromo's theft and gives a new complexion to Nostromo's later behavior. What Nostromo takes to be a theft is the result of his uncritical acceptance of the capitalist ethic which pervades his own working class, though it is an ethic produced and promulgated by the capitalists for perpetuating their own status in society. Nostromo has now acquired an insight into the exploitation of his own class, and the sense of his true bond with his class, however paradoxical in view of his changed identity as Captain Fidanza, gives him a revolutionary aspiration formerly lacking in him when he was primarily a factotum of the capitalists.

Those who see an affirmation in the ending of *Nostromo* are, deliberately or unwittingly, taking a Hegelian view of the Cunning of Reason triumphing for the general good in Sulaco. The narrative does end with a reign of stability and progress, but it is here that Conrad's art takes on powerful resonances distinctively its own. Although Conrad impresses one, in his essays and prefatory notes, as a political conservative, and an affirmative reading of *Nostromo*'s ending would seem to confirm the view,[11] the fates of the major protagonists suggest a profoundly skeptical vision of history and human passions which an emphasis on a temporary economic and political stability cannot dispel.

Conrad's imagination takes, however, a characteristically antithetical turn by showing that the historical process itself cannot be evaluated in terms of the protagonists' fates as such. The novel articulates a radical critique of the economic and political stability by revealing it to be illusory. What projections of hope and change are made in its final pages occur in the form of young revolutionaries engaging in activities calculated to reunite Sulaco to Costaguana and to wrest Sulaco's wealth from the grip of Western imperialists. If Nostromo, for all his confusions endemic to his exploited class, attends clandestine gatherings of workers he himself has organized, and gives them money to help build the opposition Republic Party, Father Corbelan emerges as a luminous figure of radical activities. Corbelan, who had earlier joined forces with Charles Gould and the mine, has been disillusioned with the illusory economic changes presented in the form of a specious political stability. It is this aspect of the novel which charges with Utopian hope an otherwise gloomy and negative picture of history and the political process.

The lives of the three main protagonists do, indeed, end in failure, their desires unfulfilled, abandoned, or perverted. Nostromo, suddenly overcome with bitterness at the exploitation he has suffered and his possible penury should Montero's rebellion succeed, finds the very foundations of his illusory, unexamined sense of self left in ruins. When Decoud's romantic passion for Antonia fails to keep his skepticism at bay, that skepticism turns inward, devoid of its rhetoric of mockery and the epistemological parody once directed at others; it overpowers him and its final consequence is suicide. The career of Gould, the pragmatic idealist, founders on an unholy mix of compromise and contradiction; he erects an empire which brings neither private happiness nor equality, justice, and freedom in the public realm. He moves steadily toward that point where the mine all but obliterates his humanity. To his wife he "seemed to dwell alone within a circumvallation of precious metal" (222). Gould's failure is the most shattering and the most suggestive because he dreams of uniting middle-class morality and capitalist economic practice: this dream is a mystifying moral event, cast far into the future, which legitimizes the capitalist in the present. *Nostromo* thus has the structure of a myth that has failed to be mythical; it retains the bitterness and failure of history.

VI

The zigzag sequence of events which so complicates the time-scheme in *Nostromo* suggests that Conrad is interested less in the chronological record than in the disclosure of the tangled forces of history.[12] Conrad's is a framework of "monumental history", to borrow a phrase from Nietzsche, a framework which is turned inside out, a meditative record of both the making and the dissolving of a phase of social-political history.[13] This begins, as the novel opens, with the narrator recounting the Azuera legend of the souls of the three adventurous gringos who "cannot tear themselves away from the bodies mounting guard over the discovered treasure" (5). This legend hangs as an ominous inscription over the entire narrative, suddenly erupting in historical form when Nostromo and Decoud take the silver to the Golfo Placido, to begin the process of separating Sulaco from the republic.

The narrative that follows discloses the process that makes the legend emblematic of history: the legend signifies the entrapment of the human souls who pursue material wealth for the sake of personal and social welfare. Thus the legend is a kind of forbidding folktale, not so much an enigma as an omen. The San Tomé silver is allegorized as the forbidden treasure of the Azuera legend; it is forbidden, in different ways, to both Gould and Nostromo. Conrad's suggestion is that the self may gain, in relations with others, an identity which sustains it; Gould and Nostromo are denied this sustenance because they are possessed by the silver.

This linking of the Azuera legend with larger historical and political perspectives in *Nostromo* creates a distance between Conrad and his narrative; it is an innovation that alters and raises to a different plane the great narrative accomplishments of *Lord Jim* and *Heart of Darkness*, which are given shape by the figure of the storyteller, Marlow. The fictional concerns of *Nostromo* are larger, encompassing a crucial phase of a society's history in the making; there is, in *Nostromo*, no one individual described in the lived intimacy of his predicament as there is in *Lord Jim* and, in a somewhat different sense, in *Heart of Darkness*. The closest we come to this is the portrayal of Doctor Monygham, who has endured a failure like Jim's, though without self-mystification. The narrator of *Nostromo*, however, constructs an allegory in ironic terms, but he experiences none of Marlow's anguish. Whereas Marlow sees his own moral hope turn into despair, *Nostromo*'s narrator remains imperturbably detached. It is as if the disturbing experience of *Heart of Darkness* and *Lord Jim* have become so integral to history that Conrad no longer needs the anguished human voice of a Marlow. That voice is now replaced by the detached, ironic commentator on history.

The use of the impersonal narrator, as well as Doctor Monygham and Decoud, suggests the distance between *Nostromo*'s moral and political trajectory and those of the two Marlow novels. The world-historical hope that gives momentum to the Marlow narratives, however problematically rendered, shrinks to personal subjective hope: that of Doctor Monygham in securing Gould's safety for Emilia's sake; of Decoud's supporting Sulacan independence because of his love for Antonia; of Nostromo's plan to become rich slowly. Moreover, neither the narrator, nor Monygham, nor Emilia Gould toward the end, has any illusion about the successful turn of events in Sulaco. For Conrad, the individual is destined to contradiction and failure. Moreover, if he is not the bearer of a transcendental telos, neither is history nor society. In this Conrad reveals himself as a Schopenhauerian rather than a Hegelian writer.[14] For Hegel, as we know, the failure and contradictions experienced by individuals are necessary for the larger whole of society to achieve its synthesis. For Conrad, on the contrary, individuals, driven by private passions, are thwarted by the contingencies of history; and history, driven by its own unpredictable forces, thwarts any possibility of social harmony.

On the face of it, Decoud, Captain Mitchell, and Don José Avellanos figure as storytellers; all keep or recite records.[15] Mitchell's record of the confusing welter of events in Costaguana is amusingly stolid, complacent, and finally ignorant; it conveys a series of facts, but at the level of naïve interpretation. Don José's history *Fifty Years of Misrule*, though more deeply informed, serves a similar purpose; his history is filled with moral democratic passion which, from the skeptical perspectives of both Decoud and the narrator, is naïve. He refuses, even after the political failure in Costaguana, to reexamine his moral passion, for he, too, wants to control history for his own reasons; his immersion in it has consequences which he himself could not have foreseen. His chronicle is destroyed, however, by the rioting mob that scatters its pages in the street—disclosing, as it were, the futility not merely of the record but of the moral passion behind the record. And, though Don José dies of old age, his death is connected to his apprehension that the brutal and tragic events of the past are now repeating themselves as farce. The scattering of his pages is emblematic of history's indifference to his judgment, albeit in a way which would have pained him.

The fate of Decoud has been treated by critics as the fate of skepticism itself.[16] Such a reading, however, uncritically accepts Decoud's insights into the idealizing and self-deluding projects of others. The repudiation of Decoud is a repudiation only of a certain species of skepticism, for a skeptical and finally ironic narrative stance is taken toward Decoud. The narrative irony toward Decoud is most striking, as Decoud attributes Nostromo's incorruptibility not to disinterestedness, as the Europeans do, but to "his enormous vanity, that finest form of egoism that can take on the aspect of every virtue" (300). For Decoud, Nostromo is like Gould, Holroyd, and others, but his uncomplicated, almost natural egoism separates him from these self-deceiving idealists. On this view Nostromo is, unself-consciously, free from self-mystification. He is in unmediated contact with his natural ego, a "natural man" as Decoud calls him, while the egos of others are connected to their deepest urges through mystifying ideals. Thus Nostromo represents a concrete embodiment of what Decoud believes to be his own skeptical stance; Nostromo seems to validate Decoud's skepticism. Decoud thinks that Nostromo, "like me, has come casually here to be drawn into events for which his skepticism as well as mine seems to entertain a sort of passive contempt" (246). But Nostromo's pure egoism, naïvely idealized by Decoud, is a focal point of the narrator's irony; Decoud identifies with Nostromo, making himself vulnerable to an irony to which he believes he is immune. Nostromo has no critical detachment from his own egoistic desires, and Decoud, the antithetical complement to Nostromo, is too self-assured a skeptic to realize that his skepticism defines and limits the knowledge he has of his own self as well as of others. Thus when Decoud and Nostromo join forces to bring about the independence of Sulaco, neither has any real interest in ideas as such. Decoud has his own romantic reasons, whereas Nostromo discovers he has no reason at all. Interestingly enough, Nostromo does become skeptical, though in a sense that Decoud could not have anticipated. Nostromo's disillusionment with his public identity propels him on a course of manipulation and deceit, ending in death. But Decoud mistakes the fateful change in Nostromo for a revelation of his pure egoism which had always existed, concealed only by the distance between them. It is a measure of the distance and radical alienation underlying their closeness that Nostromo leaves Decoud to starve and then feels very little remorse; it is a measure of the distortions in Decoud's perception that in his most deeply felt judgment of Nostromo he is wrong.

In *Nostromo*, then, Conrad carries out his subtle meditation on the relation of his narrator to the story by putting a certain distance between Decoud and the impersonal narrator. For neither Decoud nor the impersonal narrator is a diminished version of a Marlow. The narrator of *Nostromo* manifests little anguish or moral passion over the spectacle of humanity, but his capacity for comprehending the larger sweep of history is enhanced by this attitude. His irony, unlike Decoud's, is that of a detached, analytical consciousness devoid of illusions about itself or others, though a sympathetic interest in Monygham and Emilia Gould reveals an emotional delicacy that even Marlow does not possess. The passion and anguish with which Marlow probes the meaning of his experience commits him to a moral stance, though his narrative is an overwhelming testimony to the evils that undermine that moral stance. The narrator of *Nostromo* writes with a transcendental dispassion that distinguishes his irony from Marlow's irony in both his narratives. Decoud's fate in love does not so much condemn him as a skeptic as it reveals the tragic vulnerability of love in its difficult relation with intellect and despair.

The complexity of this relation emerges most compellingly in the narrator's treatment of Doctor Monygham. If, as Fredric Jameson has said,[17] Monygham is virtually generated by the very text of *Nostromo*, it is because Monygham's life offers a commentary which neither the self-proclaimed skeptic nor the novel's impersonal narrator could provide. The metaphysic of Decoud's stance is too murkily romantic to allow for the delicate morality of Monygham's sentiment for Emilia Gould. And the impersonal narrator is too concerned with the absurdity of history to allow a place of centrality to Emilia's nobility. Monygham's is a civilized response wrought by personal suffering; it bespeaks values for which the narrator has profound regard, yet this regard does not culminate in an affirmative view of history. The sense of failure which pervades the feelings of both Doctor Monygham and Emilia Gould is emblematic of this negative vision of history. Consider, for instance, the implications of Emilia's refusal to confirm Monygham's suspicion regarding Nostromo's dealings with Decoud and the treasure. Though he doesn't believe her, Monygham experiences utter defeat: "But her word was law. He accepted her denial like an inexplicable fatality affirming the victory of Nostromo's genius over his own. Even before that woman, whom he loved with secret devotion, he had been defeated by the magnificent capataz de cargadores, the man who had lived his own life on the assumption of unbroken fidelity, rectitude, and courage" (560—61). Though it is Monygham rather than Nostromo who has shown "unbroken fidelity, rectitude, and courage", neither his integrity nor his urbane skepticism earns him her confidence. For, from the narrator's skeptical perspective, what would be the point of morality if it resulted in the slighting and betrayal of another human being in his extremity?

As for Emilia, though her terrible knowledge is not betrayed, neither her conversation with Nostromo nor the course of events in Sulaco gives her any comfort. The sorrow of Giselle Viola over Nostromo's death reminds her of the desolation of her own life with Charles: "And Mrs. Gould, feeling her suppressed sobbing, nervous and excited, had the first and only moment of bitterness in her life. It was worthy of Dr. Monygham himself" (561). Her response to Giselle's words that "Nostromo loved me as no one had ever been loved before" provokes the bitter memory of Charles's love: "I have been loved, too" (561). Her sense of Charles's betrayal is as strong as her sense of Nostromo's betrayal of Linda's love.

Thus, the ending of *Nostromo* is marked by a sense of bitter personal losses and failure, and the signs of history with its terrible contingencies prowl in the background. Young radicals are, of course, preparing for a revolution that they hope will bring an epoch of justice and liberty, replacing what

Monygham has called the illusory stability and peace of independent Sulaco. It is appropriate, in this context, that Monygham should consider Giselle's mourning to be Nostromo's final triumph, "the greatest, the most enviable, the most sinister of all" (566). Thus Monygham's career questions the varying embodiments of greatness in Gould and Nostromo, as well as the romantic skepticism embodied in Decoud; Nostromo's career, especially in its final moments, complicates any sense Monygham may have of his own personal heroism. Given the problematic nature of history and society, which leaves public and private lives profoundly distorted, neither the spectacular heroism of Nostromo nor the triumph of Monygham's integrity can provide sustaining values for the community. The novel depicts the fall of a romance hero, and the unlikely rise of a cynical old doctor whose public life is suspect because of a transgression committed in his youth. It is this disposition of events in *Nostromo* that reveals Conrad's stance as a skeptic for whom heroism, even if it is privately viable as it is for Doctor Monygham, remains essentially cut off from the romance paradigm in which it has its ontological grounds.

CHAPTER FOUR
Irony and Morality:
The Secret Agent

If in *Heart of Darkness*, *Lord Jim*, and *Nostromo* Conrad explores and questions the romance paradigm and its dependence on an affirmative vision of individual greatness and heroism, it is not strange that critics should expect him to write a novel that would provide some vision of moral hope and regeneration, some dramatic containment of irony by certain moral principles. It is not surprising, then, that *The Secret Agent* did not elicit much enthusiasm for Conrad's treatment of modern urban civilization. Writing in the early 1950s, Irving Howe, for instance, was critical of Conrad's treatment of "the political spectacle from a great and chilling distance". *The Secret Agent* is flawed as a literary work, he argued, because "one misses some dramatic principle of contradiction, some force of resistance; in a word, a moral positive to serve literary ends".[1] Conrad's irony, in other words, is so relentless that it subverts any moral positives a work of art may be presumed to suggest. Albert Guerard, in substantial agreement with Howe, says that Conrad's irony is "not conducive to serious psycho-moral involvement".[2]

Nevertheless, *The Secret Agent* has grown in stature during the last twenty years, though in 1948 F. R. Leavis had already called it, along with *Nostromo*, "one of Conrad's two supreme masterpieces".[3] Leavis's valuation, however, did not establish this novel as one of Conrad's greatest works, because the novel's irony has inspired profoundly antithetical responses. If Howe and Guerard found the novel deficient in moral energy, other critics have considered the presumed absence of moral energy itself to be a product of the unqualified success of the novel's irony. J. Hillis Miller, for instance, considers *The Secret Agent* as the paradigmatic instance of Conrad's negative vision of human existence. In a phenomenological reading, Miller characterizes Conrad's vision in these terms: "Conrad's view of human life apparently depends on two notions of nothingness—the nothingness of consciousness, and the nothingness of death."[4] Avrom Fleishman, who places the novel in a large social-political context, considers its vision as a "vision of the world in a state of fragmentation—as if by explosion".[5] There are, of course, studies which examine the historical context of the Greenwich Observatory explosion and show its relevance to an adequate grasp of *The Secret Agent*'s treatment of social-political issues.[6] Ian Watt, who examines and questions several of these views and the assumptions underlying them, argues that Conrad's ironic humor operates "as a moral energy" which examines the life of men in modern urban civilization; that, though the novel "stacks every possible card against human freedom and happiness", it nevertheless provides a bracing experience for the intelligence.[7]

These critical views seem to be divided on the question of how we are to understand the novel's irony. I want to argue that the relation between irony and morality is enormously complex in *The Secret Agent*, and that part of this complexity derives from Conrad's insight into modern society. In *The Secret Agent*, Conrad sees man's social and personal life as necessarily a form of political existence, and suggests that an understanding of this life depends on our grasp of how social-political institutions determine and limit the kind of life, with all its range of emotions and attitudes, possible for us in modern urban civilization. The critique of morality, in this novel, is largely a critique of bourgeois political morality, and of the forms of ideological conflicts this morality generates. This critique cannot be reduced to a nihilistic rejection of life as such but, rather, reveals the ways in which irony itself can be seen as an instrument of serious moral, social, and political criticism of our institutions of family and state.

I

The Secret Agent is not primarily an exploration of radicalism or conservatism, though it treats both stances with considerable insight. Its real significance resides in Conrad's exploration of the relations between these two stances as they affect individual lives in society, especially the institution of the family as represented by the Verlocs. If in *Nostromo* Conrad gives rather sketchy portrayals of the Violas and Goulds in terms of their representative status as families, it is because there he is more immediately concerned with the process of composition and decomposition of history in its political-economic nexus. Similarly, in *Under Western Eyes* the portrayal of the Haldin family exemplifies, as we shall see, the classic Conradian technique of narrative reduction in order to dramatize the larger confrontation between historical forces and the individual. Razumov, for instance, struggles blindly with the social stigma of illegitimacy until he begins to grasp the contradictory nature of his society which has distorted his own relation to it. The Verloc family is not, of course, an autonomous unit, since the conditions of society determine the nature of its members' activities. Winnie, Stevie, and to a lesser extent Verloc undergo experiences that show them in their moment of crisis (as with Winnie and Verloc) or moral insight (as with Stevie). Conrad's portrayal in *The Secret Agent* of the family is more distressingly grim than that in *Under Western Eyes*.

Winnie Verloc's life is predicated upon a denial of her self, of her legitimate aspirations as a young woman. Given the conditions of her life, the whole moral force of her existence is reduced to her protecting affection for Stevie. Winnie cannot be credited with having truly chosen her course of life, though her attitude reflects the deeply binding sentiments which members of a family can have for one another. My interpretation seeks to show how Conrad explores in this novel the relations within a representative lower-class family in modern society, and how he discloses the nature and possibility of sentiment in such a family, and its implications for grasping and defining the conditions of modern social life.

Winnie is denied the freedom her mother has. Being young and marriageable she can provide shelter to her retarded brother, though she does not make this choice consciously, for she does not know what her choice will mean for her own life. Her choice is, rather, an instinctive, unreasoning response of sentimental sisterly affection; it suggests the extent to which morally binding feeling is not a matter of deliberate choice. Her sentimental bond with her younger brother, however, has its origins in a problematical situation. Her father was deeply embittered that he had produced a retarded son. He hated his son, and hated Winnie as well because she protected the object of his loathing. Winnie grows up to be Stevie's surrogate mother and her deepest instincts are to protect him at whatever cost to herself. The abuse she suffers in consequence so limits her response to the world that her selflessness, however morally praiseworthy it may appear on a first reading, is not the result of mature understanding. Winnie's mother, on the other hand, has chosen to go to the poorhouse, a choice which has the appearance of great self-sacrifice, though it burdens Winnie with the total responsibility for Stevie's care. Since her early adolescence, Winnie has made so many self-sacrifices that it is easy for her to accept her new role. Her self-sacrifices reveal the ultimately distorted nature of her feelings.

In this context, Conrad's statement to Edward Garnett that Winnie's mother is "the heroine" needs to be questioned.[8] The novel does indeed describe Winnie's mother as a "heroic old woman" who resolves "on going away from her children as an act of devotion and as a move of deep policy" (162). She is repeatedly referred to as heroic (161–63). Some critics think that Conrad here is serious, that he considers her genuinely to be "the heroine".[9] This reading, I believe, errs; for if, as I shall argue, the whole perspective of the novel is ironic one could not validly hold that the mother is altogether free from that ironic treatment. The novel's ironic treatment is not of just one or another character but of the entire network of relations between people and social institutions. The mother's excessively sentimental love for the son prevents her from loving the daughter; the daughter is to be a surrogate mother for the son, and is taught to sacrifice her life to that end. Winnie's denial of her own life thus springs from her mother's destructive, uncritical sentimental love as well as from her father's abusive treatment of her and Stevie. Only in a bitterly ironic treatment might a "heroic" mother accomplish what Winnie's mother has: that is, so to program Winnie that when Stevie is destroyed Winnie goes insane.

Yet the critique of the institution of the family in *The Secret Agent* is primarily an indictment of the society which creates and sustains the conditions that generate self-destructive families such as the Verlocs. This indictment acquires its full and terrible significance when we realize that society, for all its privileging of the family, remains largely indifferent to the destruction of the Verloc family. The story of Winnie and her mother is the story of a poor family in modern industrial society, a story in which the mother must sacrifice her own well-being to assure her helpless son's welfare, and the older sister must do the same. Their protective sentiment has its own moral justification, but neither Winnie nor her mother could understand the implications of their sacrifice, which are obscured by the amorphous, ever-present threat of poverty. Each must fight against this threat in order to provide for Stevie, and each takes recourse to actions that are deceptive and self-destructive.

A species of megalomania haunts many of Conrad's major characters, and this is overwhelmingly so in *The Secret Agent*, especially in the portrayal of Winnie and her husband. Lesser characters partake of it as well, however; one thinks of Winnie's mother's silent brooding, the idiotic condition of Stevie, the tenacity of the Professor and other anarchists. The Verlocs' delusions are perhaps the most tragic, for once the veneer of stability is wrenched from their relations and Winnie has her moment of insight into Verloc she reaches a pitch of fury and inner blindness that completely negates the point of her sacrifice. And here Conrad's treatment of Winnie is done with consummate artistic skill; he shows that in Winnie's loveless marriage there can be no moral restraint once Stevie is gone. Her response is, of course, psychologically intelligible, for she was taught not to look into things: when circumstances force her to look, she loses control.

It is a condition of Winnie's life in society that her understanding be tangled, confused, and bitter, rather than sane and clear. Her personal relations are based on blind sentiment and manipulative considerations. However deceptive the origins of her relation to Verloc, her knowledge that she has been exploited, and her brother sacrificed by Verloc for his own anarchistic ends, outrages her. Winnie can have no philosophical or detached understanding of a world rent by strong and destructive ideological wills, in which the hopes of the individual are well-nigh unrealizable. She cannot comprehend the possibility of her own happiness: she is a surrogate mother and she cannot think of being daughter, sister, or wife. Thus the normal relations on which traditional society prides and sustains itself are not possible for her; in this sense the argument that *The Secret Agent* is a tirade against *ressentiment* must be questioned. In examining the family, supposedly the most cherished institution of bourgeois society, Conrad reveals its inner workings, its ideological foundations, its distorted and self-destructive relations, all of which are sustained by its willingness to ignore that which might disturb its placid outer surface. For Conrad's discrediting of the radicals does not imply a defense of the status quo; his exposure of the workings of the lower-class family in modern society is radical and unsparing. *The Secret Agent* is a critique of radicalism, though it understands how radicalism is nourished by the distorted nature of the family.

II

Everything occurs secretly in *The Secret Agent*. "Secrecy" penetrates to the very core of each character's essential mode of being.[10] Secrecy as well as ignorance of each other's real actions or motives characterizes relations in the world of the novel. Its inhabitants do not converse with one another; they, rather, talk at one another. Their utterances and intentions are manipulative rather than moral. Verloc is a double agent with no genuine allegiance to either side. He loves commanding attention at radical gatherings, but he has little grasp of the values he shares or rejects in his activities as a spy. His ventriloquist-like speeches to Winnie when she discovers that Stevie has been the victim of his own plot shows he has no understanding of his grievous wrongdoing. But Winnie, too, is caught up in her own form of ventriloquism.

Secrecy permeates the lives of the novel's characters, contaminating even the most deeply felt or crucial moments. Verloc, for instance, tries to keep Winnie from learning about Stevie's death, and when he does tell her he treats the event as if it were a minor irritation to be recognized as such and put aside. Thus secrecy becomes solipsistic, perverse, exploitative; it is not the result of the hidden, inexorable forces as in a Greek tragedy. A peculiar consequence of this secrecy is that Verloc's death is not directly connected to his espionage activities. Moreover, if the radicals do not know the truth about Verloc's activities as a double agent, neither do they know about Verloc's trip, with Stevie, to the Observatory. When the Professor tells Ossipon that Michaelis "didn't know anything of Verloc's death" (302), he himself does not know the facts. Similarly, the Assistant Commissioner, not knowing about Verloc's death and Winnie's escape with Ossipon, characterizes events as a "domestic drama"; he cannot know that the domestic drama is also a social-political tragedy whose full significance escapes all but the narrator.

In this world of destructive self-alienation it is Stevie alone who sometimes speaks with sincerity. But he is the vulnerable child of a society ridden with conflicts and contradictions which destroy all but a trace of his identity. What survives of his identity comes to haunt Verloc, as an ironic confirmation of Winnie's innocuous prophecy that if Stevie should get lost he will manage to return: all that returns of him is the label that Winnie had stitched on the inside of his collar. Thus the meaning of Winnie's action returns misshapen and distorted; her goal is realized, but it is also thwarted in its very realization. Winnie's action is complicated and undermined by a whole multiplicity of actions by others. Vladimir's interest, for instance, in shocking the British society by an attack on the very citadel of modern scientific achievement, the Greenwich Observatory, prompted him to assign the task to Verloc; this double agent, however, is afraid of carrying on the task by himself; and then there is the element of contingency which intervenes in the form of Stevie stumbling against the root of a tree leading to his tragic destruction.

Perhaps the most powerful metaphor in *The Secret Agent* is Stevie's "drawing of circles, circles, circles; innumerable circles, concentric, eccentric; a coruscating whirl of circles that by their tangled multitude of repeated lines, uniformity of form, and confusion of intersecting lines suggested a rendering of cosmic chaos" (45). While the novel need not be reduced to the symbology of circularity, it is nevertheless significant that its narrative takes the path of circles coiling and doubling back upon itself, extending to the outermost areas of its world and returning to the center of the story which is occupied by the shop. And the shop itself serves a double function: superficially it is a means of livelihood for Verloc, while in fact it provides a cover for his clandestine activities; it enables him to win trust and evade suspicion. The comings and goings at the Verlocs' accomplish little. Similarly, in the world of the novel, the characters are continually in motion but getting nowhere;

theirs is a form of motion powered by a kind of emptiness which reveals its true nature in the deaths of Winnie, Stevie, and Verloc. It is significant that the reader is present only at Verloc's death, that only Verloc dies in the shop, whereas the deaths of Stevie and Winnie, occurring elsewhere, are reported to us. The significance inheres in the ironic narrator's suggestion that the shop, a physical embodiment of the rottenness of Verloc's life, and Verloc are indissolubly linked together, and that Verloc is as much a spy as he is a representative of distorted bourgeois morality. One of his functions as an *agent provocateur*, we remember, is to delude those who are willing to be deluded into thinking that destruction is a proper means of regenerating society.

III

The most significant moments in *The Secret Agent* occur in chapter 8, which describes the cab-ride with Stevie, and the disintegration of the last vestige of Winnie's moral emotion in chapter 11, which depicts as well Verloc's apalling indifference. It is around these episodes that the narrative weaves a series of circular movements, from different trajectories, that reveal in totality the protagonists' fragmented lives. These episodes give the fullest phenomenological accounts of the mental lives of Stevie, Verloc, and Winnie, accounts which reveal Conrad's deepest interest in *The Secret Agent*: that is, to illuminate the desperate condition of the institution of the family as it is besieged by material and ideological forces.

Stevie's spiritual nature is profoundly antithetical to that of the Professor. As we shall see, the Professor's integrity and sincerity stem from a relentless, negative attitude toward self and society, while Stevie's integrity and sincerity stem from his instinctive compassion. The Professor's language is devastatingly clear and precise, while Stevie's shows that he "was no master of phrases, and perhaps for that very reason his thoughts lacked clearness and precision" (171). The Professor has no feelings; his attitude amounts to the utter rejection of the world and self. Stevie's feelings of bewilderment and rage, on the contrary, constitute elements of a rudimentary moral system. As the narrator says, Stevie "felt with greater completeness and some profundity" (171). These words suggest the narrator has taken a moral stance toward Stevie's capacity to feel: it is the same stance taken in *Lord Jim*, where Jim is valued for his capacity to feel. But in *Lord Jim* the concern was directly with the implications of a quest for grounding identity in transcendental ideals; in *The Secret Agent* that concern has been, as we shall soon discuss, replaced by a relentlessly negative irony which not only opens the novel but ends it as well.

For Stevie words and feelings are profoundly connected ·to concrete experience. He does not manipulate words for specific purposes. He is incapable of the perception that words are arbitrary linguistic signs that allow for the infinite manipulation of themselves and of human beings. Thus Winnie tells Verloc: "He isn't fit to hear what's said here. He believes it is all true. He knows no better. He gets into his passions over it" (59). On this view, an aspect of maturity is the ability to hear words without feeling; it is to live life in such a way that one's words and actions need have no connection. For Stevie, however, abstractions involve moral judgments, and they must make sense in a specific, understandable fashion. This is why the anarchist talk about the burning flesh is unsettling to Stevie; his response is instinctively human, unlike the profoundly alienated responses of nearly all the other characters in the novel.

The moral indignation Stevie feels, and occasionally succeeds in expressing, springs from his capacity to experience sympathetically the events that happen around him; it is a sign of the self-alienation of those around him that they lack this capacity. Thus he is upset by the cabman beating the horse, not because of the abstract moral norm it violates, but because he "knew what it was to be beaten" (171). Yet Stevie has developed intuitions so that he does not rigidly adhere even to the implications of his own experience of having been beaten. His feeling that the cabman committed a wrong in beating the horse gives way to more complex feelings when he learns that the cabman's family is very poor, that his work is a terribly inadequate means of livelihood for his family. Stevie's reponse, "Bad world for poor people" (171), which appears to be a mere stammer of words, captures his deeply felt judgment, and it represents extraordinary moral understanding in an otherwise distorted and brutalizing landscape of human relations.

Stevie's madness is not a repudiation of the moral judgments he makes, so much as a repudiation of the world which allows for moral judgments only at the price of madness. It is in this context that Stevie's destruction makes compelling artistic sense. Adapting Stein's words in *Lord Jim*, one may say that Stevie has come into a world where he is not wanted, where he has no reason to be. It is true that Stevie's mother gives up her home for him, that his sister gives up her sweetheart for him, and that she finally murders to avenge him. But this view isolates Stevie's family from the larger social nexus within which the lower-class family such as Winnie's is reduced to living an agonizing and self-destructive life. For this larger nexus in which Stevie lives allows for being only in the sense of an essential non-being. When Stevie is destroyed, what is snuffed out is an anomalous life; his very existence defies the world he can neither understand nor control, though unknowingly he exposes it in all its grim horror. From the perspective of Winnie, Stevie is upset by the world because he does not understand it; she assumes that to understand the world is to accept it. The other alternative is to condemn it without taking any real responsibility for changing it, as the anarchists do. In this sense, Stevie's madness is connected to his trustfulness, since in the world of *The Secret Agent* trustfulness has no place except in the lives of the mad. From the ironic perspective of the narrative, Stevie's compassion for the oppressed derives from his madness, for the real world is so completely a world of convenience and manipulation that in it moral feeling bears the mark of corrosive, irrational sentimentality. This is a grim and distressing diagnosis of modern society, in which integrity and sincerity exist only in a crazed nihilist like the Professor, or a congenitally defective boy like Stevie.

If Stevie's madness reveals a deeply felt moral stance, Winnie's disintegration upon learning of his death reveals the madness underlying her former composure. With Stevie's death she has lost her reason for living, especially the reason for honoring the marriage vows. Verloc, her husband, no longer presents the aspect of a husband: "Her contract with existence, as represented by that man standing over there, was at an end" (207). Her factitiously constructed identity has been organized around Stevie's needs; with his death, that identity is fragmented. It is a tragic paradox in her life that, though now she "is a free woman", she does not "exactly know what use to make of her freedom" (254). Her freedom is terrible in its suddenness, and is the cause of her undoing. Her sudden brief glimpse of freedom becomes terrifying, for the desire for freedom rests upon a conception of the self and its relation to communal life foreign to Winnie.

Through the portrayal of Winnie, then, the novel explores the genesis of suffering, self-sacrifice, and moral distortion. Since her childhood of abuse and suffering, she has internalized a system of self-exploitation which leaves her totally unprepared for the crisis which befalls her. Not looking into things leads her to not looking into her own self, or her relations to others. When the crisis suddenly erupts in her life, she is made to look beneath the placid surface of events; the vision of futility that arises bears down upon her with a relentlessness that drives her mad. It is precisely this kind of looking beneath the surface that Winnie, given the nature of her self, cannot endure; hers is a will to suffer which makes her incapable of confronting her past.

The distortion of sentiment and self latent in Winnie for so many years at last appears in all its destructiveness. Her entrapment in life has been so profound that her discovery of the truth about Stevie's death leaves her shattered; the course of her life seems merciless and implacable, beyond her control, culminating in suicide. It is thus that Winnie becomes mad in a way Stevie was not; for Stevie's madness allowed for moral emotion lacking in others, whereas Winnie's madness was the consequence of a summing up of life resulting in self-alienation and despair. Thus the ostensible justification for her desperate crime reveals itself as madness. At the moment of her most passionate identification with Stevie, she not only seems mad but also assumes her brother's facial expression; yet she also unleashes forces that would have apalled Stevie, and in that sense severs her real bond with him. Stevie's trustfulness is, of course, a part of his madness; his trustfulness has no place in the society portrayed in *The Secret Agent*. Thus it is that Winnie experiences the full force of the alienation she has ignored for so many years in her real relation to Verloc.

Complete indifference is the defining emotion in the moral life of Adolf Verloc, the secret agent. This qualifies him to be the clandestine purveyor of pornography, a spy of a foreign embassy, an informer to the police, and an underground organizer of anarchist activities. This same indifference allows him to marry Winnie, and take over, along with her, her brother, her mother, and their furniture. He callously employs Stevie in the task he himself dreads, and feels so little remorse over Stevie's death that he talks volubly to Winnie, worrying more about his possible ill-treatment by the revolutionaries than about his part in Stevie's death. Yet he remains preeminently a functionary of the petty bourgeoisie. His capacity in this regard constitutes a denial of moral feeling in bourgeois society more devastating than in all Conrad's other fiction. Fat, indolent, married, loving comfort, wanting to protect the edifices of society, Verloc is a representative of the status quo rather than an angry idealist driven to anarchism:

> Mr. Verloc surveyed through the park railings the evidence of the town's opulence and luxury with an approving eye. All these people had to be protected. Protection is the first necessity of opulence and luxury. They had to be protected; and their horses, carriages, houses, servants had to be protected; and the source of their wealth had to be protected in the heart of the city and the heart of the country; the whole social order favourable to their hygienic idleness had to be protected against the shallow enviousness of unhygienic labour. (12)

It is significant that Verloc, who exemplifies unhygienic idleness, should think these thoughts which the narrator repudiates. Verloc's thoughts here, though seemingly reflective, are paradoxically devoid of the anarchist insight as well as the conservative insight he espouses in a moment of idle expansiveness and self-justification. *The Secret Agent*, of course, repudiates the social order Verloc seems so anxious to protect here. After this moment of unwitting self-revelation, Verloc slumps into his habitual torpor of mind, though later he will be shocked out of it, not so much by Stevie's death as by Winnie's terrible response to the circumstances of his death: the narrator's uncovering of Verloc's state of mind is a formidable piece of phenomenological probing.[11]

The tragedy of Verloc is that he has no moral sensibility. He does not understand Winnie's rage and despair, nor does he understand the political and moral conflict between the anarchists and conservatives. His revolutionary commitment is empty of meaning; it was little more than his love of his own resonant voice. Verlos is a lower-class version of Kurtz, a pedestrian and denatured version of Nostromo, whose career reveals the distressing problem of trust and betrayal in modern society. Verloc tells Vladimir that people trusted him because of his voice, that because of his voice he had no need of sincerity. The persuasive powers of his language and voice, however, fail Verloc the one time he speaks to Winnie in perfect sincerity. His "revolutionary" speech until then had nothing revolutionary about it, for it was not connected to the ideal of liberation which is the goal of revolution; he had only used his voice to secure his position among the anarchists. He now thinks that he was neither mistaken nor guilty in any way: that is the most damning feature of Verloc's consciousness after Stevie's death. Thus he remains incapable, even at this terrible moment in his married life, of reciprocation or understanding with Winnie.

When he sees Winnie's agonizing rage over Stevie's death, Verloc is, for the first time, freed from his characteristic inertia, and begins a process of psychological reflection. In a stroke of consummate art, Conrad's narrative shows Verloc reflecting about his own self, rather than the consequences and meaning of his conduct and his relations to others. He is vindictively angry at the anarchists, though he has no right to make moral criticisms of others: one must possess the capacity for self-criticism in order to know what it is to criticize others, and Verloc does not possess that capacity. This tendency, however, to see oneself in isolation is peculiar not just to Verloc and Winnie, but to nearly all the characters in *The Secret Agent*.

IV

Conrad claimed, in a letter to Cunninghame Graham, that he admired the Professor's integrity: he had given him "the note of perfect sincerity".[12] The narrative, however, does not allow for this in a straightforward fashion, since the Professor's integrity, sincerity, and self-confidence are problematized as well. This occurs several times in the novel: first during the conversation with Inspector Heat; second, while walking with the multitudes around him; and, finally, at the very end when, in the city full of men, the Professor is characterized as a mere pest. This is not to deny that the Professor is more sincerely committed to the values he professes than nearly all the others, nor that he is the only one who makes a genuinely devastating criticism of society. But the discomfitures he experiences cannot be construed as manifestations of a mere *ressentiment*, though, as Fredric Jameson suggests, Conrad's radicals embody a *ressentiment* which is not the mark of a true revolutionary.[13] *Ressentiment*, of course, is at the origin of the Professor's radical posture: the origins of his radical discontent put into question his sincerity and integrity. His sincerity consists in having worked out the logic of his commitment, and in having modeled his behavior on the conclusions of that logic. Conrad's subtle analysis here of the Professor's conviction is based on the nineteenth century's great methodological and conceptual fiction that human personality and social phenomena (as well as works of art) are best understood in their essential nature by an adequate grasp of their origins, or the forces which gave birth to them.

The origins of the Professor's *ressentiment*, however, shed a compromising light on his revolutionary idealism. His "imagination had been fired early by the tales of men rising from the depths of poverty to positions of authority and affluence" (80). The Professor has gained his title as a nickname, for he was only "an assistant demonstrator in chemistry at some technical institute", who had early in his career begun struggling "to raise himself in the social scale" (75). But society had never rewarded his "genius" and his bitterness at this had perverted his original virtues of integrity and sincerity:

The extreme, almost ascetic purity of his thought, combined with an astounding ignorance of worldly ambitions, had set before him a goal of power and prestige to be attained without the medium of arts, graces, tact, wealth—by sheer weight of merit alone. On that view he considered himself entitled to undisputed success. His father, a delicate dark enthusiast with a sloping forehead, had been an itinerant and rousing preacher of some obsure but rigid Christian sect—a man supremely confident in the privileges of his righteousness. In the son, individualist by temperament, once the science of colleges had replaced thoroughly the faith of conventicles, this moral attitude translated itself into a frenzied puritanism of ambition. He nursed it as something secularly holy. To see it thwarted opened his eyes to the true nature of the world, whose morality was artificial, corrupt, and blasphemous. The way of even the most justifiable revolutions is prepared by personal impulses

114

disguised into creeds. The Professor's indignation found in itself a final cause that absolved him from the sin of turning to destruction as the agent of his ambition (80—81)

Thus the Professor's response to society is highly egocentric: society's legitimacy depends on whether or not it recognizes his worth. Though egoistic like Lord Jim, the Professor is not a youthful idealist. Jim's failure leads him to a denial of that failure, to an assertion of his essential purity. All his actions after the leap from *Patna* confirm his allegiance to the legitimizing values of society. For the Professor, on the other hand, the very concept of legitimacy has lost its meaning because of his failure. Yet his implicit critique of society, though extremist, solipsistic, and finally self-destructive, contains an element of truth, which accounts for the admiring interest Conrad took in the creation of the Professor. And, beyond that, Conrad is profoundly sympathetic to the frustrating plight of an intelligence unable to develop a critical yet also sustaining relation to self and society. The Professor's dilemma is inevitable in a society whose moral nihilism breeds, on the one hand, indifferent, life-denying institutions and, on the other hand, anarchists whose revolutionary passion paralyzes their moral sense.

The Professor, however, is very much a product of a Protestant bourgeois conception of life. He works fourteen hours a day, and sometimes goes hungry (69—70). He remains fiercely dedicated to the work he most values, the creation of a perfect detonator. His criticism of the anarchists derives from that maniacal dedication: "You [revolutionists] plan the future, you lose yourselves in reveries of economical systems derived from what is; whereas what is wanted is a clean sweep and a clear start for a new conception of life. That sort of future will take care of itself if you will only make room for it" (73). He believes that the anarchists' preoccupation with a new conception of life prevents them from acting in the present; for, as he sees it, what matters is the swift destruction of what is. Yet what justifies the assumption that destruction will lead to a clean start? Why would it be clean? The Professor lives in the grip of the fiction of immaculate origins, a fiction which is vaguely theological in the question it begs. For who would create the world anew after its total destruction? What knowledge would exist to guide this future state? And what can be the meaning of hope after such destruction? It is hard to escape the conclusion that, though he has not yet evolved a perfect detonator, the Professor is a perfect nihilist, whose vision is clouded, vague, and ill-conceived.

The Professor represents the destructive power of logic in certain forms of radical ideology. His vision is perfectly logical and brutal, and so thoroughly nihilistic that not even he escapes its consequences. Yet his logic is cut off from any understanding of the moral relations among human beings. Like Verloc he cannot be self-critical, and his completely coherent and self-consistent vision has no ethically viable relation to the world as it is. This is the consequence, of course, of his nihilistic belief that destruction is the only alternative to the painful nature of reality which he must otherwise endure. The Professor does not believe that society is devoid of value and meaning, or that its talk of value is an illusory veil thrown over a stark hollowness which he might cast aside and bring on the millennium. Yet he believes society can be destroyed and made over again, founded on perfect justice. For all his opposition to the radicals, he, too, is in the grip of an idealist illusion which inspired, in the nineteenth century, several revolutionary philosophical and political systems. In his fierce and unsparing condemnation of all political systems devised to reconstitute society, he appears to resemble Nietzsche; but Nietzsche, who also celebrates life's creative possibilities, would argue that the Professor is the product of a thwarted bourgeois passion for success and domination, that his grim and undeterred self-confidence in his vision suggests an altered exteriority which barely conceals his messianic vision of a future paradise. Nietzsche, with his profound understanding of illusory and factitious values, sought to prevent values from hardening into absolutes which destroy what is vital for human life.

This image of the Professor is not so admirable, then, as the one suggested in Conrad's letter to Cunninghame Graham. Yet the Professor's criticism of the anarchists suggests the direction that serious self-criticism on the part of the anarchists might take. But the Professor's nihilistic stance cannot be the source of redeeming illumination. In so far as the Professor, the only bearer of an authentic insight into certain aspects of society, is correct, the novel dramatizes—and castigates—the triumph of a certain kind of nihilism. His insights are acute, but partial, and finally despairing. As he explains, liberal democratic institutions sustain all forms of radicalism but they deprive the radicals of any genuine passion for revolutionary action. The Professor's sardonic advice to Ossipon to take advantage of Winnie's helplessness captures the young anarchist's basic desires. His insight into the essentially identical nature of the terrorist and the policeman is uncanny: "Like to like," he says. "The terrorist and the policeman both come from the same basket. Revolution, legality—countermoves in the same game; forms of idleness at bottom identical" (69).

Yet, in spite of himself, the Professor is an anarchist. He is too fanatically committed to his ideology to place it in critical perspective. The narrator's comments, interspersed throughout the novel, leave no doubt about this.

For example, the Professor's nihilistic idealism, though seemingly logical, is rendered dubious by the narrator's comments about its origins in his academic and financial failure. His detachment from all mankind conceals a corrosive, frustrated passion which blinds him to his own brutality. His satisfaction in being a moral agent depends on a delusion which cloaks "his vengeful bitterness" (81). And he remains cut off from the saving intuitions that occasionally spring to his mind: though he meditates "confidently on his power" he also feels "a sense of defeat before the mass of mankind mighty in its numbers (80–81). Yet the Professor's sincerity makes him "respectable" because, with the exception of Stevie, he is the only character whose ideas and actions are straightforwardly connected. Here Conrad's appreciation of sincerity links him to the great romantic poets such as Wordsworth, for whom virtue resided in acts of feeling and integrity.[14] By making the Professor incorruptible rather than merely despicable, Conrad invites reflection on the possibility of moral feelings in the world of *The Secret Agent*. In so doing, Conrad takes up the peculiar moral task of the novelist; he severely judges a society that can allow its members a measure of coherence and sincerity only after such deformations of feeling.

A conversation between Ossipon and the Professor deepens the question of sincerity, of the relation of words to action, bringing out the full distortion of the Professor's integrity. Ossipon calls the bombing incident "criminal" because he fears it will create difficulties for the anarchists.[15] The exchange is worth quoting at length:

> The little man lifted his thin black eyebrows with dispassionate scorn.
> "Criminal. What is that? What *is* crime? What can be the meaning of such an assertion?"
> "How am I to express myself? One must use the current words," said Ossipon, impatiently. . . .
> ". . . The condemned social order has not been built up on paper and ink, and I don't fancy that a combination of paper and ink will ever put an end to it, whatever you may think . . . I am not taking my cue from the Red Committee. I would see you all hounded out of here, or arrested— or beheaded for that matter—without turning a hair. What happens to us as individuals is not of the least consequence." (71–72)

Given a society whose foundations are unjust, ordinary notions of legality and crime mean nothing to the Professor. Indeed, for the Professor, the concept of crime as it is held in the novel's society legitimizes a false system of legality; it derives authority from institutions whose means as well as ends are often unjust. But the concept of crime invoked here is divorced from any

117

credible notion of justice. Shocked by the Professor's perverse logic, Ossipon defends the ordinary use of language. Yet, as the Professor suggests, Ossipon's ordinary use of language repudiates the anarchist view that ordinary language sustains the status quo by sustaining the whole network of arbitrary institutional concepts. Thus, in the Professor's view, Ossipon's anarchistic view is self-contradictory, one that he can maintain only in ignorance of its implications.

Are we to say, then, that the Professor's attitude to language, conventions, and society is essentially correct? It seems to me that Conrad here elaborates, through the figure of the Professor, the problem of sincerity and logical consistency in all its horrific moral implications; and it is connected, at a different level, to the same problem in the career of Lord Jim. Both Jim and the Professor are committed to the same absolute logic, though the content of that logic differs in each case. Jim's idealism is, as it were, inverted by the Professor's bitterly cynical assessment of society's inner contradictions. He therefore evolves a logic that will enable him to live in perfect sincerity and without illusion. Thus the Professor, taking pride in his consistency and sincerity, can say: "It is I who am the true propagandist" (70). It is also a consequence of his pride in this brutal logic that he entertains no false hope for himself; thus he says in his last conversation with Ossipon: "I remain—if I am strong enough" (304). He renounces his own self as well as the world, since to his logical mind one cannot truly renounce one without the other. This virtually commits him to silence, though he speaks to castigate others, and to denounce language itself. Such a commitment cannot allow for hope or nostalgia, except for the hope for the destruction of society and an ill-defined nostalgia for a hypothetical world. Thus to Ossipon's exasperated question "what do you want from us?" the Professor answers, "A perfect detonator" (69). This desire for the means of total destruction reveals the Professor's distressing awareness that the vastness of the multitude makes it indestructible, and that he can never be strong enough. Hence his conditional reply, "I remain—if I am strong enough"; he will not forsake the logical consistency of his plan for destruction, though he admits he is not strong enough, for he is not, in the end, omnipotent. Thus his interest in the perfect detonator is a joke which he cannot, in his sincerity, recognize. His sincerity, however purely it connects his values and his conduct, is a terrible parody of sincerity, for it has no relation to realizable moral values. The Professor's values cannot be expressed in lived relations, for he denies the legitimacy of all relations. His attitude is that of a brilliant and impotent megalomaniac, whose extremist views are striking for their fragmentary insight, though his perverse pursuit of logic destroys his understanding of what it *means* to affirm or deny something; for his dream begins and ends with the perfect detonator, cutting him off from the very concept of hope.

V

In his "Author's Note" to *The Secret Agent* Conrad describes the novel as "telling Winnie Verloc's story to its anarchistic end of utter desolation, madness, and despair" (xxv). It is society that produces its anarchists and conservatives alike: the Verlocs, Vladimirs, Professors, and Ossipons. This is why Conrad remarks, "Ironic treatment alone would enable me to say all I felt I would have to say in scorn as well as in pity" (xxiii). Conrad's statement seems to suggest that his irony is connected to moral judgment, though in Conrad this judgment seldom implies the possibility of a simple moral affirmation. Yet Conrad's irony is indissolubly bound to a moral conception of life, though the characters of *The Secret Agent* are generally incapable of mature moral emotion. His irony essentially derives from his observation that modern society promotes its own forms of nihilism, and that morality, as it is allowed to exist, denies the aspirations of those who are capable of moral emotion.

In *The Secret Agent* Conrad once again grapples with the problematical relation between morality and experience; he ends in an attitude of deep skepticism. Yet there is a strong distinction to be drawn between the moral nihilism of the Professor and the skeptical stance of the narrator. The Professor believes that the world can be made over in the image of justice, if only it can first be destroyed. The narrator, however, knows the world cannot be destroyed. As he sees it, society will continue on its presumably endless, uncertain journey, and evil, exploitation, injustice, and suffering will continue to prevail. Those in power may not always be evil, but even their good intentions will provide little relief for those caught up in a system of suffering.

The repudiation of the Professor is the repudiation of bottomless nihilism that ends in a program for total destruction and the quasi-religious renunciation of real life. But the narrator cannot set forth a list of moral positives. That society goes on, that the Professor is no more than a mere pest in the city full of men, does not mean society is redeemed in defeating nihilistic pests like the professor. The relation of the narrator to the repudiation of the Professor must be placed in the larger context of Stevie's death, Verloc's murder, Winnie's disintegration and suicide, and the society's general unawareness that a family has been destroyed. The pervasive indifference to the destruction of Winnie and her family is perhaps the novel's greatest indictment of conservatism; no reading of *The Secret Agent* as a tirade against *ressentiment* or as an unqualified defence of conservatism can account for the critical doublings that undermine all self-serving visions of hope entertained by either the conservatives or the anarchists. It is in order to write without such consolation that Conrad took recourse to the highly impersonal narrator, who is able to do justice to the moral feelings of the only person—Stevie—deemed unfit to live in the novel's society.

It is Stevie's great misfortune to live in a world which does not value those who live by the intensities of felt experience. It is in the portrayal of Stevie that Conrad listens to the discourse of madness and castigates the madness of the larger world. Conrad listens to Stevie just as Freud, the first modern man, according to Foucault, tried to listen to the neurotic.[16] Though neither Winnie nor Verloc nor even Ossipon, the medical student, listened carefully to Stevie, the narrator pays minute attention to Stevie's inarticulate but penetrating remarks about the life around him. In *The Secret Agent* Conrad involves the sympathetic reader in his radical criticism of the conventional perception of things. In the novel's world where empty oratory operates in the place of action and idealistic pretense masquerades as sincere conviction, even the surface details of life are difficult to interpret, since the "normal" characters are caught up in duplicity, shallowness, and calculation.

Stevie's madness does not imply the narrator's repudiation of the moral judgments Stevie makes; it is, rather, a repudiation of the world which allows for moral judgments only at the price of madness. Stevie's trustfulness is part of his madness as well, and from the ironic perspective of the narrator Stevie's pity and compassion are inconceivable apart from madness, since the world he lives in is so completely a network of convenience and exploitation that any moral feeling in it bears the imprint of a corrosive sentimentality. In the world of *The Secret Agent*, integrity and sincerity are to be found only in the utterly crazed anarchists like the Professor, or in a helpless boy like Stevie. The moral judgments made by the anarchists, however, have little bearing on their real actions. Indeed, their denunciations, instead of inspiring constructive action, release them from any need of it; rhetoric becomes a substitute for work. But any account of the narrator's perspective on the anarchists must clarify the ambiguous status accorded the Professor.

As we have seen before, the Professor sees injustice and suffering, and wishes to destroy the world in the hope that a just and perfect world will follow. Stevie, on the other hand, sees the same suffering and is moved to profound compassion. He is, of course, no visionary and could never provide a theoretical charter for the reconstruction of the world. Yet Stevie's "supreme remedy", for "all pain and misery", which is to take all the afflicted parties "to bed with him" (167), may be as valid to the narrator as the remedies of the novel's self-appointed thinkers. For the Professor is a visionary who wishes to destroy not only the oppressors who have created the illusion of legality but also the oppressed who remain caught in that illusion. The narrator's stance, if it is not an endorsement of Stevie's uncomplicated humanism, is not exactly a repudiation of the Professor and his vision, either. For from the narrator's perspective the tragedy of human existence is that, for mature response to be really consequential, violence must, in some instances, be justified. Thus the comment: "To destroy public faith in legality was the imperfect formula of [the Professor's] pedantic fanaticism; but the subconscious conviction that the framework of an established social order cannot be effectually shattered except by some form of collective or individual violence was precise and correct" (81). If the first sentence captures acutely the limitations of the Professor's attitude, the second leaves no doubt about the narrator's essentially negative assessment of the social order. The narrator, of course, does not claim to possess an insight into the ways by which the social order might be shattered and replaced by something more wholesome and just. But he does believe that violence is a tragic necessity for bringing about genuine revolutionary change. Unlike the anarchists and the Professor, the narrator has no formula for social change; it is as if morality in *The Secret Agent* finds its most congenial abode in the figure of a retarded child.

It is this helplessness of morality in effecting real social change that Conrad discloses in the complex mediations and entanglements in the world of *The Secret Agent*. These mediations are directly at work in the apparatus of the state which maintains the status quo. Inspector Heat not only employs informers, like Verloc, who are in the pay of foreign governments, but also keeps that fact secret from higher authorities within his own department. Conrad's treatment of the Home Secretary, Sir Ethelred, though mildly amusing, shows the political process itself to be a parody of its ideals. Sir Ethelred has no patience for details, and wants to know only the final result of any inquiry. All his political energies are directed toward nationalizing the fisheries, an act he considers revolutionary. Conrad completes the political parody by showing Sir Ethelred's incomprehension at the idea that there can be anything wrong with the world.

The internal workings of the state institutions are put in some difficulty but not jeopardized in any way by the clandestine activities of foreign governments. Thus Vladimir, a Russian *agent provocateur*, is engaged in provoking the British government into passing repressive legislation. Like the Professor, Vladimir attacks all forms of democratic moderation; Vladimir wants to eliminate radical movements and hence freedom altogether, and the Professor wants to eliminate all government to bring about absolute freedom. If the Professor considers England "dangerous with her idealistic conception of legality" (73), Vladimir considers it "absurd with its sentimental regard for individual liberty" (29). What the Professor and Vladimir consider dangerous is normal for the Home Secretary, the Assistant Commissioner, and Inspector Heat. Seeing the Professor, "the unwholesome-looking little agent of destruction" (83), Heat thinks, almost nostalgically, of the ordinary housebreaker as "a tribute to what is normal in the constitution of society" (93). Heat and his superiors all believe in the essential justice of democratic political institutions; they also believe in the possibility of social life created by such institutions. Anarchism and autocracy, on the other hand, are at one in their rejection of the idea of social life based on the political institutions that guarantee what one might call a kind of situational freedom.

The parody of the political figures such as Sir Ethelred is balanced by the parody of the ordinary anarchists whom the professor condemns as "the slaves of social convention" (69). The old terrorist Karl Yundt, dependent on the care of an old woman, bellows an extravagant rhetoric of violence: "I have always dreamed of a band of men absolute in their resolve to discard all scruples in the choice of means, strong enough to give themselves frankly the name of destroyers, and free from the taint of that resigned pessimism which rots the world" (42). Ossipon, a medical student and scientific materialist, exploits girlfriends for money as he later exploits Winnie. And Michaelis, the ticket-of-leave apostle, is patronized by a wealthy lady; he spins out a sentimental rhetoric advocating patience because "revolutionary propaganda is a delicate work of high conscience" (50). With the exception of the Professor, these anarchists are all lazy, depending on the normality of ordinary social life they condemn.

Thus, if the institution of family is rendered impotent before the conflict of opposed ideological forces, the radicals themselves do not escape such impotence. Each radical criticizes society and its institutions in a different way, and none sees in the activities of others his own project and goals. This lack of reciprocity is the product of atomization, isolation, impersonalization, and distortion characteristic of the relations within the family. The radicals themselves constitute, as it were, a family analogous to the traditional family in the novel. Their presumed common goal is outweighed by the kind of relations obtaining among them; very much like the Verlocs, they live an atomized and distorted life in their solipsistic isolation from each other.

The family, constituted by the official bureaucratic apparatus, in its very sluggishness, in-fighting, and mutual distrust, resembles the radicals, albeit as one positive element within an otherwise grotesque situation. The Home

Secretary and the Assistant Commissioner believe in the gradual amelioration of social suffering, but they contribute little toward real improvement. In their ignorance of the real tragedy in the Verlocs' domestic life, they are as removed from social reality as are the anarchists. Inspector Heat's interest in the fragment of Stevie's coat does not extend to Stevie's human identity and the tragic story of his total innocence. The fact that Heat considers these considerations extraneous and that the public agency which Inspector Heat represents is likewise unconcerned with personal, psychological issues seems to be the mark of detachment, perspective, and common sense. Yet Conrad reveals the apalling nature of such detachment, and calls into question the morality of this common sense. The Inspector's response should be placed, then, in the context of his professional obligations, which resemble, all too much, the inner character of society.

The apparent self-sufficiency and isolation of characters in *The Secret Agent* conceal their profound dependence on one another. It is a dependence marked by a radical self-alienation which makes reciprocity impossible; it is a dependence that spawns all forms of manipulative exploitation, though it also obscures what might be characterized as legitimately human self-interests. Yet this does not imply a clear moral alternative, one that Conrad indirectly defends and elaborates.[17] The novel's ironic detachment is the product of a moral intelligence, and a despairing critical consciousness. Indeed, the degree of ironic narrative detachment suggests a moral force that has realized the futility of its own passion. "True wisdom, which is not certain of anything in this world of contradictions" (84) may well describe the essential virtue of the narrative voice. Conrad combines pragmatism and skepticism in a manner so strikingly original that skepticism is more than a rugged element of pragmatism itself, as it is for proponents of "common sense". Normally, to be pragmatic is to entertain a skeptical attitude which opens one to possibilities one might otherwise ignore. But the world of *The Secret Agent* is not a world of possibilities. Yet Conrad does not celebrate nihilism, for what would be the point of celebrating destruction as such when society itself is viewed as a complicated mechanism of destructive forces operating at a variety of levels? What would be the point of celebrating nihilism when the reason for dismay is the extent to which versions of nihilism implicate much of what society has evolved as civilized life?

VI

The Secret Agent departs radically in one important respect from *Heart of Darkness*, *Lord Jim*, *Nostromo*, and *Under Western Eyes* because it is unconcerned with the concept of quest. It is Conrad's most thoroughgoing critique of modern industrial society, directing its criticism simultaneously at the embattled ideologies this society spawns, the tangled, confused, and corrupt network of bourgeois economy and politics, as well as the institution of family that this society undermines while claiming to cherish it. This society gives rise to the pieties of conservative moralism and the inflammatory rhetoric of a variety of radicals. The defeat of the Professor or his sense of insignificance before the multitude does not imply a victory of conservatism, since the real, though unconscious, representatives of conservatism— Stevie, Winnie, and their mother—are the most tragic victims of this society. The novel's bitter parody of anarchism does not signify any residual faith in the eventual moral regeneration of conservatism, since conservatism blinds its supporters to the possibilities of regeneration. *The Secret Agent* thus is not an ideological weapon for any party. Conservatism in *The Secret Agent* cannot comprehend the forces that alter the relations of past and present, and radicalism cannot comprehend that many of its representatives are disaffected authoritarians with a tyrannical passion for power.

Conrad deals with man's historical, cultural, and political being in ways that must not be reduced to the illustration of a political program or theoretical system, though he dramatizes the often unforeseen implications of political and theoretical programs. For example, the anarchists in *The Secret Agent*, with the exception of the Professor, are trapped in contradictions in their actual practice. Their theoretical tirades are projections, in ideological form, of this entrapment; the tirades are resolved only at the level of fantasy. Their theorizing is an instrument of concealment and mystification which makes their impotence respectable. For Marx and Engels, the sharper the contradictions in society, the greater the tendency for ideology to descend "to the level of mere idealizing phrases, conscious illusion, deliberate hypocrisy".[18] This insight applies equally well to the conservatives and the anarchists in *The Secret Agent*. The practice of both groups manifests the unity of their consciousness and their specific reality, and shows this unity to be inevitably degraded. Conservative ideology helps establish a certain stability in society, though it cannot entirely obscure the repression that ensures that stability. Like Marx, Conrad recognizes the gap between actions and ideas. For Marx this gap was a consequence of specific historical conditions and contradictions which he believed could be overcome, but for Conrad this gap is endemic to human existence. Whereas Marx might be, for all his remarkable analyses of the history of society, a romantic visionary, Conrad despairs of the possibility of overcoming man's alienation both within himself and in his relation to other men. Conrad remains a constantly resourceful skeptical critic of man in his social-political aspirations. Yet he is not opposed to revolutionary practice, though he is dismayed by those who profess revolutionary action while remaining in dependent complicity with a social system they despise. In Marx, the critique of ideology exposes distorted forms of consciousness which conceal the interests of the ruling class. Conrad reveals the distorted consciousness in the radicals themselves, though *The Secret Agent* can be considered a defense of conservatism only if one denies the centrality given to the gross and unrelenting suffering occurring, almost systematically, in the institution of the family. *The Secret Agent* examines the institution of the family, especially the lower-class family, in modern urban civilization, and finds it besieged by ideological and material forces it is powerless to control or even understand. The *apparent* critique of the family as an institution, however, is an indictment of our civilization whose abstract ideological conflicts all but squelch the possibility of mature acts of feeling and integrity.

The Secret Agent, then, differs from *Nostromo* in several significant respects. *Nostromo* dramatizes the history of events in a fledgling and underdeveloped nation. Its technical resources are therefore necessarily broad in scope, and the narrative itself does not engage the explicit ideological conflicts that characterize the world of *The Secret Agent*. For this world is besieged by self-conscious political commitments which are mutually opposed. In *Nostromo*, on the other hand, Conrad depicts a society in the process of change, and the difficulty and confusion it experiences in defining its own aspirations and identity. The ideological conflicts in *Nostromo* are relatively concealed and remain at the level of hopes and frustrations men experience through their personal lives. In *The Secret Agent* these conflicts are overtly thematized, since they not only inform the structure of the society but determine the very conditions of life as it is lived by the individual members of this society. If many of *Nostromo*'s characters are self-deceived and do not understand the workings of the historical process by which their own desire manifests itself as the desire for power, the characters of *The Secret Agent* are caught in a structure of deception and duplicity which is the defining feature of life in their society. In *Nostromo* the confused perspective of a nation being thrust into the modern world by industrialization and capitalism affords Conrad the opportunity of revealing the historical process in all its bewildering aspects. In *The Secret Agent* society enjoys a specious stability and self-confidence which appears to be the result of civilized values and democratic liberties. But *The Secret Agent*, as much as *Nostromo*, is Conrad's diagnostic history of contemporary society, one greatly unsettling in its negative force.

125

CHAPTER FIVE

Ideology and the Self: *Under Western Eyes*

"*Under Western Eyes* with its rendering of political intrigue and really aching passion has always seemed to me by a long way Conrad's finest achievement . . . if I were asked to name the book by which I was sure . . . that Conrad would go down to posterity this is the book that I should name."[1] Ford Madox Ford made this statement in 1928. Ford's notorious exaggerations do not make him a reliable guide to what posterity may or may not like, though this is one of the novels which has grown in stature rather belatedly.[2] Several leading Conrad critics consider the narrator of *Under Western Eyes* to be its major artistic flaw. Irving Howe, for instance, maintains that "the narrator is not simply an awkward intrusion; he signifies a wish on Conrad's part to dissociate himself from his own imagination".[3] Albert Guerard, too, while appreciating many of the novel's stylistic virtues, considers the narrator simply inadequate to the challenge presented by the novel's material.[4]

At least part of the reason for this kind of critical response has to do, I think, with the extraordinary innovations of narrative technique in *Heart of Darkness* and *Lord Jim*. These innovations, together with the subtle and dark reflection in his major fiction up to *The Secret Agent*, obscure Conrad's remarkable handling of the power and limits that characterize the understanding of the liberal conservative narrator of *Under Western Eyes*. As he said in his "Author's Note" to the novel, the narrative works through the implications of a course of action that "has suggested itself more as a matter of feeling than a matter of thinking" (xii).[5] I attempt to show in this chapter that in *Under Western Eyes* Conrad seeks to render the moral texture of human relations and actions in the complex and antithetical context of revolutionary action and daily living. And he does this partly by developing the figure of a narrator in some ways as interesting and original as the Marlow of his earlier great novels.

Conrad's avoidance in *Nostromo* and *The Secret Agent* of a Marlow-like figure enables him to employ narrative strategies important to capture the workings of social-political institutions in modern society. Thus in *Nostromo* and *The*

Secret Agent no single character embodies the powerful and self-blinding idealistic drive of Lord Jim. The closest we come to this is Doctor Monygham, who is a superannuated version of Jim. He is self-deprecatingly mature in a way Jim could never be. His maturity, tempered by a deeply skeptical grasp of human motives, prevents him from idealizing his own self, though in an almost fatally Jim-like endeavor he, too, is driven by a desire to regain a modicum of self-respect through a heroic act. *Nostromo*'s skeptical protagonist, Decoud, castigates all who act because of the ideas they hold; yet he, too, is mystified by ideas and acts because of them. During his island solitude he commits suicide, not because he is fully conscious of his desires, but because his skeptical stance has alienated him from them.

Conrad's critical attitude toward historical and ideological forces operating in modern social institutions, his great insight into the creative and self-destructive potentialities in his characters, and his general pessimism concerning the turn of events in history—these are subtly explored in *Nostromo* and *The Secret Agent*. They have equipped him to invent a narrator who can be placed in the highly charged ideological atmosphere of *Under Western Eyes*. The narrator's insight and failure are, as we shall see, necessary to an examination of the relations between self and community in the context of ideological conflicts. As in the preceding two novels, *Under Western Eyes* dramatizes the Hegelian idea that social and personal relations cannot be conceived of apart from their existence in the political life of a community. Conrad, however, explores this idea without Hegel's world-historical conviction of the eventual triumph of reason, a conviction based on his belief in the ultimate identity of history with reason. *Under Western Eyes*, as I shall try to show, is a highly complex and sophisticated novel which demonstrates the interdependence of political and moral questions, though it insists that neither the political category nor the moral one is simple, allowing for pre-packaged theoretical solutions.

I

For the first time in Conrad's major fiction, the narrator of *Under Western Eyes* seems, or professes, to dislike the major protagonist of his narrative. This is also the first instance in Conrad's fiction when a narrator explicitly expounds and defends his views. The Marlow of *Heart of Darkness* and *Lord Jim*, of course, holds views, but the dramatic interest of his holding them derives from his losing confidence in them as he confronts experiences he has not envisaged. In fact, the power of Marlow's language derives from its recurrent and instinctive recognition that his experience cannot be communicated in language, that his language, in straining to characterize his experience, distorts it; his narrative acquires its magic from his intense endeavor to bring the subjective and private nature of his experience within the bounds of language. Hence Marlow often employs lexical, semantic, and temporal dislocations to render the bewildering nature of his experience. The narrator of *Under Western Eyes*, too, protests that he can't understand Razumov's conduct or views. Almost like Marlow, he asserts that "Words, as is well known, are the great foes of reality" (3). But this admission does not undermine his confidence in his reasoning and values. He instead digresses for a moment to specify his prejudices and offers them as objectively valid notions. Jacques Berthoud is right in saying that the "narrator's function in the novel is not so much to interpret a predicament as to represent a point of view". The point of view he represents is, of course, "the tolerant conservatism" that he professes "as a reasonable liberal Englishman".[6]

No doubt the narrator's values derive from the explicit defense of democracy and reason that he weaves into his narrative of Razumov and Russian social and political life. His defense, I shall argue, is certainly powerful, but fundamentally questionable since it cannot comprehend how vulnerable a society without longstanding, efficacious democratic traditions is to destructive, antithetical ideologies. Consequently, the narrator's mock-modesty about his not understanding Razumov or Russian reality possesses an ironic force he does not intend: what he jokingly says about his failure to understand is literally true. It will be part of my argument in this chapter that the narrator fails to grasp the complex and contradictory moral and political life in Russian society, and that this failure is owing to his inability to understand the nature of revolutionary hope. This implies that the limits of the narrator's understanding are the limits of his conceptual categories or presuppositions. It is appropriate, then, that Conrad should have his narrator come into possession of Razumov's diaries, that the narrator should give a verbatim account of his conversations with Razumov, that he should be unwittingly present at Razumov's heartrending confession to Natalia. It is appropriate, too, that the narrator should be shown as a fussy old Englishman and that he come in for indirect authorial drubbing. Razumov at one point calls him a "devil" (360), and certain narrative moments suggest that the narrator's interest in Natalia derives from his impotent and jealous romantic love for her. While these moments are not serious, they qualify the reader's trust in the narrator and encourage a reading that finds the narrator's understanding to be seriously limited. Moreover, the relation in *Under Western Eyes* between clarity and obscurity is crucial to an understanding of the novel. In *Heart of*

Darkness and *Lord Jim*, the narrators speak in a language that is tentative, one that does not claim ontological security for the world it portrays, and does not suggest that the propositions it is constrained to offer are stable or enduring. In *Under Western Eyes*, Conrad has forsaken the skeptical stance, yet the power of the novel derives at least partly from Conrad's abandoning his narrator at those moments when his rational liberalism will not bear self-reflection. Conrad thus exploits the resources of a clarity that the narrator's stance affords, yet reveals its limitations in the context of an alien and bewildering experience.

First, for the cogency of the narrator's democratic reasoning. Knowing Natalia's passionate and ardent nature, the narrator says: "I knew her well enough to have discovered her scorn for all the practical forms of political liberty known to the western world" (104). This provides him with an occasion to clarify his general point of view, one which governs his narrative: "I suppose one must be a Russian to understand Russian simplicity, a terrible corroding simplicity in which mystique phrases clothe a naïve and hopeless cynicism. I think sometimes that the psychological secret of the profound difference of that people consists in this, that they detest life, the irremediable life of the earth as it is, whereas we westerners cherish it with perhaps an equal exaggeration of its sentimental value" (104). The cogency of the narrator's point of view here derives from a solid common sense that eschews extravagant metaphysics in favor of a homespun skeptical stance. For the narrator, neither a transcendental metaphysic with its denial of ordinary life nor a romanticization of ordinary life with its implicit devaluation of critical reasoning can satisfactorily respond to the exigencies of existence.

The narrator's stance makes immediate good sense as a comment on Natalia's vision of concord in Russia: "There must be a necessity superior to our conceptions. It is a very miserable and false thing to belong to the majority. We Russians shall find some better form of national freedom than an artificial conflict of parties—which is wrong because it is a conflict and contemptible because it is artificial. It is left for us Russians to discover a better way" (106). To Natalia's vision of "concord" (104) and her insistence on the "necessity" (106) of her Utopian vision which is "inconceivable to the strict logic of ideas" (106), the narrator's response is the epitome of rationality: "I suppose that you will be shocked if I tell you that I haven't understood—I won't say a single word; I've understood all the words. . . . But what can be this era of disembodied concord you are looking forward to? Life is a thing of form. It has its plastic shape and a definite intellectual aspect. The most idealistic conceptions of love and forebearance must be clothed in flesh as it were before they can be made understandable" (106). This is, of course, the clearest statement of the logic of rational understanding, "rational" meaning here the narrator's liberal democratic understanding. On this view, one can understand words in any statement individually, though that doesn't mean that *any* statement makes good sense. For words to make sense they must relate to concrete social reality, communicating that reality to human beings; the narrator suggests that the Utopian vision of Natalia and the revolutionaries is beyond the limits of the conceivable, and has no relation to the historical, social experiences of human beings. The narrator, appropriately a teacher of languages, seems to be right in saying that ideas in their abstract forms have no relation to life, that their value resides in their capacity to be concretized in real life.

A careful probing of the novel's main actions will show, I shall argue, that the narrator's view is inherently limited, for he implicitly conceives the model of liberal democracy to be the crowning historical development of any society; thus the Russia of the novel must founder until she embraces this unquestionable mode of social existence.

That the narrator's view is inherently limited on philosophical and political grounds does not make the novel in any way suspect. After all, Natalia looks to the teacher of languages for support and understanding, and since the Russians, including Natalia, indulge in explicit and overbearing metaphysics, it is useful to have a narrator who is wary of all metaphysics. Though a representative of democracy and reason, the narrator is nevertheless different from the complacent and unthinking bureaucrats of *The Secret Agent* whose defense of autocracy provokes its impersonal narrator's and readers' skeptical derision. The teacher of languages, on the other hand, is ruefully aware that liberal democracy is tending toward "the perfection of mediocrity". He calls Geneva "the respectable and passionless abode of democratic liberty" (357), and the average Swiss citizen one who is "made secure from the cradle to the grave by the perfected mechanism of democratic institutions" (175). The narrator thus maintains his critical detachment, without recognizing that it is in the nature of institutions to simplify and mechanize ideas, often emptying the highest ideals of their content. Thus even the values of the narrator's beloved democracy degenerate, at times, into sheer mediocrity.

So, then, what authority can the narrator claim for his criticism of the Russian social and intellectual ethos with its violent conjunction of cruel autocrats and radical revolutionaries? The narrator's authority derives from, and is limited by, his understanding of Western history in its progress from monarchy and feudalism to liberal democracy in the modern age. It is an understanding that derives its hope from the liberties wrested from the past, yet it sees some aspects of the present in the light of intelligent skepticism.

In Natalia's irrationalism, for instance, he detects the proclivity for morally dangerous and obscurantist political programs; he understands that Natalia's insistence on the special destiny of the Russian people is a sort of national and cultural narcissism that blindly proclaims its moral superiority.

The narrator's insight, none the less, is limited to his specific locale, and to the moral characters of the individual revolutionaries. Both Natalia and the exiled revolutionaries engage in a rhetoric that is far removed from action. The revolutionaries, especially their leader Peter Ivanovitch, seek greater prestige in associating with the Haldin family because Victor Haldin has assassinated the Minister in St Petersburg and has been executed by the authorities; their revolutionary commitment is to prestige and not to the compassion by which revolution may claim its justification. For Ivanovitch, the Haldin family not only enhances his prestige, but also helps him in consolidating his leadership among the revolutionaries. The rhetoric of revolution blinds the exiles to the tragic consequences of the loss of a son and brother to an aging mother and a youthful sister. The politics of autocracy and revolution are embattled theoretical wills in which human life itself becomes mere ideological raw material. Both sides claim to use reason, but reason of neither is founded in the practical necessities of daily living. It is against the brutal nature of the political process which reveals itself in the conflict of ideological wills that Conrad's skepticism is directed. For such politics, social history is an arena of intrigue, secrecy, violence, and subversion. Both ideologies act in the name of the highest values, though both spawn leadership that is always suspect.

The narrator's exposition of the cynicism latent in the Russian ideological conflict is confirmed in Razumov's words: "We are Russians, that is—children; that is—sincere; that is—cynical" (207). The sincerity of a child is such that he will not recognize the pointlessness or absurdity of his action, nor tolerate any criticism of it. Criticism makes him even more tenacious, though this is not a tenacity of purpose, but pure unreasoning willfulness. The child flaunts the meaningless, and his action, will, and reason become inseparable from sincerity, and, oddly enough, his sincerity becomes inseparable from his cynicism. Yet the child's cynicism is playful or at worst irritating; in the adult, in the general mentality of a whole society, this cynicism manifests itself in the violent destruction of all opposition. Razumov's words sustain the narrator's view of Russian reality, though it cannot explain the profound moral agony that drives Razumov to his confession not simply to Natalia but also to the revolutionaries. But this will require some careful study of Razumov, who, I may assert here, is the most fully developed and sustained character in all of Conrad's major fiction.

Contrary, then, to the narrator's confidence in the power of reason and its capacity to evolve and control language, Conrad often insists that language is inadequate to capture the complexity of human experience. From *The Nigger of the "Narcissus"* to *Heart of Darkness*, *Lord Jim*, *Nostromo*, and *The Secret Agent*, Conrad is always aware that the writing of fiction rests upon the illusion of meaningful human relations, though aware at the same time that it is in fiction that the ephemeral and questionable nature of the illusion is revealed. The teacher of languages is thus very different from the narrators of all Conrad's works we have examined so far. He exudes a confidence and rationality that enable him to criticize shrewdly the radicals and embattled autocrats; and his intelligent skepticism and democratic reasoning provide us with a subtle critique of the Russian political situation. Yet his rationality is inadequate to the texture of experience as it is lived by Razumov, Tekla, Natalia, and Sophia Antonovna. It is the last three who are ultimately betrayed by Razumov's betrayal of Victor Haldin. And in betraying Haldin and the revolutionaries he betrayed his own self; his confession is an attempt to end his self-alienation and self-betrayal. These are the things that the teacher of languages does not understand. He, of course, says that he does not understand Razumov or Russian reality, but he says this not from the perspective of the Marlow of *Heart of Darkness* and *Lord Jim* who has been profoundly shattered by the irrationality that lurks beneath the surface of stability and order. The narrators of the previous works subvert the world of stable meanings and translucent clarity, but the teacher of languages remains captive to his categorical confidence; yet the novel questions this reason, this language. In *Under Western Eyes*, Conrad employs conservatism to deal with ideological conflicts to which it is radically opposed. Conrad uses a double perspective so that the narrator may speak with authority and intelligence about events which are not accessible to him. The consequence of juxtaposing the narrator's intelligibility against the conflict between autocracy and revolution, however, is that the narrator's liberal conservatism is shown to be inadequate to grasp the aspirations of those who are committed to revolutionary action; the ideas of democratic freedom, order, and reason cannot explain either Razumov's confession or the novel's confirmation of the concept of revolutionary hope, a hope that is shared by Razumov, Tekla, Natalia, and Sophia Antonovna.

II

When Razumov discovers the reasons for Haldin's presence in his room, he senses the collapse of his carefully planned future. Haldin, however, means to express his instinctive though misplaced trust in Razumov. Razumov instinctively reciprocates his trust when he agrees to carry his message: "depend on me" (21). What follows is the story of transgressions against the pact and Razumov's troubled attempts to restore his sense of self and his clarity of vision, as well as the independence which is bound up in inter-dependence. With his betrayal of Haldin, however, seeing clearly becomes an act of duplicity, for he must lead others to misperceive him in order to maintain his distance from them. Yet Razumov is entrapped in his own falsehood: in deceiving others he becomes alienated from any clear under-standing of himself. His initial alienation, before Haldin has entered his life, has now deepened and become more desperate. The irony of his previous situation was that his intellectual endeavor, however arduous, could not compensate for his illegitimacy, or his lack of social standing. And, unlike his compatriots whose passion is expressed with great volubility, Razumov is sparing with words. But he puts his faith in reason—his Russian name signifies "reason"—and hopes to overcome his namelessness by intellectual efforts. And "he is easily swayed by argument and authority" (5). Aware of his lack of family ties he reflects that "his success would matter to no one" (11). Yet he hopes to realize his identity in the only moral terms that are available to him: "A man's real life is that accorded to him in the thoughts of other men by reason of respect or natural love" (14). Razumov is thus trying to live by the light of reason, and his reason, at least on the surface, is morally informed. In Conrad's major fiction, however, life is never conceived as a progression of ordinary happenings in which men perform their duties. For Conrad, life becomes worth dramatizing because of the contingencies that disrupt the placidity of events. Razumov of course does not understand that the concept of honor or identity has no moral content *per se* in an autocratic society, since an honorable identity is maintained there by supporting, consolidating, and serving the oppressive institutions of the autocracy.

By placing trust in Razumov and by his remark about his sister's trustful eyes (22), Haldin establishes a link between Razumov and Natalia, and his arrival in Razumov's room unleashes forces which Razumov cannot control. His desire to conquer Natalia's soul is part of his struggle with the event that has so far determined the course of his life. To possess Natalia is to exorcize Haldin, to believe that, despite everything, he still has control over his life. Yet this is only another delusion, for he has never had control over his life. He lost it perhaps most dramatically when Haldin entered his room, but, as Councillor Mikulin tells Razumov, in an autocratic state one is free to think as long as one knows it is permissible.

Autocracy's absolute control over its citizens, its tendency to generate ideological violence, is playing out in the tragedy of Razumov. Forced by the autocracy to be a secret agent among the exiled radicals in Geneva, Razumov sends his secret letters to the Russian authorities. This subjugation to authority undermines his moral self-consciousness, and to regain some measure of integrity and composure, he writes his secret diary. The diary is a form of self-indictment which he knows may prove dangerous to him: "He was aware of the danger of that strange self-indulgence. He alludes to it himself, but he could not refrain. It calmed him—it reconciled him to his existence" (339). His life is thus founded on a contradiction, one of which he is aware though he has not willed it. Paradoxically, the diary, the repository of his true feelings, enables him to live with his duplicity. When, however, he does tell Victor's mother the *coherent* story that he pieced together with Sophia Antonovna's unwitting assistance—a coherent but not truthful story—his experience proves to be shattering. His "fifteen minutes with Mrs. Haldin were like the revenge of the unknown" (340). He could retain neither his composure nor his sense of coherence; his words "troubled him like some strange discovery" (340). The words indeed do not tell the story. In the sorrow of Victor Haldin's mother Razumov perceives "a secret obstinacy . . . something he could not understand" (340).

Razumov tries to shake off the incomprehensible nature of a mother's sorrow for her son, and he makes a determined effort to tell and live the lie: "Nothing could touch him now; in the eyes of the revolutionists there was now no shadow on his past. The phantom of Haldin had indeed been walked over, was left behind lying powerless and passive on the pavement covered with snow" (340). Caught in the defensive movement of his rationalizations Razumov tries to repeat, in a concentrated moment of bitter reflection, his betrayal of Haldin. He fights back his "pitying suprise": "Mothers did not matter" (340). Not having experienced the love of a mother, Razumov has only an abstract relation to the very idea of maternal love. But, faced with the concrete reality of a sorrowing mother, Razumov's abstract denunciation of the concept of maternal love loses its power. He finds himself reflecting on her love:

> What did it mean? Before its incomprehensible character he became conscious of anger in his stern mood, the old anger against Haldin reawakened by the contemplation of Haldin's mother. And was it not something like enviousness which gripped his heart, as if of a privilege denied to him alone of all the men that had ever passed through this world? It was the other who had attained to repose and yet continued to exist in the affection of that mourning old woman, in the thoughts of all

these people posing for lovers of humanity. It was impossible to get rid of him. "It's myself whom I have given up to destruction," thought Razumov. "He had induced me to do it. I can't shake him off." (341)

Razumov has thus lost not simply the coherence of his story, but also his belief that reason might justify his betrayal of Haldin. In this sense, *Under Western Eyes* is a complex reworking of *Lord Jim*, in which Conrad examines the consequences of a betrayal in relation to the self and the possibilities of moral action. If it does not have as its narrator a deeply ambivalent Marlow to represent the complexities of experience, Conrad compensates for it by thematizing the same concerns in the context of ideological conflicts in which moral impulses are thwarted or compromised by the inauthentic life of the protagonist. If at first Razumov felt "Nothing could touch him now" (340), he now feels himself in the clutches of his past, and the dead Haldin remains an intransigent psychological force. And Razumov, despite his abstract rejection of mothers, bitterly and acutely feels the loss of his own mother's love.

A profoundly shattering consequence of this moment is that Razumov has lost the support of his confident rationalizations. They had enabled him to reason without seeing reason's relation to emotion, to lie about Haldin's betrayal and death. Now he is unnerved: privately he articulates to himself a story which contradicts the one he has just told Mrs Haldin. He has known this story since the moment of the betrayal, though he had explained away his own culpability. If he had questioned the validity of Haldin's ideological commitment, he had also refused to allow Haldin to thwart the ambitions he had set for himself. But in the course of lying to Mrs Haldin, Razumov perceives a truth that hasn't yet affected his life: Razumov's betrayal of Haldin was in fact a self-betrayal. He is "alarmed by that discovery" (341), and he strides out of the room where he has told the story: "It was frankly a flight" (341).

In Razumov's consciousness, disjointed as it is from the story he is telling Mrs Haldin, there begins a process of reinterpretation of his initial response to Haldin, one which undermines the factitious coherence of his story. This experience leads to his recognition of the essential falsehood of his constructed identity. At this moment, he begins to appreciate his complete isolation from the rest of humanity that experiences love, sorrow, and pity, and he also begins to yearn for integration into the web of humanity which his betrayal and rationalization have made impossible. Through his failure to justify the betrayal of Haldin he experiences a desire that he cannot understand; his "flight" is a flight against his own deeper yearnings. He is profoundly fragmented; his rationalizations condemning Haldin's revolutionary ideology are unsatisfying attempts at self-justification. The factitious coherence of his story leaves him profoundly isolated, and makes him feel mentally unhinged. But his "flight" does not help him escape. Just before he strides out of Mrs Haldin's room, Natalia returns home with the English teacher. This second irruption of chance, like the first, unleashes forces he cannot control. While the first drove him to betrayal and rationalization, the second brings him to a denial of his moral rightness. Even so, Razumov is not in control of himself. His experience in Mrs Haldin's room has so unnerved him that he cannot bring himself to repeat that "silly story" (341) to Natalia Haldin. The confession that he begins now is a protracted and oblique expression of his guilt and moral responsibility.

The suddenness with which he begins his confession suggests this loss of conscious control. Just as his betrayal had been spontaneous and unpremeditated, his confession also seems unself-conscious. Conrad's understanding of the will is a profound one; he seems to imply here that the will cannot guarantee that its intentions will be carried out. It is not in the will, but in experience, discipline, and dedication to work that morality finds its best support. As I said, Razumov begins his confession obliquely; while seeming to interrogate Natalia, he conducts a severe interrogation of himself. To Natalia's expression of gratitude for coming to see her mother, Razumov responds: "In comforting a bereaved mother? . . . But there is a question of fitness. Has this occurred to you?" (343) The process of self-interrogation leads to a moral perplexity Razumov has never before experienced: "But how to prove what you give me credit for—ah! that's another question. No one has ever expected such a thing from me before. No one whom my tenderness would have been any use to. . . . You come too late. You must expect nothing from me" (344). The confidence Natalia puts in Razumov is, of course, a continuation of the trust Haldin had put in him before. Even if Haldin's trust compromised Razumov's safety by bringing him within the sphere of his own revolutionary violence, Haldin's trust nevertheless possesses a certain moral power, for under torture and despite his knowledge of Razumov's betrayal Haldin never betrayed Razumov. That the authorities remained suspicious of Razumov suggests only the climate of fear and duplicity maintained by the autocracy. It was in such a moral climate that Razumov blundered and lost control; but any control he formerly had was already fragile. Its fragility derived from the nature of his society, his own dearth of love and friendship and trust whose foundation is the instinctive knowledge that betrayal of another's trust involves the moral isolation of the man who betrays. Razumov feels guilt but seeks to smother it with reason. He succeeds only in distorting the reasoning which is at the basis of his being a double agent. Thus he becomes an instrument of the autocracy he hates and a hero for the radical exiles he detests. Neither the autocrats nor the radicals seem morally justified to him, but he serves autocracy and endures the admiration of the radicals.

Razumov's demonic desire to conquer Natalia's soul is, as we have seen, part of his continuing attempt to overcome the event which controls the course of his life. Referring to Haldin's remark that his sister has trustful eyes, Razumov tells her, "It meant that there is in you no guile, no deception, no falsehood, suspicion—nothing in your heart that could give you a conception of living, acting, speaking a lie, if it ever came in your way. That you are a predestined victim" (349). It is Razumov's feeling of love for Natalia, together with his awareness of the love of her sorrowing mother, which allows him the first movement toward liberation from the captivity to the past. Love does not liberate him from guilt, so much as it brings him to a full consciousness of his guilt, so that he can affirm his love only through renunciation. Thus for Razumov to love Natalia is to disclose those secrets which would make impossible her reciprocation of his love. To love her genuinely is to be forever deprived of her love, though this loss is not without recompense.

It is important to remember that Razumov's spoken confession to Natalia is quite oblique, unlike the direct confession he will soon make to the revolutionaries. But between the oblique and direct confessions Razumov returns to his hotel room and begins writing the confession in his diary. "He produces a page and a half of incoherent writing where his expression is baffled by the novelty and the mysteriousness of that side of our emotional life to which his solitary existence had been a stranger. Then only he begins to address directly the reader he had in mind, trying to express in broken sentences, full of wonder and awe, the sovereign (he uses that very word) power of her person over his imagination" (357). This initial incoherence is the logical consequence of his having lived the truth of his betrayal in his secret notes to himself. Until now, Razumov has lived a painfully duplicitous life, agonized over his insight into the folly of both autocrats and revolutionaries. Once he recognizes that his continuing dissimulation entails further betrayals of those whose purity and integrity he respects, he can no longer maintain his self-control. The resources of cunning and duplicity are no longer useful when he decides to write the confession. The dislocation of self here is also that of his writing, since the self and writing constitute the kind of relation to the world he thought was possible for him. Razumov's emergence into a morally viable public self depends on an experience of love, which allows him to speak without irony or dissimulation. Formerly his language was fissured: his words had an immediate meaning which was always false. His strategy of disclosure remained an act of concealment. His earlier conversations with Antonovna, Ivanovitch, and Natalia tended to be indirect and suggestive, and in that sense obscurely confessional. But the confession was done in bad faith since his expression obscured what it pretended to confess.

When Razumov began his confession to Natalia, he conveyed the gist of the matter, but not the depth of his remorse. Since the betrayal his speech has become an elaborate means of cunning and dissimulation: he tells Natalia that "in order to speak fittingly to a mother of her lost son one must have had some experience of the filial relation" (344). Razumov, a man without a name and without a family, is suddenly to blame for the tragic grief of a family, and his act of violation has implications more brutal than the act of random violence that the sentimental idealist, Victor Haldin, committed. Razumov's words thus contain a profound truth, but the words, even as they verge on confession, also seek to mitigate the evil they disclose. His spoken confession, from its very beginning, is caught up in a form of reasoning which evades responsibility, yet within the context of his baffling experience his reasoning has its own legitimacy. How can one learn to love without having experienced it? Thus the story he tries to tell Mrs Haldin leaves him more embittered than before, for he has not performed an act of conscience. His act was meant to gain security, to free himself from any suspicion the revolutionaries might have had about him. He overcomes his hesitations to visit Mrs Haldin as soon as he is in possession of a credible story about the betrayal and execution of her son. Ostensibly he goes to see Mrs Haldin to offer consolation, but his visit only compounds the first betrayal. As he tells the story Razumov repeats the old rationalizations, though he cannot rid himself of Haldin, for the consequences of the betrayal are profound and far-reaching, depriving him of any sincere expression. Only an admission of guilt can restore his sense of sanity, which his reason denies him. What unnerves Razumov is his utter loneliness before Haldin's mother, his sense that the meaning of Victor Haldin is in the love his mother and sister feel for him, and that, though dead, he lives in that emotional force denied to Razumov himself. Moments such as this one enable Conrad to reappropriate for modern literature certain disturbing elements of tragedy unmitigated by confession or forgiveness.

Once Razumov's spell of incoherence is past, he does write a confession. In the past, writing had a private significance for Razumov, for he wrote secret notes partly to tell himself the truth and partly to regain his composure, without which he could not have continued his public dissimulation. This time his writing is not a private disclosure to himself, but a disclosure of the truth to Natalia. It is a public act that liberates him from the entanglements of deception and self-alienation: "Now I have done it; and as I write here, I am in the depths of anguish, but there is air to breath at last—air" (361). His sense of relief and liberation is the release as well from rationalizing prevarication; he is free from the sense of irony and derision that has tainted all his relationships since the betrayal. Consequently he writes with deep feeling: "In giving Victor Haldin up, it was myself, after all, whom I have betrayed most basely. You must believe what I say now, you can't refuse to believe this" (361). Having overcome for the moment the schism between his private and public selves, and having taken upon himself the burdens of his past, Razumov is now able to talk. He decides to go to the revolutionaries' meeting where he can confess his betrayal of Haldin, and he talks with the composure of a man who has penetrated his own self-deception and now talks with tragic self-knowledge.

Marlow in *Heart of Darkness*, we recall, tries to describe Kurtz's "ability to talk", but his description begins with a series of antithetical words unrelated to the concept of description; it initiates and sustains an impression of disintegration. Marlow cannot really describe Kurtz's "ability to talk" which, interestingly enough, he has only heard of. His attempt to capture what he hasn't experienced ends with his insistence on the necessity of deferral, though his retrospective account seeks to capture the complex process of anticipation, experience, and disillusionment that is the crux of his story. Just as Kurtz is presumed to have the "ability to talk", Razumov is presumed to have the ability to reason. Paradoxically, however, this man of reason is best known among his fellow students for his ability to maintain silence. When he breaks this silence, he is driven into deception, irony, and derision. His confession frees him from this stranglehold and he begins to speak. Jim, too, we remember, was incapable of talking, and Marlow interpreted him continually without receiving an adequate response from Jim himself. Thus, after his mishap with Gentleman Brown, Jim was unable to write a letter home; his ideals had no relation to human affairs. His ideals were manifestations of his egoistic self-entrapment that deprived him of ordinary human language, of its imperfect, provisional, and necessary concepts.

Czarist autocracy, Haldin's mystical populism, Peter Ivanovitch's theory of history (211—12)—all are at base identical. As Avrom Fleishman has noted, all these forms of Russian thought are undergirded by "a conception of society as an organism, a real unity of its members".[7] This unity, however, is a unity of sentiment deriving its force from contradictory ideals: it is the terror of history disguised in apparently beneficent forms of ideology. The critique of revolution in *Under Western Eyes* is primarily a critique of absolutism which manifests itself in various forms such as Ivanovitch's nihilism which is based on a theory of history requiring mass human sacrifice, Victor Haldin's crazed populism which contends that his "spirit shall go on warring in some Russian body till all falsehood is swept out of the world" (22), and General T's extreme rightist position which prompts him to want to destroy rebels of every kind (50). The rhetoric that the representatives of each ideology employ always sacrifices the present to the future, a future that depends on the violent removal of social and ideological contradictions. In this sense, *Under Western Eyes* is the story of a young man caught in the violent contradictions of obscurantist ideals. From General T to Peter Ivanovitch to Victor and Natalia Haldin, all Russians seem to hold views that require a total subordination of the individual to the state or a collectivist dream. Nor can Razumov forsake the dream, though he is aware of its dangers. As he says to Natalia: "Ziemianitch ended by falling into mysticism. So many of our true Russian souls end that way. Very characteristic" (283). He seeks to avoid this pitfall of simplification which is part of his Russian spiritual inheritance; he wishes to forestall the interpretation of his life history in terms of an inherited political allegory. Yet he remains a captive to it, and the narrative delineates the great difficulty entailed in escaping one's unconscious national and racial heritage. Thus at the moment of his confession to Natalia he admits: "I have the greatest difficulty in saving myself from the superstition of an active Providence" (350). And his remark to Natalia about the English teacher illustrates his captivity to this inheritance: "every word of that friend of yours was egging me on to the unpardonable sin of stealing your soul. Could he have been the devil himself in the shape of an old Englishman? Natalia Victorovna, I was possessed" (359—60).

In one sense Razumov's words above simply rationalize his intention to steal Natalia's soul, a continuation of his rationalizations about his betrayal of her brother. His present intention is no doubt complicated by his appreciation of Natalia's difference from the radical exiles he meets at Ivanovitch's gatherings. His admiration motivates him to regain the integrity he has lost through the betrayal of Haldin. His conflict springs, nevertheless, from an obscure but tenacious feeling of a heinous wrong done to him. His vilification of the English teacher derives from his naïve political allegory which so influences his understanding. The teacher seems diabolical to Razumov because his is a reflective, though reticent, consciousness capable of penetrating Razumov's darker motives, as well as his intentions toward Natalia. And at a subtler, displaced level Razumov's attitude to the English teacher is a reenactment of his response to Victor Haldin. Besides dramatizing the individual in the arena of embattled ideological wills, the novel also dramatizes the conflict of wills between Razumov and the English teacher, and between the English teacher and Peter Ivanovitch, for the possession of Natalia's soul. The teacher's intention makes sense because his interest is in Natalia's personal safety, in getting her to dissociate herself from the revolutionary activists whom he considers fated to self-destruction. Ivanovitch, too, though differently motivated, shares the teacher's appreciation of Natalia's purity of intention.

III

A predominant concern of *Under Western Eyes* is with the concepts of understanding and communication as they are entangled with the self. Though at the beginning Razumov is excessively self-confident and rationalistic, he is also confused about his relation to his country. By identifying himself exclusively as a Russian he cannot comprehend the peculiar fashion in which others perceive him. Lacking any filial ties, Razumov is subject to the caprice of both state and individuals. There is a depressing similarity in the responses of both Haldin and Councillor Mikulin to Razumov: Haldin had decided that because Razumov had no family no one else would suffer should he get caught. And, in asking Razumov the question "Where to?" (99) after the interrogation, Mikulin suggests that Razumov may not decide what to do with his life; the state will. It is then that Razumov understands that his betrayal of Haldin has made him a servant of the autocracy.

But it is not Razumov alone who remains cut off from a proper appreciation of the self and its context. For instance, Victor Haldin's act of assassination is done in the name of revolution, though he recognizes the brutality of the act itself. What is worse, in the name of revolutionary commitment, he sets loose forces in Razumov's life which enslave him for many years. Haldin's idealism is a sentimental one, and Conrad's treatment of it is profoundly ironic. If Haldin chooses Razumov because he has no filial relations, his own act of bombing is profoundly indifferent to the filial relations he himself does have. Haldin conceives the suffering that his family might endure in terms of the state's oppression of them, but he is not deterred by the psychological suffering that his possible capture would cause. Razumov has not understood love and the suffering of those who love, because he has no family; Haldin has felt the deep bond of filial relations and we are left puzzled at his understanding of love. It is true that the rhetoric of ideology has blinded him to the deep and complex bonds he shares with his mother and Natalia, yet it is also true that autocracy calls forth a political response from the oppressed, who must put aside their personal ties. It is Conrad's distressing insight that autocracy complicates, and even destroys, the personal integrity of its subjects, whether they be obedient or rebellious.

Of all Conrad's novels, *Under Western Eyes* is the most resolutely tragic in the Greek sense; its modernity derives not from an attitude verging on nihilism, but from its skeptical rejection of the comforting illusions of ideology as well as those comforting illusions derived from even the purest filial love. *Under Western Eyes* exposes the fissure between the private and public domains and the consequent distortions in both; yet it denies any easy relationship between them. The novel insists that the private domain is sustained in part by the public, though it clearly fears the triumph of the public domain. For once the public domain, with its impersonal institutions, controls the lives of the individuals it becomes an inhuman machine with an oppressive rhetoric of order and control antithetical to the ideals of disclosure and understanding. For Conrad, a meaningful public domain consists of the relations among individuals, relations free from exploitation and from the obfuscation of systematizing ideology. But, as we saw in our discussion of *The Secret Agent*, Conrad has little hope for the future. For Conrad the life of the individual caught up in the confrontation between autocracy and revolution is inevitably tragic.

When the revolutionaries at last ask the mutilated and deaf Razumov for advice and he begins talking well, we know that the destructive urge that drove him into isolation as a secret agent for the Russian government has finally taken its leave of him. How one learns to talk well, without duplicity, falsehood or guile, is one of the great concerns of the novel. In the beginning Razumov's talk was veiled; he said what he didn't mean, and he left unsaid what he did mean. Razumov's overcoming of the schism within himself, however, does not imply that the novel is a saga of hope, for his release is purchased at a hideous physical price. It is in this context that some of Natalia's conversations with the narrator should be placed. When Natalia quotes her brother's words to the English teacher—"Unstained, lofty, and solitary existences" (135)—she adds: "These are the words which my brother applies to a young man he came to know in St. Petersburg" (135). At this moment the reader's knowledge of Razumov's betrayal of Haldin and his subsequent rationalizations leads to an overwhelming sense of Razumov's moral failure. And because this conversation occurs after Natalia's rebuff of Ivanovitch one knows that Natalia's is no empty rhetoric, although it is filled with Utopian idealism which is perhaps naïve. The teacher's observation, for instance, does have the force of historical truth: "The scrupulous and the just, the noble, humane, and devoted natures; the unselfish and the intelligent may begin a movement—but it passes away from them. They are not the leaders of a revolution. They are its victims: the victims of disgust, of disenchantment—often of remorse. Hopes grotesquely betrayed, ideals caricatured—that is the definition of revolutionary success" (134–35). Revolutionary success tends to make the innocent its victims, and the teacher wants to save Natalia from being one. Despite his limitations, the teacher has a subtle grasp of the nature of revolutionary action, but given his commitment to liberal values he cannot see that Natalia must participate in some form of revolutionary activity.

To participate in revolution is to endanger one's own life, though to think of safety is tantamount, for Natalia, to the betrayal of her ideals, which were her brother's ideals as well, however naïvely he may have pursued them. Natalia's answer to the English teacher, in this sense, is unassailable: "I would take liberty from any hand as a hungry man would snatch a piece of bread" (135). It is significant that Conrad uses Natalia's words as the epigraph to *Under Western Eyes*, for his critique of revolutionary ideology and action, as I see it, does not blind him to the power of revolutionary hope, even as it threatens the ideal of political liberty. Yet he knows that revolutionary hope may be betrayed by a demagogue and phony spiritualist like Ivanovitch, that the most noble and sincere may be victimized by the power-hungry, and that the rhetoric of ideology may conceal the social conditions that make the idea of revolution compelling. One of Conrad's most powerful achievements in this novel is his linking of two radically opposed aspects of man's historical experience and aspirations: that is, the link between the teacher's essentially valid historical statement and Natalia's compelling moral-psychological assertion. On the teacher's view it seems that a hungry man should not be allowed to snatch a piece of bread whether he is living in a democracy or in an autocracy, though the teacher would imagine the democracy offering some relief to the hungry. Autocracy, on the other hand, deals a harsh blow to the hungry and the innocent and renders its own power inherently unstable. Natalia, if she is to maintain her revolutionary hope, must reject the teacher's view because his view is historical with regard to democracy, but not so with regard to revolution. For revolution is a relatively modern phenomenon and, while its ideologies and actions are often self-defeating or irrelevant, the oppressed cannot do without revolutionary hope. The alternative is to live in abject submission to the ghastly reality of oppression. Natalia's words thus must be judged in terms of their relation to her actions. On these terms, her words have the ring of sincerity which Razumov's have lacked until the moment of his confession.

IV

Much of the interest of *Under Western Eyes* derives from Conrad's interweaving of two apparently different stories within the story of Razumov, stories which explore the connection between sincerity of expression and action. The first is the account of Ivanovitch's escape from the Siberian prison and his leadership of the radical movement in exile. The tale of his inhuman suffering might have made a moving saga of horror and redemption, but Conrad's treatment of Ivanovitch is unsparingly derisive.[8] Ivanovitch has written several self-serving volumes about his escape and the woman who helped him to release his chains: he has fallen into what the English teacher would call the mystic female worship, and his autobiography becomes a monument to "the cult of woman" (125). In both writing and speech, Ivanovitch is incapable of straightforward expression. His purpose is to present himself as the revolutionary hero who will lead a nation out of its appalling subjection. But in truth Ivanovitch remains deeply alienated from any true understanding of his experience. His life as a revolutionary leader in Geneva is a betrayal of his past suffering, and the narrator takes him as a parody of revolutionary leadership.

The story of Tekla's life, on the other hand, is what one might call a low-mimetic but deeply touching repetition of Razumov's own life. Conrad lets Tekla recount her own life story, and her transparent sincerity strikingly contrasts with the narratives of Ivanovitch. Her story in itself takes the opposite course from Ivanovitch's, for Ivanovitch escapes the tyranny of autocracy only to become a tyrant in his own right; Tekla, on the other hand, has escaped from her autocratic family, though she has remained essentially humble and sincere: "I tried to make myself useful to the utterly hopeless. I suppose you understand what I mean? I mean the people who have nowhere to go and nothing to look forward to in their life" (150). The real interest of Tekla's story, however, is in her depiction of Ivanovitch dictating his revolutionary prose to her. Because Tekla would look out the window for a moment's relief while Ivanovitch paced to and fro straining after his rhetoric, he forced her to sit in front of the wall and forbade her to move. What rhetorical eloquence Ivanovitch achieves involves this brutality capriciously inflicted on Tekla, a member of the lower class, for whose liberation Ivanovitch has ostensibly been working. Tekla's story differs from the main story because, unlike Razumov who did not share Haldin's revolutionary commitment, Tekla is betrayed by the man she serves. And, unlike Victor Haldin, the burly feminist spews forth a rhetoric unconnected to the actions he considers necessary for social change; Ivanovitch's revolutionary stance is essentially

144

self-aggrandizing. Despite his experience of suffering, his status as a leader involves no compassion for those who suffer, which alone would justify his revolutionary hope. His daily life has become a parody of revolutionary zeal; he was once a victim denied humane treatment who has become the ludicrous victimizer of his own frail secretary.

Tekla's own moral integrity allows her an instinctive grasp of Ivanovitch's fraudulence: "To have one's illusions destroyed—that is really more than one can bear" (125). When she finally leaves Ivanovitch to nurse the mutilated Razumov, who has by now learned to *talk well*, she regains the revolutionary hope she had lost in her enslavement to the phony revolutionary.

V

The English teacher and Razumov are both engaged in a kind of reading and writing, in a hermeneutic project in which interpreter and text have changing relations.[9] The teacher seeks to read the political situation and to make a coherent story out of the baffling reality of Russian life, whereas Razumov seeks to *write* a coherent life for himself which can confound the dark fatality that has destroyed his sense of purpose. What the English teacher does is, in a sense, both quasi-referential and quasi-performative. At the level of overt intention he seeks to invest his narrative with objective validity and authoritative referential content; yet because at the level of experience he does not penetrate the tangled knot of problems which determines Razumov's life his account becomes a performative act, a rhetorical enterprise whose full significance remains obscure to his own understanding. Razumov's career, on the other hand, reaches from the writing of abstract academic essays to deliberately misleading conversations and letters while secretly writing the truth to himself, and it culminates in his confession.

Though radically different in outlook and emotions from both the English teacher and Razumov, Victor Haldin possesses a self-confidence which perhaps exceeds theirs. Haldin's tenacious belief in the rationality of the historical process prevents him from imagining that his particular act of assassination might be irrational or absurd even though he assassinated not only the minister, but also his own accomplice, as well as a number of innocent bystanders. He cannot conceive of his action as destroying the lives of specific individuals while having little impact on the historical process itself. In the grip of his conviction, he has thrown himself into the future where he

145

is freed from the complex and dismaying recognition that revolution requires a conjunction of many elements, and entails compromises and at times deferral of action.[10] Haldin is what Marxists might call an adherent of Utopianism who sacrifices himself for a future projected by desire. Conrad converts Haldin's revolutionary Utopianism into a bitter paradox by turning loose upon him what his plan had no use for: that is, contingency. When he takes refuge in Razumov's room, hoping for sympathy and support, he does so because he has so unquestioningly subordinated Razumov's life to his Utopian plans. Thus he is deeply shocked to see Razumov doesn't fall into the pattern he had constructed in his dreams. Perhaps the most brilliant stroke in Conrad's brief portrait of a sentimental revolutionary is in Haldin's emotional integrity toward Razumov, an integrity that will haunt Razumov until the moment of his confession.

Lord Jim does not understand—and given his transcendental concept of the self it is inevitable that he should not—that even the unwitting betrayal of another means self-betrayal. Razumov's moral self-discovery is in his gradual awareness that his betrayal of Haldin also entailed a betrayal of his own self. If Razumov eventually recognizes that the betrayal of Haldin has alienated him from society and self, Jim's final act is a romantic affirmation of self and of the unlimited possibilities of goodness which he conceives the self to embody. Razumov's confession is an act of repudiation that releases him from the cycle of fatal repetitions, but Jim's blindness to evil engulfs him. If Razumov's confession halts the cycle of repetition, Jim's admission of his responsibility for Dain Waris's death only accelerates its deadly force. For Jim confession becomes the moral triumph of the self, whereas for Razumov confession becomes a release of the self from the process of self-destruction. For Jim confession leads to a final denial of life, though his romantic pursuit of his ideal already had effectively cut him off from life. For Razumov, on the other hand, confession reintegrates him with the community, such as it is. And it grants him a sense of serenity denied him while he could still act and respond. It is, of course, a tragic serenity; he is deaf but not tormented, mutilated but spiritually at rest because he has escaped the repetition which Jim, the ultimate idealist, for all his triumphant self-assertion, could not escape. Razumov's reintegration, however, should not be construed as a moral possibility that conclusively redefines the world for us. For a world in which action, hope, and failure are always intertwined, Razumov's wholeness can have no enduring value. Like *Lord Jim*, *Under Western Eyes* reappropriates the concept of the tragic. The earlier novel portrays the tragic consequences of a naïve, romantic imagination; the later portrays the tragic consequences of a betrayal forced upon a man caught in the battle of ideological wills. For

Conrad, idealists such as Jim, Razumov, and even Natalia and Tekla do not inherit the earth, though through their struggles they suggest the beauty and possibility of acts of feeling and integrity, even as they bring to our attention the forces that operate against this possibility.

CHAPTER SIX
Skepticism and Experience: *Victory*

I

Many critics have held that *Victory* must be classed with the works of Joseph Conrad's decline, as one of a series of radically inferior novels sharing deficiencies absent in the best of Conrad's early novels.[1] One major break from the concerns of Conrad's great works consists in the development of what Albert Guerard has characterized as the "sentimental ethic", a cluster of thematic elements which suggest a "new cleansed moral universe" and a repudiation of the earlier skepticism. In consequence, Conrad's later works, including *Victory*, are no more than forays into mawkishness, complacency, and simplistic plot-structure.[2] There are, of course, others who argue that *Victory* is a modernist allegory whose value depends on a shift in Conrad's "thematic interests away from the essentially inner psycho-moral perplexities of his early work toward the external conditions which define the status of the moral agent".[3]

These two presumably different interpretations are not really opposed, though their value judgments of *Victory* certainly are. Indeed, those who castigate *Victory* for its sentimental ethic recognize its obvious formal structure, which, construed as allegorical, lends credence to their perception of a new optimism in Conrad. Both these readings are plausible in their analyses of much specific detail in the novel: the allegorical readings focus on symbolic structures that transform the realistic beginning of *Victory* into a "core of allegory",[4] whereas the "sentimental ethic" reading focuses on the scenes, especially the voyeur scenes, that are badly executed.[5]

The opposition between these two readings is revealed in responses to Heyst's final words to Davidson: "woe to the man whose heart has not learned while young to hope, to love—and to put its trust in life" (410). Several critics have argued that the value of the human bond is asserted, and skepticism repudiated. Other critics have argued that Heyst's final words convey only a sentimental affirmation, not an artistically realized affirmation. The allegorical reading shows that Heyst's skepticism fails miserably in crisis, that his final act, his burning of himself with the house, is a symbolic repudiation of his former life, an "existential affirmation".[6] The other reading shows that "Heyst emerges as neither a romantic nor a skeptic, but as a good man brought down by chance and 'other people,'"[7] that "Heyst's flaw is never made real".[8]

There is no doubt that Heyst's final words encapsulate the general movement of the story, that they express Heyst's wish that he had "learned" love and trust earlier in life. Yet, if placed in the total context of the novel, Heyst's words reveal a despair and bitterness that are powerful psychological adjuncts of his deep-seated skepticism. The deeper resonances of meanings in Heyst's words spring from his attribution of an incapacity for love and hope and trust—all of which are interdependent—to the older man who had not learned them in the naïveté of youth. Hope, love, and trust, in this view, are learned attitudes; they are neither spontaneous nor natural; they are learned at a time when one is impressionable, when one has not had the disillusioning experience of the world. Naïve learning may be a snare or an illusion which makes possible the attitudes of love and hope.

Heyst's final act is therefore a rejection of the world, since the only alternative available to him is an illusory certainty stemming from the naïveté of youth and inexperience. This reading of Heyst's final words does not cancel, though it certainly contradicts, the immediate response that construes them to mean a repudiation of his skepticism. The novel thus invites contradictory readings at crucial moments and generates a textual ambiguity that is not resolvable into a final thematic meaning.

A careful reading of *Victory* will, I believe, show that both the allegorical and the sentimental readings, despite their immediate plausibility, fail to take into account several crucial and problematic features of the novel.[9] For, rather than constituting a shift from the vision of Conrad's best novels, *Victory* retains earlier themes, though in an altered context. This altered context has implications for the form of *Victory*, a form which certainly differs from the recurrent formal features of the earlier novels. In *Victory* the tragic implications of a skeptical attitude to life are forcefully depicted. Yet this attack upon skepticism does not generate a new, more positive metaphysics. Indeed, there are implications for a less negative portrayal of life, but there are also a refinement and an extension of Conrad's earlier bleak vision. As I shall try to demonstrate in this chapter, the novel allows for (or oscillates between) two contradictory readings of skepticism and thus problematizes any reading that seeks to resolve *Victory* into either an allegorical structure of formal constraints or a propositional reduction of themes.

Guerard has complained that *Victory* panders to adolescent fancies: "the simple yet vague erotic fantasy of the island shared with a grateful uneducated girl".[10] However, as Guerard himself notes in another context, Conrad through most of his creative phase met with consistent success in bringing to bear serious and complex themes upon the framework of the exotic novel of adventure.[11] *Victory* is but another case in point: Conrad's imagination transmutes the rudiments of popular romance, lending them new significance. Heyst, the man of "tired eyes" (15), of whom "the last vestiges of youth had gone off his face and all the hair off the top of his head" (8), hardly fits the stereotype of the swashbuckling adventurer. Instead, he is "enigmatical and disregarded like an insignificant ghost" (24). Further, the narrative's climax transpires within a complex matrix of deception, reticence, and isolated motives; Heyst's final confrontation with Mr Jones proves abortive, the evil trio turns out to be oddly inept, and Heyst remains enmeshed in tragic immobility. Such elements do not define popular adventure romance.

Those who find *Victory* genuinely deficient in artistic powers and sentimental in its ethos argue that evil here springs from outside rather than from within as in the early novels. As a result, in Guerard's view, Mr Jones's assertions of "spectral fellowship" (393) with Heyst—"you and I have much more in common than you think" (321)—are false. For Heyst, the innocent, paralyzed in will and shrinking from any crime, cannot have any true connection with Jones.[12] If this characterization is correct, then it constitutes a serious charge, since it questions Conrad's very ability to construe or realize Heyst's relationship with Jones.

Guerard accurately describes Heyst's personality but misreads its implications in the world of the novel. It is significant and ironic that Heyst consistently engenders tragic "criminal" results no matter whether he remains frozen in the paralysis of his skepticism or is driven to action by love. He becomes linked in a subtle, unknowing alliance with Jones, though their motives remain poles apart. The allegorical figures of Jones, Ricardo, and Pedro only serve to externalize the evil "within"; they are, in a sense, the means of displacement of this evil for the purpose of fictional representation. Conrad has thus readapted, rather than abandoned, his earlier concerns. Skepticism, initially engendered out of a sense of the evil of the external world, finally leads its adherent to discover that evil within. The movement of the narrative in *Victory* thus dissolves a simple dichotomy of outer and inner as the source of evil and shows the ways in which each is implicated in the other.

Heyst's primary bond with Jones, however, arises through his skepticism. Both are wanderers "coming and going up and down the earth" (317−18) with a shared contempt for life. More important, Jones's rabid misogyny is subtly echoed in Heyst's reactions to Lena. Beneath the flood of romantic ardor the detached, mistrustful side of Heyst's nature prompts undercurrents of aversion to Lena's presence which culminate in his willingness to believe her unfaithful. Thus Heyst both loves and feels subtly threatened by Lena. Her presence seems "to infect his very heart" (84), with the result that "weaknesses are free to enter" (210). He feels himself "enveloped in the atmosphere of femininity as in a cloud, suspecting pitfalls . . . afraid to move" (221–22), and reflects that "no wonder . . . women can deceive men so completely. The faculty was inherent in them" (81). In her supposed treachery with Ricardo, Heyst sees her "as if enthroned" (391), the sole point of immobility in a trembling universe, a goddess of infidelity cloaked in innocence. Such impressions link Heyst to Mr Jones and undermine his bond with Lena. Hence Jones's vile intimations of fellowship have genuine, though obscure, substance.

Consistent with his skepticism, Heyst refuses all communal ties, a refusal that already establishes a connection with his negative double, Jones. No human being, however, has his meaning or identity without some sort of tie with the community. Heyst is, in effect, named and given an identity by others. Thus it is that he has come to be known as "Enchanted Heyst", (7), "Hard Facts" (8), and "Hermit" (31). He possesses for others an identity which circulates in the form of rumor and takes on the forms desired by those who make or spread the rumor. First there is Morrison, then Lena. For them identity is constituted by reciprocity, which Heyst, by his withdrawal and evasiveness, has denied. And now, when the world presents itself again, it is in the form of Jones and his accomplices. For one who neither acts nor communicates in a resolute way, the world is necessarily that which is constituted and presented by others. This is why Jones can say, "I am the world itself, come to pay you a visit" (379), and thus differentiate himself from Heyst. Jones can affirm his "spectral fellowship" with Heyst because he is, like others, free to remake Heyst in his own image. Jones's conception of Heyst, though undeniably malevolent, is nevertheless not without a psychologically compelling element.

There are undeniable weaknesses that pervade *Victory*, and they enter the narrative quite early—with Schomberg in fact. The Schomberg scenes begin with his malignant rumors about Heyst, become bizarre with his furtive pursuit of the helpless Lena, who has arrived with the Zangiacomo orchestra to perform at Schomberg's hotel, and culminate in a farce when Lena is known to have fled with Heyst. Schomberg faces a worse predicament when Jones and his accomplices arrive to stay at his hotel. Even if Conrad depicted the Schomberg scenes with genuine relish, they cannot be construed as a significant allegorical dimension in *Victory*. Jones and his accomplices have a more immediate dramatic relevance, for Jones is a representative of cynical and destructive skepticism, a logical culmination of Heyst's urban and inexperienced skepticism. But the desperadoes are described in painfully obvious symbolic terms: critics have noted the "archetypal" animal imagery that portrays their savage motives.[13] The symbolism is strained; the conversations between Ricardo and Jones deal repetitively with their ruthless plot against Heyst, relieved only by Jones's petulance and Ricardo's sly praise of his boss.

Yet it will not do to say, as Guerard does, that *Victory* is set in a "new cleansed moral universe", for malevolence remains immanent both in nature and within the hero's personality. As in the earlier novels, nature in *Victory* is alternately depicted as blindly indifferent or as actively sinister. Samburan is an island of "general desolation" above which the coal company's blackboard sign hangs "like an inscription stuck above a grave" (42). Overhead, the sun bursts upon the island like "the eye of an enemy" (185); the surrounding sea is a "flaming abyss of emptiness" (216). Humanity, as embodied in Lena and Heyst, appears as "two remote white specks against the sombre line of the forest" (189), negligible motes within an "oppressive infinity . . . without breath, without light" (373). Such statements explicitly link *Victory* to earlier bleak depictions of the universe in Conrad's work.

Both the allegorical and the "sentimental ethic" readings of the novel neglect those moments in the narrative that reveal Conrad's powerful treatment of the complex interaction between skepticism and experience, between an abstract denial of life and the contingencies of life as they erupt into and complicate the skeptic's detachment from the world of action and suffering. The very crux of the narrative turns upon the conflict generated by Heyst's divided loyalties. He is a man torn between allegiance to the self of universal detachment implanted in him by his father and his spontaneous adherence to the call of the human community as it is embodied in Lena and Morrison—the same moral challenge of response to human suffering thrust upon Razumov in *Under Western Eyes*.

II

Before probing the implications for Heyst's skepticism of his twin rescues of Morrison and Lena it will be useful to observe that Conrad had successfully dramatized, in *Under Western Eyes*, the difficult relation between action and intention, and that in *Victory* he is once again grappling with the same problem. Yet the handling of this problem is now mediated by Conrad's earlier treatment of the relation between skepticism and values in *Heart of Darkness*, *Lord Jim*, and *Nostromo*. While in these works skeptical reflection emerges as a result of confrontation with the darker possibilities of the self as it attempts to assert its own intrinsic moral principle against the evil of the universe, in *Victory* skeptical withdrawal is a constitutive element of Heyst's identity which poses difficulties for both his actions and intentions, thereby not only making them mutually antithetical and irreconcilable but making each internally divided.

Conrad has interwoven throughout *Victory* narrative statements which bear the stamp of skeptical withdrawal. The first chapter describes "the persistent inertia of Heyst" (3), and calls his "most frequent visitors" "shadows" (4). While still a boy, Heyst developed "a profound mistrust of life" (91) and decided to "drift" as a "defence against life" (92). Such a skeptical rejection of the world Heyst learned from his father. Yet the tragic irony of this lesson in Heyst's life stems from the fact that his father's skepticism had its origins in his anger at the world "which had instinctively rejected his wisdom" (91). Embittered, the elder Heyst had withdrawn from active participation in the world's affairs and had admonished his son "to cultivate that form of contempt which is called pity" (174). Since humanity is an object of pity through contempt, the elder Heyst had also taught his son that he, too, was as pitiful as the rest of mankind. This conflation of pity and contempt makes it impossible for the son to experience an emotion without being critically aware of it. Thus at his father's funeral, when Heyst becomes "aware of his eyes being wet", this awareness does not reflect the bond of a son to a father but, rather, makes him realize that the "dead man had kept him on the bank". And now, "alone on the bank of the stream", he has the responsibility to abide by his father's gospel of skeptical withdrawal: "Look on—make no sound" (175). Heyst's rescues of Morrison and Lena occur in this context of skeptical detachment contaminated only by a pity that does not engage a deeper commitment to life. The original Adam in him—"There must be a lot of the original Adam in me, after all" (173)—at best prompts his instinct and remains powerless to affect his skeptical perception of things.

It is, I think, a measure of Conrad's grasp of the complex nature of intentional action that the ultimate failure of Heyst's twin rescues lies in his incapacity to feel friendship or love except through the alienating medium of pity. These failures inhere in the intense mistrust Heyst projects for all action—"the barbed hook, baited with . . . illusion" (174)—even when benevolently intended. His mistrust of all action is bound to make any action he performs formless, enigmatical, and finally a matter of free interpretation by others.

And in the exotic world of adventure and exploitation his actions are bound to be named and interpreted by desperate characters like Schomberg. Heyst's alliance with Morrison, for example, ends by giving rise to the fatal rumor of hidden money on Samburan and the death of Morrison. Later, Heyst's theft of Lena is the stimulus goading Schomberg's unreasoning hatred into active malevolence. Thus enmeshed in the obscurities of both chance and the irrationality of others, Heyst's apparently well-intentioned actions end by subtly linking him to the malignance of Jones.

As the rescues of Morrison and Lena suggest, Heyst's instinctive and unacknowledged allegiance to human community—in radical contradiction to his consciously held skepticism—has existed from the beginning. Moreover, critics have usefully discussed a Conradian reworking of the Eden myth and emphasized the repetition of Adam's primeval naming of things in Heyst's christening of the nameless girl as "Lena".[14] What no one has considered is the reason for the conjunction of the two contradictory attitudes, one involving a metaphysical denial of life, and the other an affirmation of it. Whether or not skepticism is a sustained philosophical logic, in Conrad's fiction it is complicated—as it is bound to be in any lived experience—by the contingencies of human response, and not simply by the contingencies of chance and irrationality that suddenly invade the lives of Jim and Razumov, but by the felt responses of specific individuals in their particular historical situations.

These responses are likely not only to differ from consciously held beliefs but to contradict them, undermining the possibility of a clearly defined logical concept of human action or expression. This is not to deny the value of logic but, rather, to underline the peculiar depth in human response at which logic and value, or reason and emotion, become entangled. This is why Heyst can consciously deny both love and murder—"I've never killed a man or loved a woman" (212)—and at the same time feel outraged at Lena's suggestion that there was anything morally wrong in his construal of the rescue of Morrison. Consider, for instance, Heyst's characterization of friendship: "The people in this part of the world went by appearances, and called us friends . . . Appearances—what more, what better can you ask for? . . . You can't have anything else" (204). Taken on their own terms, Heyst's words are incontrovertible. Yet they cannot touch the actual experience of living; they are too theoretical. They cannot explain Heyst's anger that his relation with Morrison should be construed by the world in a negative light. Heyst's anger, initially directed at the malignant world, finally culminates in the impasse in communication with Lena, an impasse which repeats, in a more heightened and complicated form, the impasse which must have occurred in his communication with Morrison. Once again, the momentary resentment he feels toward Lena becomes a generalized feeling "against life itself—that commonest of snares, in which he felt himself caught, seeing clearly the plot of plots and unconsoled by the lucidity of his mind" (215).

Heyst's rescue of Morrison involved no real comprehension of the nature of his act and its implications for the nature of his self. As an external action it is certainly within the bounds of his skepticism, though at a deeper level it already contradicts the dictates of that philosophy. The rescue of Lena, too, involved no real comprehension of his action, though Lena's probing of his rescue of Morrison forces Heyst to enter into the circuit of communication that his skepticism would impede and complicate. At the very moment when communication begins to take place Heyst's philosophy causes a rift in the process of reciprocity. Heyst is therefore forced to respond in a contradictory fashion: on the one hand, he defends his rescue of Morrison against the negative characterization of it by others and wishes that at least Lena would see the benevolent nature of his act; on the other hand, he at the same time defends his skeptical commitment by reducing friendship to mere appearance. The first response attempts to reappropriate the rescue of Morrison and put it in a context of intersubjective relationship, whereas the second response explodes that relationship as an "appearance", as an illusion which is stripped of contaminating power by skeptical withdrawal. Nevertheless, Heyst's philosophy is already contaminated by its antithetical possibility in the actions he performs. He at once persists in uniting his actions with his philosophy and drives a wedge between action and intention.

The arrival of the intruders poses a threat to the illusory security of Heyst with Lena on the island, and reveals the impossibility of a genuinely vigilant hold on skepticism. His reassurance to Lena that "nothing can break in on us here" (223) is a consequence of his skeptical rejection of the world. Yet the belief that he could be secure from the evil of the world entails the view that evil is external, that other people constitute one's hell, and that in the privacy of one's interior one is free from the encroachment of evil.[15] The movement of the narrative in *Victory* does not really invert this notion but, rather, situates it alongside its inverse. A simple opposition of good and evil is not dramatized but, rather, the disclosure that Heyst's skeptical mind, despite the apparent purity and rigor of its logic, cannot really comprehend the ways in which good is entangled with evil.

The novel embodies Heyst's rescue of Lena as a repetition of his earlier rescue of Morrison and adds commentary which puts into question both rescues and reveals, at the level of the meaning of Heyst's actions, the figurative resemblance between Morrison and Lena. The resemblance claimed here is, of course, formal, just as Heyst's own account of the Morrison rescue formally suggests the nature of his response to Lena's plight and his rescue of her. When Heyst is forced to deal with the evil trio, it is not simply a question of his rescuing Lena once again. Indeed, his crisis is compounded in that the intruders have come because of their conviction that Heyst's wealth stems from his ill-treatment of Morrison. And he is forced to attempt another rescue of Lena in a context of suspicion by others, a context in which Jones and Ricardo as well as Lena have questioned his response to Morrison. Heyst's situation is further complicated by the intruders' suspicion that there may not be real love between Lena and Heyst, that Heyst may indeed be a desperado like them. However erroneous this suspicion may be, their design is connected to their uncanny insight into Heyst, one that is a psychological correlative of their insight into their own selves. Conrad is here redoing, albeit at a much simpler level, the great confrontation between Lord Jim and Gentleman Brown. As we recall, Brown is morally wrong but psychologically right; it is in that sense that Jones, though morally wrong, is right in his psychological assessment of Heyst. The point of Conrad's treatment of both pairs is that psychological responses and tendencies have moral consequences, and that our strictly ethical categories of good and evil may obscure rather than clarify the meaning and consequences of the ways we understand our actions. Heyst's attempt to deal with the intruders is a concentrated form of rescue in which not only Morrison and Lena are at stake but also Heyst himself. It is an unconscious endeavor on his part to reconstitute his identity by placing it in the context of love and friendship, by reclaiming for himself what he has rejected as mere appearance. His attempt must be characterized as unconscious because at the level of overt action and intention the allegiance to skepticism remains for Heyst the defining mode of response and therefore subverts any possible reconstitution of his self. The self-rescue, repeating at a higher level the rescues of Morrison and Lena, is in contradiction to his skeptical commitment, though the moral significance of this rescue is also compromised because of that commitment. It is in these disabling ramifications of skepticism for action and intention that the dramatic interest of *Victory* resides.

It is inescapable for Heyst that love, too, like friendship, should be mere appearance and that Lena should find him devoid of feelings of love for her. For Heyst, love, being grounded in reciprocal relationship, is impossible because his skeptical conception of life cannot liberate a response antithetical to itself. This is neither to deny Lena's love for Heyst, nor to deny Heyst's unconscious though perhaps deep feelings for Lena. It is, rather, to suggest the obstacles generated by Heyst's skepticism and to show how these obstacles compel Lena to devise a sentimental and finally self-destructive mode of action to "prove" her love for Heyst. Heyst, on the other hand, not having had the experience of genuine attachment for another person, cannot trust the novelty of his feelings for her. He therefore responds to her in a complicated and misleading way. Thus, to Lena's comment, "you can never love me for myself", Heyst says, "it looks as if you were trying to pick a very unnecessary quarrel with me" (221). Lena's statement, as his answer affirms, puts Heyst in an uncomfortable light. Yet Lena's intuition that Heyst is being evasive is unfailing. In order to deal with Lena's feelings, Heyst would have to confront and understand more fully his own state of mind. However, the responses of both Lena and Heyst are, to a great extent, determined by their past experiences. Given his tendency to be skeptical and detached, Heyst generates feelings of uncertainty and confusion in Lena's mind. Lena, on the other hand, owing to her unfortunate past, questions Heyst in a way that complicates his responses.

Consequently, for the skeptical Heyst the moment conversation begins to turn on love it ceases to take place. This failure to communicate here is a moral one; it cannot be remedied by an endeavor he might make better to explain to Lena his view of life. Heyst's discomfiture is described as an impasse in communication:

> That girl, seated in her chair in grateful quietude, was to him like a script in an unknown language, or even more mysterious: like any writing to an illiterate. As far as women went he was altogether uninstructed and he had not the gift of intuition which is fostered in the days of youth by dreams and visions, exercises of the heart fitting it for the encounters of a world in which love itself rests as much on antagonism as on attraction. His mental attitude was that of a man looking this way and that on a piece of writing which he is unable to decipher, but which may be big with some revelation. He didn't know what to say. All he found to add was:
>
> "I don't even understand what I have done or left undone to distress you like this." (222)

Lena's expectation of love is an "unknown language", something that does not have a vital relation to his perception of life. It therefore becomes a mystery to be deciphered, a revelation that amounts to totally radical experience, leaving him speechless or dumbfounded. Heyst's discomfiture, which is also a discomfiture of his skepticism, operates at such a profound level that he can obscurely experience the complexity and novelty of his feelings for her but cannot comprehend them. His experience, in other words, reveals the dominant pattern in *Victory* of the skeptic facing those moments which put into question his mode of defining and defying the world and lapsing at the same time into a response which prevents him from recognizing those moments. The moment when his skepticism faces its own failure is also the moment when Heyst is impelled by the same *learned* attitude to be blind to its disabling nature. The remark he makes to Lena is a classic moment of such a blinding avoidance of her plea for love.

Almost from the beginning several misunderstandings drive a wedge between Lena and Heyst, misunderstandings complicated by the antithetical responses that divide Heyst within himself. Lena is constantly confused by Heyst and, though she has learned in the naïveté of youth to hope and love, she lives in virtual bewilderment of Heyst. She finds him "too wonderfully difficult to know" (246), misinterprets his devotion to her—"she had a sense of having been for him only . . . a thing that passes" (394)—and ultimately acts in secrecy. Correspondingly, Heyst finds Lena inscrutable, "like a script in an unknown language". The "grey veil of her eyes" (330) baffles his efforts to understand her. Moreover, each occasionally loses confidence in the other's reality. Lena at one point reaches for Heyst's hand "as if only to make sure that he was there, that he was real and no mere darker shadow in the obscurity" (372) in much the same way that Heyst "within a foot of her person . . . lost the sense of her existence" (248).

This experience of the ephemerality of the other is portrayed in such a psychologically compelling manner that the protagonists' earlier experiences are not falsified but are given a strange power, with paradoxical resonances for both of them. For example, Lena's memories of her early destitution and exploitation by others make her sensitive to the morally invidious implications of much of Heyst's discourse. Repeatedly, though no doubt unwittingly, she brings Heyst up against the psychological dead end of his skeptical commitment. She is quick to question Heyst's account of his rescue of Morrison: "You saved a man for fun—is that what you mean?" (199). Later, she suddenly tells him: "You should try to love me." And this is said with a sureness of intuition that leaves Heyst completely baffled, for she explains her words thus: "sometimes it seems to me that you can never love me for myself, only for myself, as people do love each other when it is to be for ever" (221). Lena seems to recognize not merely that Heyst does not really love her but that, given his rejection of the world as evil and of friendship as appearance, he cannot possibly feel or experience love. This recognition compounds her sense that she has been liberated from her past only in a superficial sense, that she has not been really freed from the destitution and abuse that make up her life in the past, that she cannot feel the security of the self deriving from a knowledge of genuine human reciprocity. As she tells Heyst: "I can only be what you think I am" (187). Lena's sentimental desire for love here occurs in a context where she has an unfailing sense of obstacles against it.

Among the most powerful features of *Victory* is Conrad's remarkable conjunction of murder and love for the skeptical mind. Heyst's conjunction of these passions has serious ramifications for his relation with both Lena and the intruders, and for the final scenes of the novel as well. For the skeptical Heyst, love and murder imply passions that keep one ensnared to life. Both passions, however extreme and unrelated they might appear, encompass a complex range of human response. Implicitly, these passions evoke the whole context of human actions and obligations and the problems that attend it; Heyst's alienation from this context reveals the deformed nature of his response to Lena and the trio, and hence it reveals his own self-alienation. Thus Heyst separates himself from others who are ensnared in such passions: "I was simply moving on, while others, perhaps, were going somewhere. An indifference as to roads and purposes makes one meeker, as it were. . . . I never did care, I won't say for life—I had scorned what people call by that name from the first—but for being alive" (211—12). From his consistently skeptical viewpoint the concept of purpose is devoid of any meaning or value. Love signals for him a series of weaknesses—"shame, anger, stupid indignations, stupid fears" (210). Rather than accepting love's strength as inseparable from potential weaknesses, Heyst has chosen to be "meek". Yet Heyst's meekness as a lover borders on the unethical when he confesses to Lena his indifference to the threat the intruders present: "They ought to have aroused my fury. But I have refined everything away by this time—anger, indignation, scorn itself. Nothing's left but disgust. Since you have told me of that abominable calumny, it has become immense—it extends even to myself" (329—30). The calumny Heyst refers to is Schomberg's lie about Heyst's treatment of Morrison (258).

Heyst's rationale for his lack of anger at the evil trio prevents him from acting in the present and thereby contributes to the final tragic outcome. Since his dislike of the trio is not connected to a passionate love for Lena, he cannot prevent them from carrying out their design. An attempt, moreover, to protect her, or even himself, may involve an act of murder that would confirm his love for her and for living; and it would compel him to see that life is an arena of ethical choices, a rejection of which might be both murder and suicide. Yet if he had been able to overcome the disabling nature of his skeptical commitment it would not have implied a simple and uncomplicated possibility of love in life. Conrad is far from writing a transcendental or sentimental hymn to love in *Victory*.

Heyst's animadversions against learning to hope and to love have an ironic significance in that they themselves spring from a prior negative learning, imparted by his father. The irony is compounded when we realize that Heyst learned this attitude when he was young and naïve. Throughout his maturity Heyst is forced to pose obstacles to specific contexts and experiences of life by framing and distorting them through the skeptical commitment of his youth. The adult Heyst thus remains caught in the prisonhouse of his youth and has as his condition of understanding not various problematic features of experience but an overtly unswerving allegiance to a doctrine. The doctrine, moreover, is not grounded in his own experience but in the disillusionment of his father. Heyst's father's moral fervor, when rejected by the world, turns upon itself in a rejection of life, and has its logical culmination in Heyst's suicide. Yet the suicide is also the result of Heyst's assumption of guilt and responsibility as well as his recognition that the supposedly moral basis of his rejection of the world and action is profoundly immoral. Heyst's final words thus signify both a repudiation of the consequences of skepticism and a repudiation of life itself. But they do not signify a repudiation of skepticism itself because to do so he would have to entertain a positive conception of life.

The narrative, of course, undermines Heyst's skepticism in a variety of ways. The most direct contradiction of skepticism occurs through Heyst's rescues of Morrison and Lena. More subtly, however, this undermining occurs when Heyst feels that his attitude of withdrawal only entraps him in irrevocable isolation:

> Not a single soul belonging to him lived anywhere on Earth. Of this fact
> . . . he had only lately become aware. . . . And though he had made up
> his mind to retire from the world in hermit fashion, yet he was irrationally
> moved by this sense of loneliness which had come to him in the hour of
> renunciation. It hurt him. Nothing is more painful than the shock of
> sharp contradictions that lacerate our intelligence and our feelings.
> (66–67)

To characterize the "sense of loneliness" as irrational is to deny the value of human feelings or human fellowship. The skeptic's embrace of his view stems from the impossibility of ever capturing the world in clear definitions and coherent doctrines grounded in a positive perception of it. The negative posture gives him a conceptual apparatus which he hopes will enable him both to eliminate all contradictions and to apprehend the world in a sustained and coherent manner. But that cannot happen. Heyst has only substituted coherence grounded in the negative for coherence grounded in the positive. The movement from a metaphysical affirmation of life to a metaphysical denial of life simply leads to an inversion of concepts; it cannot change the formal conditions present in both doctrines, conditions that simplify and distort the complex and irreducible features of human experience. It is inevitable that Heyst's loneliness, a logical outcome of his position, should hurt him, generating in him a contradictory response to overcome that feeling.

Later, after his unsuccessful pleading with Wang to return the revolver, Heyst discovers that he cannot successfully renounce the world. He thus says to Lena:

> "I don't know how to talk. I have managed to refine everything away. I've said to the Earth that bore me: "I am I and you are a shadow." And, by Jove, it is so. But it appears that such words cannot be uttered with impunity. Here I am on a Shadow inhabited by Shades. How helpless a man is against the Shades. How is one to intimidate, persuade, resist, assert oneself against them? (350)

This is a revealing admission of the inefficacy of Heyst's skepticism. His philosophy has taught Heyst to drift through life inconspicuously, not to "intimidate, persuade, resist, assert". The active verbs imply a whole series of actions and are grounded in moral discourse, though they need not lead to morally positive responses. His spiritual inheritance, however, bars Heyst from engaging in these actions. Not having learned the moral value of action, Heyst cannot attempt a deliberate defiance of the evil trio. They simply become elements within his generalized concept of the world, the "Shades".

Counter to these moments that tend to undermine Heyst's skepticism are other moments that not only contaminate the positive moments but generate meanings which culminate in the ambiguity of Heyst's final words to Davidson. The conversations between Lena and Heyst, discussed earlier, provide a striking evidence of Conrad's ability to dramatize the debilitating power of both skepticism and the past. These negative moments have existed from the very beginning, at least since Heyst's first determination never to enter "the stream". Consider, for instance, his state of mind after the seemingly romantic escape with Lena. When he signals to Davidson's boat in order to return Mrs Schomberg's shawl, among his first words to Davidson are these:

> I suppose I have done a certain amount of harm, since I allowed myself to be tempted into action. It seemed innocent enough, but all action is bound to be harmful. It is devilish. That is why this world is evil upon the whole. But I have done with it. I shall never lift a little finger again.

At one time I thought that intelligent observation of facts was the best way of cheating the time which is allotted to us whether we want it or not; but now I have done with observation, too. (54)

It is not surprising that the narrator should describe these words, coming after an apparently romantic rescue, as "enigmatical" (53) or that Davidson should momentarily think Heyst "mad" (54). The strangeness of Heyst's words can be shown by clarifying their various implications. These words express and reaffirm his adherence to skepticism; they even make that adherence stronger by his repudiation of "intelligent observation of facts", the only means he had initially allowed to sustain his skepticism. They suggest that Heyst's philosophy implicitly contained the moral difficulties which he would face in his relations with Morrison and Lena. Moreover, they foreshadow Heyst's immobility in the face of crisis, a foreshadowing which will prompt Lena to jeopardize her life in order to "prove" her love as well as the value of responsible action. But, more important, they disclose the madness in the logic of Heyst's skepticism, a logic for which actions and intentions have a perverted relationship. They disclose a logic which implies both the inevitability of discomfiture for Heyst's skepticism and the powerlessness of his experience before that commitment. These words suggest, in short, the ambiguity of Heyst's experience that will be captured only in his final words to Davidson. The final words, however, are an embittered response to his experience, for which neither life through hope, trust, and love nor detachment through pity and contempt for the living (including himself) are viable alternatives. Heyst's suicide, needless to say, is more complex than an allegorical repudiation of skepticism.

III

At the basis of Heyst's discomfiture is an insuperable difficulty for the skeptical mind. Rejection of the world as evil springs from the skeptic's failure to capture the phenomena of life in clear and indubitable definitions. Rightly aware of the impossibility of absolute eradication of the negative in life, Heyst is driven by his spiritual inheritance both to embrace the negative itself as the principle of all life and to reject love, friendship, and their correlates as appearances. He cannot accept the premise that for love or friendship to be meaningful one must allow for the liability that love may be betrayed, that friendship may run into difficulties that bring failure or subordination to other inexorable demands of life. To the extent that *Victory*

162

succeeds as a novel, it does so, I think, in its dramatization of the complex modes which characterize the phenomena of life, where intentions may become perverted either in one's mind or in one's actions, where genuine love may be blocked and transformed into a harbinger of crime by excessive pursuit of the logic of ideas in relation to actual living, and where self and community have no clearly definable boundaries, and responsible action no single meaning.

The critical search for the meanings of *Victory* is, then, futile if it turns into a search for the victory of specific characters. To say that Lena emerges finally as victorious, or that Heyst emerges as victorious through his supposedly symbolic repudiation of his former self and his assumption of guilt and responsibility for Lena's death, is to sentimentalize *Victory*. Because of the claim for a modernist secularization of allegory in the novel, such an allegorical reading must accept the obvious case of Schomberg left to his desperate scheme. And it must emphasize the deaths of a good man and an innocent woman brought to their ruin by chance and the irrationality of others. Though it is true that an allegorical reading of *Victory* seems to be more satisfactory than one that judges it by some strict standards derived from Conrad's earlier great works, the allegorical reading solves the thematics of skepticism much too readily. It imposes a neat schema and thereby fails to account for those features that problematize our reading of *Victory*. Thus, while the apparent simplicity of *Victory* tends to invite an allegorical reading, it ends by confirming the interpretation that finds the novel a mere sentimental adventure romance. In other words, the reading that castigates *Victory* for its sentimental ethic already allows for the allegorical reading rather than contradicting it.

No doubt the texture of *Victory* is not as rich as that of the earlier major novels. There is in *Victory* a relaxation in the quality of writing; the power of imaginative invention is not as energetic as in the previous great novels; the symbolic trappings that characterize the evil trio are tedious; and Lena's plan to save Heyst through self-sacrifice is dangerously close to adolescent romance. There are, none the less, powerful moments in *Victory*, which both probe the problematic nature of skeptical consciousness in Heyst and articulate the complexities that make it impossible to reduce human response to a final, univocal meaning. The texture of the novel is psychologically fully compatible with the demands of the problems set by a direct confrontation with skepticism, for whenever skepticism is a given of one's perception of the world it limits the possibility of action and commitment. Indeed, skepticism makes it impossible to exorcize the evil of the universe which impels the skeptic to its rejection. And it poses insuperable difficulties in the path of a desire to separate oneself from that universe. The thinness of *Victory* thus has to do with a metaphysical denial of life which ostensibly operates as the novel's inaugurating premise, and its success consists in Conrad's ability to dramatize the unforeseen ways in which contradictory responses reveal an unbridgeable gulf between the hero's actions and intentions.

Conclusion

Throughout Conrad's major fiction the problematical relation between action and intention, language and experience, threatens the supposed coherence of a character's or a narrator's action or understanding, and opens the complex play of antithetical meanings. From *Heart of Darkness* through *Lord Jim*, *Nostromo*, *The Secret Agent*, *Under Western Eyes*, to *Victory*, Conrad's narratives dramatize the enigmas which represent, for him, the deepest questions of existence. This is not to suggest that Conrad's novels follow a single pattern of meanings. Far from it. The novels begin at different points of departure, even as some of them recharacterize his previous novelistic preoccupations. Thus, if Lord Jim's final act in Patusan remains in the problematical area of antithetical consequences of intentional action, Razumov's double confession in *Under Western Eyes* frees him from repeating his terrible betrayal of Victor Haldin, and Heyst, the protagonist of *Victory*, remains mired in his skeptical inheritance even at the moment of his renunciation of it.

In *Lord Jim*, Marlow, as he tries to understand Jim, finds language inadequate to the task, and consequently feels that his experience has left him "strangely unenlightened". This experience is given a new twist in *Nostromo* in the context of political-economic forces. Conrad accordingly shifts his narrative strategy in order to combine various stories that would elucidate the history of Costaguana; he discloses certain fundamental tensions between ideal and action, knowledge and experience, and prepares the stage for *The Secret Agent* and *Under Western Eyes*. These two novels reveal a fissure in the institutions of both family and state, and question the network of central concepts that lie at the heart of Western culture. This kind of questioning Conrad had, of course, already begun in *Heart of Darkness* where, by employing the figure of the storyteller, he had woven a magic web of words that draws attention to itself by its stark assertion that value and "magic" are absent from the concepts of culture that at first seem to motivate the act of storytelling.

For Conrad, unless actions spring from human intentions, they are liable to have their own inhuman momentum. Inasmuch as intention is subjective whereas action is intersubjective, there is always the possibility of divergence between intention and action. There is, in effect, no guarantee that intentional actions will not engender unfortunate and even criminal results, that intentions will not be perverted by actions and expressions. The narrative of *Victory*, from beginning to end, traces Heyst's skeptical inheritance, and discloses the problematic relationship between actions and intentions. Thus one's intentions are complicated or undermined by social-political reality or by the circumstances of one's upbringing. Charles Gould clings to his intentions, at the risk of perverting the very values which initially motivated his interest in operating the mine.

In both *The Secret Agent* and *Under Western Eyes*, the destiny of a human being is shown to be entangled with the destiny of a nation. Individual lives, though they seem to manifest themselves in isolation, are held together in the genealogical network of society. The story of Winnie Verloc is one of disintegration of a consciousness that has suddenly lost its precariously held reason for living, whereas the story of Razumov is one of the gradual emergence of a consciousness that had taken pride in an unexamined and questionable belief in rationality and benevolent autocracy. Winnie's life may be characterized as a form of unconsciousness promoted and sustained by modern conservative society. Razumov's life, on the other hand, represents the aspirations of an alienated intelligence unable to reflect for long on the nature and meaning of his constructed identity.

Conrad's major fiction, then, becomes far more compelling when one begins to ponder the important and difficult questions that it articulates and dramatizes. The power of his fiction does not derive from a skepticism verging on futility and despair but, rather, from its radical confrontation with both hope and failure. It is in this confrontation that the originality of Conrad's skepticism resides; it is not the skepticism of some abstract philosophical stance, but a skepticism concretized in language, action, and character. Conrad dramatizes action and idea in terms of the felt experience in the lives of human beings. His art leaves us with the unsettling knowledge that there is no guarantee that men of extraordinary integrity, who may be emblems of a whole civilization, will know how to act with moral insight. And it describes the shattering paradox that such men may indeed become so entrapped within their ideals that they may destroy the meaning and possibility of moral insight. Interpreting Conrad is not a matter of finding a kernel of philosophical truth, because when an effort of this nature is made it is liable to arrive at E. M. Forster's famous but utterly wrong judgment that "the secret casket of his genius contains a vapour rather than a jewel".[1]

The irony of Conrad's political novels is not the nihilistic irony which is indifferent to all forms of suffering, exploitation, and wrongdoing. For

Conrad the political question about the nature and conditions of modern life and the fate of the individual, the family, and the lower classes is a moral question, and it requires nothing less than a devastating criticism of both conservatives and Utopian revolutionaries. If Conrad attacked Chiliastic Utopianism, he also questioned smug conceptions of liberal democracy. The attitude implicit in Conrad's political novels would reject the Kantian as well as utilitarian principles that seek to articulate a rational plan of social action, just as it would reject the Hegelian as well as Marxist conceptions of determinate laws operating through history. This makes his vision of society deeply skeptical and pessimistic, but his vision has nothing whatever to do with the nihilism which he discovers and condemns in modern conservative democracy as well as in the Utopian rhetoric of many of his revolutionaries. Like Hegel and Marx, Conrad knows that human identity is a social construction, and that man's life has its basis in the political nature of his community. His refusal to believe that there is anything like abstract meaning or value in reality apart from man's social-political life does not make him a nihilist, except in the view of those who believe in absolutist transcendental ideals of objectivity, truth, and meaning.

Conrad's fiction is, in a radical sense, antitheoretical. Its devastating critique of anarchism, for instance, underpins a liberal democratic faith in individualism, but this faith is always counterbalanced by a relentless scrutiny of individualism as it manifests itself in various forms of egotistical projects. Conrad's skepticism, then, inheres in his tendency to explore the maladies of various entrenched perspectives in our social-political life, and it contests the general philosophical or ideological impulse to abstract from any particular political or moral situation. Its abstractions give moral concerns a moralistic form and political concerns the form of propaganda. To Conrad, the moralist wants to impose his standards on everything else, and the ideologue wants to impose his system and beliefs on others, and they exempt themselves from the criticism they make of others. Conrad's fiction explores with intense thoroughness particular situations in which the self finds itself, and their implications for community, even as the self finds itself in a given situation because of its formation in community. The vision Conrad has of our collective lives, as represented in a given community whether in the world of *The Secret Agent* or in that of *Nostromo*, is in no doubt marked by despair, but the point of his critique of society is not meant to compound our sense of fragmentation and helplessness. Its very questioning of various ideological projects and their practical consequences enables us to distance ourselves from them and thus liberates us from the paralyzing weight of their importance in our social-political life.

Like Aristotle, Conrad insists on the indissoluble link between the human capacities for speech and political action. Aristotle rejected any meaningful relation between political action and violence. Conrad's fiction, however, shows an uncanny insight into the historical necessities of political action which call for violence. While Doctor Monygham is distressed, toward the end of *Nostromo*, by the signs of revolutionary activities he sees in Sulaco, the Conradian narrator knows the economic and political stability of Sulaco to be specious and illusory, founded on an expedient separatist politics, one that has deprived the natives of Costaguana of the rightful share of their national wealth. Razumov's confession, in *Under Western Eyes*, to the revolutionaries, even after having known the vulgarity and phoniness of Ivanovitch's revolutionary stance, is an acknowledgement of the affirmative dimension of revolutionary activity. Yet this is also a moment when, having recognized the truth of revolutionary aspirations, Razumov has freed his speech from its rationalizing and self-lacerating prevarications, and begun to talk well. The revolutionaries are misguided in their speech and often in their action, but not in their aspirations. Consequently, even their political action must be indissolubly linked to sincere and intelligible speech if their speech is to be prevented from degenerating into mere ideological and self-mystifying rhetoric, and if their action is to be prevented from mindless and self-perpetuating violence.

If Marx sought to make whole what history had made fragmented, Conrad tries to understand the nature and meaning of fragmentation as it operates in the various forms of modern life. It is perhaps because of his personal and historical experience as a Pole that Conrad's fiction resists the wishful thinking of Marx's predictions. By trying, however, to understand social life and its history, Conrad is at one with Marx in suggesting that moralizing in our modern situation is fraught with peril, since it is our burden as moderns to learn painfully and slowly what we are, and how we have become what we are. This entails for Conrad a recognition that neither moralizing, nor Utopian visions, nor yet the pursuit of ends we cannot place in relation to our historical experience can help us free ourselves from our inheritance or our present. Conrad's fiction resists any prescriptive attitude; this can be taken for nihilism only by those who crave moral and epistemological foundations. Such nihilism is the spiritual progeny of idealism; it abstracts moral values or dis-values, but cannot help us grasp the total configuration of Conrad's art. His fiction does not propose affirmations so much as it puts our affirmations into question. Nihilism, like every other vision dramatized in Conrad's fiction, is not yet commended, but examined and tested. The fate of a thoroughgoing skeptic like Decoud or Heyst is revealed in all its terrible implications and found to be tragic. In Conrad's treatment of the human condition, in all its bewildering complexity and variousness, we find a vision of hope and despair deeply entangled, one that yields up neither a theology of hope nor one of despair.

Notes

INTRODUCTION

1 For a discussion of the preface, see Ian Watt, *Conrad in the Nineteenth Century* (Berkeley, Calif.: University of California Press, 1979), pp.76−88. Fredric Jameson has said that Conrad's statement ("My task is to make you *see*") is "the declaration of the independence of the image as such": *The Political Unconscious: Literature as a Socially Symbolic Expression* (Ithaca, NY/London: Cornell University Press, 1981), p. 232.

2 See Watt, *Conrad in the Nineteenth Century*, pp. 169−80. See also, for a historical comment on Conrad's interest in impressionism, Eloise Knapp Hay, "Impressionism Limited", in Norman Sherry (ed.), *Joseph Conrad: A Commemoration* (London: Macmillan, 1976), pp. 54−64.

3 T. E. Hulme, *Speculations: Essays on Humanism and the Philosophy of Art*, ed. Herbert Read (London: Routledge & Kegan Paul, 1924). For a discussion of imagism, see Herbert Schneidau, *Ezra Pound: The Image and the Real* (Baton Rouge, La: Louisiana State University Press, 1969), chs 1−4.

4 *Russian Formalist Criticism*, ed. and trans. Lee T. Lemon and Marion J. Reis (Lincoln, Neb.: University of Nebraska Press, 1965), p. 12.

5 See *Joseph Conrad's Letters to R. B. Cunninghame Graham*, ed. C. T. Watts (Cambridge: Cambridge University Press, 1969); *Letters from Joseph Conrad, 1895−1924*, ed. Edward Garnett (Indianapolis, Ind.: Bobbs-Merrill, 1928); *Letters of Joseph Conrad to Marguerite Poradowska, 1890−1920* (New Haven, Conn.: Yale University Press, 1940). See also these biographies: Jocelyn Baines, *Joseph Conrad: A Critical Biography* (London: Weidenfeld & Nicolson, 1959); Bernard C. Meyer, *Joseph Conrad: A Psychoanalytic Biography* (Princeton, NJ: Princeton University Press, 1967); and Frederick Karl, *Joseph Conrad: The Three Lives* (New York: Farrar, Straus & Giroux, 1979); and Zdzislaw Najder, *Joseph Conrad: A Chronicle* (New Brunswick, NJ: Rutgers University Press, 1983). See also *Conrad's Polish Background: Letters to and from Polish Friends*, ed. Zdzislaw Najder, trans. Halina Carroll (London: Oxford University Press, 1964).

6 This is an important argument in Paul de Man, *Blindness and Insight: Essays in the Rhetoric of Contemporary Criticism* (New York: Oxford University Press, 1971), esp. pp. 17 and 135.

7 See Albert Guerard, *Conrad the Novelist* (Cambridge, Mass.: Harvard University Press, 1958), and Thomas Moser, *Joseph Conrad: Achievement and Decline* (Cambridge, Mass.: Harvard University Press, 1957). Both Guerard and Moser

170

stress the dark vision implicit in Conrad's early fiction up to *Nostromo*; the later works, they believe, suffer a decline partly because of the softening of irony and attitude and partly because of the emergence of a sentimental ethic in the works such as *Victory*. J. Hillis Miller argues for a starkly nihilistic vision in Conrad's fiction: see his *The Poets of Reality: Six Twentieth Century Writers* (Cambridge, Mass.: Harvard University Press, 1965), pp. 39–67. For a fuller exploration of the nihilistic reading, see Royal Roussel, *The Metaphysics of Darkness: A Study in the Unity of and Development of Conrad's Fiction* (Baltimore, Md/London: Johns Hopkins University Press, 1971).

8 Watt, *Conrad in the Nineteenth Century*; Jacques Berthoud, *Joseph Conrad: The Major Phase* (Cambridge: Cambridge University Press, 1978); and H. M. Daleski, *Joseph Conrad: The Way of Dispossession* (London: Faber, 1977). There are, of course, differences among these critics, as there would be between Guerard and Miller. A detailed survey and classification of Conrad criticism would have to include the work of Tony Tanner, Avrom Fleishman, Jeremy Hawthorn, Fredric Jameson, and David Thorburn, among others.

9 For the nihilistic emphasis, see William W. Bonney, *Thorns and Arabesques: Contexts for Conrad's Fiction* (Baltimore, Md/London: Johns Hopkins University Press, 1980). For the moral emphasis, see Daniel R. Schwarz, *Conrad: "Almayer's Folly" to "Under Western Eyes"* (Ithaca, NY/London: Cornell University Press, 1980).

10 See, for instance, Watt, *Conrad in the Nineteenth Century*; and Jameson's chapter on Conrad in *Political Unconscious*, pp. 206–80.

11 See Conrad's *A Personal Record*, published together with *The Mirror of the Sea* in the Kent Edition (New York: Doubleday, 1926), Vol. 12, p. 36.

12 *Metacriticism* (Athens, Ga: University of Georgia Press, 1981), chs 6 and 7; see also my "Criticism and interpretation", in Joseph P. Strelka (ed.), *Literary Theory and Criticism* (Berne: Peter Lang, 1984), Vol. 1, pp. 531–47, for a criticism of Fredric Jameson's admirable work, which seems to me hampered by the limits his Marxist methodological imperative imposes on dialectical analysis.

13 See, for instance, Edward W. Said, *Joseph Conrad and the Fiction of Autobiography* (Cambridge, Mass.: Harvard University Press, 1965), and also his "Conrad: the presentation of narrative", *Novel*, Vol. 7 (1974). See also Peter Glassman, *Language and Being: Joseph Conrad and the Literature of Personality* (New York: Columbia University Press, 1976).

14 Avrom Fleishman, *Conrad's Politics: Community and Anarchy in the Fiction of Joseph Conrad* (Baltimore, Md/London: Johns Hopkins University Press, 1967), p. 55.

15 ibid., pp. 65–66.

16 *"Autocracy and War"* appears in Conrad's *Notes on Life and Letters* (New York: Doubleday, 1926), pt 2, pp. 83–114. For a discussion of this essay, see Fleishman, *Conrad's Politics*, pp. 32–37. Eloise Knapp Hay, *The Political Novels of Joseph Conrad: A Critical Study* (Chicago, Ill.: University of Chicago Press, 1963), gives a thorough historical background for Conrad's political novels.

17 Fleishman, *Conrad's Politics*, p. 71.

18 ibid.

19 G. W. F. Hegel, *The Philosophy of History*, trans. J. Sibree (New York: Dover, 1956), p. 19. The classic discussion of the Absolute Idea is, of course, in *The Phenomenology of Mind*, trans. J. B. Baillie (New York: Harper & Row, 1967).

20 Karl Marx, *Critique of Hegel's "Philosophy of Right"*, trans. A. Jolin and Joseph O'Malley (Cambridge: Cambridge University Press, 1970), p. xlviii.

21 I use in this study the following political and philosophical terms which I want to explain here: imperialism, colonialism, capitalism, conservatism, idealism, anarchism, and nihilism. Each of these terms has a rich and at times confusing history, and the logical implications of each can be debated at great length. My use of these terms, however, is straightforward and consistent throughout this book.

Because of Conrad's own concerns, I use "imperialism" and "colonialism" as closely related notions. As Ian Watt has said, "Conrad's attitude was divided, and, like many historians, his novels present as many "imperialisms" and "colonialisms" as there are particular cases." Historically, over the last two hundred years, imperialism did not always mean the same thing, and was denounced and praised for different reasons. Both critics and supporters of imperialism saw it as expansion of a country's political control; others saw political expansion in terms of a civilizing duty toward primitive societies, and still others saw it as the logical outcome of an economic necessity. Conrad himself condemned the political and commercial motives of imperialism, while admiring the importance of British colonialism for preparing a foreign country for democracy. In his fiction, however, he is profoundly critical of imperialism and colonialism. Colonialism is imperialistic precisely because a colonizing country seeks to establish economic and political hegemony over the colonies; sometimes it may increase its power through cultural hegemony which it can establish by planting its own forms of legal and educational institutions in the colonies.

Like imperialism, "capitalism" is a difficult and controversial notion. In strictly economic terms, it means the arrangement of a market economy in which capital is in the hands of private owners who pay wages to laborers in exchange for their labor. The capitalist's primary interest is in profit. Capitalism becomes a highly complex notion as soon as we think of it in the context of Marx's thought. Marx considered capitalism to be a necessary but transient historical stage in the political economy of a society. Capitalism is the stage when society is marked by a strong internal opposition between the bourgeoisie who own property and the proletariat who do not own property. Marx, of course, believed that capitalism prepares the conditions for its own overthrow by the next historical stage, communism, when the society will become classless.

"Conservatism" is concerned with the conservation of existing institutions and values; this because it is skeptical toward proposals for radical change. Conservatives see their stance as a practical one which, they believe, resists abstract ideological doctrines; they consider existing institutions to be capable

172

of dealing with new situations as they arise. Thus Hegel's *Philosophy of Right*, and in fact the whole spirit of his philosophy, is conservative, in that he believed the contemporary Prussian state to embody the very best virtues of an efficiently functioning society.

"Idealism," "anarchism," and "nihilism" are philosophical notions which have inspired political stances of striking peculiarity and varying interests. Idealism may designate metaphysical idealism, as developed, in different ways, by Plato, Kant, and Hegel; and it may refer to moral and political idealism. When I occasionally refer, in these pages, to idealism, it is to moral and political idealism, since in the nineteenth century metaphysical idealism had its major philosophical form in Hegel's thought, and inspired, sometimes by way of opposition as in Marx, moral and political idealist doctrines of a radical cast. A consequence of Hegel's notion that the rational and the actual are in principle identical is the promotion of the state as the bearer of what is proper and rational. Moral and political idealism values ideals of conduct, even against a recalcitrant and perhaps dangerous actuality.

"Anarchism" is the belief that all forms of authority, including those of the state, are inherently evil, and ought to be abolished. Anarchism is a Utopian vision of society in which all individuals are free to live in a state of nature, and allow for spontaneous cooperation in a manner conducive to everyone's absolute freedom. Anarchism advocates the violent destruction of the state, but sometimes ends in self-contradiction, as in Bakunin's case, by setting up an elitist autocratic dictatorship which is maintained by violence. "Nihilism" is in many ways similar to anarchism and is inspired by the same extreme moral-political idealism that underlies anarchism. It is a basic tenet of nihilism that society is based on lies, that there is no such thing as truth, meaning or value. The only way one could see the world as it is, it argues, will be by the elimination of all institutions and all hope. Yet in a strange twist of logic nihilism holds that such destruction would make the world a better place to live. Nihilism need not be the same as pessimism, since a pessimistic, skeptical stance such as Conrad's derives from an extraordinarily subtle exploration of the workings of man's personal and social life. The pessimistic stance would find the nihilistic rhetoric of total destruction and absolute freedom inherently absurd.

The quotation from Ian Watt is taken from his *Conrad in the Nineteenth Century*, p. 156; see also C. T. Watt's discussion of Conrad's attitude to imperialism in his introduction to *Conrad's Letters to Cunninghame Graham*, pp. 10—24. For a full discussion of imperialism, see Richard Koebner and Helmut Dan Schmidt, *Imperialism: The Story and Significance of a Political Word, 1840—1960* (Cambridge: Cambridge University Press, 1964). An interesting psychological discussion of colonialism is in O. Mannoni, *Prospero and Caliban: The Psychology of Colonization*, trans. Pamela Powesland (New York: Praeger, 1956). For a treatment of Conrad's exploration of imperialism and colonialism, see John A. McClure, *Kipling and Conrad: The Colonial Fiction* (Cambridge, Mass.: Harvard University Press, 1981), pp. 82—170.

22 Conrad, *Mirror of the Sea*, p. 24.

23 Conrad, *Notes on Life and Letters*, pp. 190–91.

24 *The Nigger of the "Narcissus"* has been criticized for its "wavering point of view" (Guerard's phrase in *Conrad the Novelist*, p. 107). For a severe criticism of the story, see Marvin Mudrick, "The artist's conscience and *The Nigger of the 'Narcissus'*," *Nineteenth-Century Fiction*, Vol. 11 (1957), pp. 288–97. For a balanced discussion of the story's point-of-view problem, see Guerard, *Conrad the Novelist*, pp. 100–25, and Ian Watt, "Conrad criticism and *The Nigger of the 'Narcissus'*," *Nineteenth-Century Fiction*, Vol. 12 (1958), pp. 257–83. Watt's essay is a response to Mudrick's attack.

25 See *Joseph Conrad: Life and Letters*, ed. G. Jean-Aubry (London: Heinemann, 1927), Vol. 2, pp. 63–64.

26 My debts to, and differences from, Conrad criticism are more or less implicit throughout this study. My theoretical concerns are articulated in my *Metacriticism*, especially chs 6 and 7. Among the philosophers and critics I have learned from I might mention here Wittgenstein, especially his *On Certainty*, ed. G. E. M. Anscombe and G. H. von Wright, trans. Denis Paul and G. E. M. Anscombe (Oxford: Basil Blackwell, 1969), and Walter Benjamin, *Illuminations*, trans. Harry Zohn (New York: Schocken Books, 1969), especially "The Storyteller", pp. 83–109. Needless to say, what I have learned from these writers as well as the whole climate of contemporary debate is, I hope, through reflective assimilation rather than in terms of any attempt at deriving a strict methodological model.

CHAPTER 1

1 For Conrad's admiration for what he calls "militant geographers" such as James Cook, Sir John Franklin, Mungo Park, and David Livingstone, see his essay "Geography and Some Explorers", in *Last Essays* (Garden City, NY: Doubleday, Page, 1926), pp. 1–31; for a sensitive discussion of Conrad's relations to the romance tradition, see David Thorburn, *Conrad's Romanticism* (New Haven, Conn.: Yale University Press, 1974), esp. pp. 41–56 and 100–46.

2 See, for instance, Murray Krieger, *The Tragic Vision: The Confrontation of Extremity* (Baltimore, Md/London: Johns Hopkins University Press, 1973), pp. 154–65, for an existential-thematic reading; Ian Watt, *Conrad in the Nineteenth Century* (Berkeley, Calif.: University of California Press, 1979), pp. 135–253, for a historical-thematic reading; Jacques Berthoud, *Joseph Conrad: The Major Phase* (Cambridge: Cambridge University Press, 1978), pp. 41–63, for an ethical reading; Fredric Jameson's reading of Conrad, especially that of *Lord Jim*, in *The Political Unconscious: Literature as a Socially Symbolic Expression* (Ithaca, NY/London: Cornell University Press, 1981), is Marxist.

3 Here I am indebted to Watt's interpretation of Kurtz's painting, though in

placing the painting in the larger context of Kurtz's conduct my response differs from Watt's: see Watt, *Conrad in the Nineteenth Century*, p. 229.

4 See Conrad's letter to William Blackwood in *Joseph Conrad: Letters to William Blackwood and David Meldrum*, ed. William Blackburn (Durham, NC: Duke University Press, 1958), p. 154. See also Watt, *Conrad in the Nineteenth Century*, pp. 241–53.

5 Frank Kermode, *The Sense of an Ending: Studies in the Theory of Fiction* (New York: Oxford University Press, 1967), p. 18.

6 Lionel Trilling, *Beyond Culture: Essays on Literature and Learning* (New York: Viking, 1968), p. 20.

7 See Watt, *Conrad in the Nineteenth Century*, pp. 200–14, for a discussion of "Marlow and Henry James".

8 Trilling, *Beyond Culture*, p. 20.

9 Friedrich Nietzsche, *Beyond Good and Evil*, trans. Walter Kaufmann (New York: Random House, 1966), p. 89. I have modified slightly Kaufmann's translation. In Kaufmann, Nietzsche's passage in which this sentence appears is this: "Whoever fights monsters should see to it that in the process he does not become a monster. And when you look long into an abyss, the abyss also looks into you."

10 Benita Parry, *Conrad and Imperialism: Ideological Boundaries and Visionary Frontiers* (London: Macmillan, 1983). For a detailed and useful study of *Heart of Darkness*, see Cedric Watts, *Conrad's "Heart of Darkness": A Critical and Contextual Discussion* (Milan: Murisa International, 1977). See also Claude Rawson's excellent essay on Conrad and Swift, "Gulliver, Marlow and the flat-nosed people: colonial oppression and race in satire and fiction", pt 1, *Dutch Quarterly Review*, Vol. 3 (1983), pp. 162–78; pt 2, Vol. 4 (1983), pp. 280–99.

11 Quoted by Trilling, *Beyond Culture*, p. 22.

12 The phenomenological reading of Conrad by J. Hillis Miller in *The Poets of Reality: Six Twentieth Century Writers* (Cambridge, Mass.: Harvard University Press, 1965) and Royal Roussel in *The Metaphysics of Darkness: A Study in the Unity of and Development of Conrad's Fiction* (Baltimore, Md/London: Johns Hopkins University Press, 1971) is existentialist, if not Sartrean. See also Ian Watt's remarks on *Heart of Darkness* in relation to Sartre, in *Conrad in the Nineteenth Century*, pp. 166–67; Bruce Johnson's reading of Conrad, in *Conrad's Models of Mind* (Minneapolis, Minn.: University of Minnesota Press, 1971), is Sartrean; finally, Eloise Knapp Hay, "Conrad between Sartre and Socrates", *Modern Language Quarterly*, Vol. 34 (March 1973), pp. 85–97, reflects on Conrad in relation to Sartre and Socrates, while placing him close to the latter (21). I came across Parry's study when I had nearly finished my typescript for press.

13 See Nietzsche's attack on Socrates in *The Birth of Tragedy and the Case of Wagner*, trans. Walter Kaufmann (New York: Vintage, 1967), pp. 81-98. Nietzsche's reading of Socrates is radically different from the one generally held about Socrates.

14 For Freud's discussion of the origins of guilt and morality, see *Civilization and Its*

Discontents, trans. James Strachey (New York: Norton, 1961); and *Totem and Taboo*, trans. James Strachey (London: Routledge & Kegan Paul, 1950).

15 This is the point of Trilling's deeply felt essay, "On the teaching of modern literature," in his *Beyond Culture*, pp. 3–30.

16 For a remarkably insightful discussion of the relation between self and community and implications for morality, see Alasdair MacIntyre, *After Virtue: A Study in Morality* (Notre Dame, Ind.:University of Notre Dame Press, 1981), esp. pp. 30–34 and 210–6. Though I read this book after I had worked out several of my ideas explored here, I hope my study has benefited from MacIntyre's discussion. One crucial respect in which I see Conrad exploring the question of values and their implications for human action is in the fact that Conrad often dramatizes the self outside its cultural communal context, and then views its dilemmas in the context of its community's own inner contradictions. For Conrad, however, as for MacIntyre, moral questions are political in nature just as political questions are moral in nature. Both would seem to suggest that only when human action is seen atomistically, in isolation from other features of social life, one separates ethical from political questions, and treats them as matters requiring logical resolution.

CHAPTER 2

1 For a history of Conrad's composition of the novel, see many of Conrad's letters to William Blackwood, in *Joseph Conrad: Letters to William Blackwood and David S. Meldrum*, ed. William Blackburn (Durham, NC: Duke University Press, 1958), pp. 54–90; see also Eloise Knapp Hay, "*Lord Jim*: from sketch to novel", *Comparative Literature*, Vol. 12 (1960), pp. 289–309; and Ian Watt, *Conrad in the Nineteenth Century* (Berkeley, Calif.: University of California Press, 1979), pp. 259–69, and Norman Sherry, *Conrad's Eastern World* (Cambridge: Cambridge University Press, 1966), pp. 41–170.

2 J. Hillis Miller has, in a discussion of the problem of interpreting *Lord Jim*, said that Jim cannot "ever be clear to us, except with the paradoxical clarity generated by our recognition that the process of interpreting his story is a ceaseless movement toward a light which always remains hidden": "The interpretation of *Lord Jim*", in Morton W. Bloomfield (ed.), *The Interpretation of Narrative: Theory and Practice* (Cambridge, Mass.: Harvard University Press, 1970), p. 228. For a somewhat revised version of this reading, see Miller's "*Lord Jim*: repetition as subversion of organic form", in his *Fiction and Repetition: Seven English Novels* (Cambridge, Mass.: Harvard University Press, 1982), pp. 22–41.

3 The complexity of Marlow's narrative has provoked a variety of critical responses. For instance, Walter F. Wright, in *Romance and Tragedy in Joseph Conrad* (Lincoln, Neb.: Nebraska University Press), p. 118, characterizes

Marlow as a representative of the "MacWhirr tradition" who is "securely anchored in the solidarity of the captain's professional oblivion." Douglas Hewitt, in *Conrad: A Reassessment* (Cambridge, Mass.: Harvard University Press, 1952), pp. 37–38, has argued that Marlow is radically confused; the reader looks to Marlow "for a definite comment, explicit or implicit, on Jim's conduct and he is not able to give it." Albert Guerard, in *Conrad the Novelist* (Cambridge, Mass.: Harvard University Press, 1958), pp. 126–74, has provided what is certainly an authoritative discussion of *Lord Jim*. Guerard attributes Marlow's confusing narrative to Conrad's deliberate aesthetic strategy, an impressionistic technique that seeks to maintain a "balance of sympathy and judgment" (152). For a superb analysis of the narrative techniques in *Lord Jim*, see Watt, *Conrad in the Nineteenth Century*, pp. 269–310.

For some important studies of *Lord Jim*, not focusing primarily on Marlow's narrative, see Dorothy Van Ghent, "On *Lord Jim*", in her *The English Novel: Form and Function* (New York, Rinehart, 1953), pp. 229–44; Tony Tanner, "Butterflies and beetles—Conrad's two truths", *Chicago Review*, Vol. 16 (1963), pp. 123–40; Bruce Johnson, *Conrad's Models of Mind* (Minneapolis, Minn.: University of Minnesota Press, 1971), pp. 54–69; and Jacques Berthoud, *Joseph Conrad: The Major Phase* (Cambridge: Cambridge University Press, 1978), pp. 64–93.

My interpretation of *Lord Jim* can be directly characterized here by placing it in critical relation to the interpretations by Guerard, Berthoud, and Watt. Guerard has conveniently summarized his interpretation thus: "that on a first reading we are inclined to think Marlow's own judgment of Jim too harsh (since we have missed some of the evidence that led him to that judgment); that on a second reading (because we are discovering that evidence with a force of delayed impact) we may think Marlow's judgment too lenient" (*Conrad the Novelist*, p. 154). In a sense, there is no doubt that we discover, on a second reading, things that are missed by the first reading. Yet, by conceiving the question of the control on the reader's sympathy and judgment in a neat schematic fashion, Guerard's reading becomes inadequate. My interpretation seeks to show that a straightforward either/or response is not available to the reader except arbitrarily and that Marlow's own difficulty in rendering such a judgment is at the basis of both his reflection on his narrative and his adoption of his particular narrative strategy. This will, in effect, require a revision of our grasp of Conrad's impressionist technique. Watt and Berthoud read *Lord Jim* in moral terms and see an essentially affirmative, if tragic, conception of human life in the novel.

4   Edward W. Said, *Beginnings: Intention and Method* (New York: Basic Books, 1975), p. 84. However, someone else's experience is always outside one's own discourse, though the latter can seek to grasp it. This "grasping" of another's experience is always a form of interpretation.

5   Strangely enough, critical studies of *Lord Jim* have almost entirely ignored the importance of the French lieutenant to Marlow's narrative. This is no doubt because critics have considered the lieutenant to be a vehicle of ordinary

consciousness undermined by Marlow's deeper preoccupations and by Stein's philosophical stature. Guerard (*Conrad the Novelist*), however, has rightly praised the "natural unreflective heroism of the French lieutenant" (159), but he does not pause to inquire into the lieutenant's specific remarks or his larger role in Marlow's narrative. Berthoud (*Conrad: The Major Phase*) has carefully examined the French lieutenant's role; his discussion identifies that role as constituting "one of the two fundamental moral premises of the novel" (71). My interpretation, while sharing Berthoud's view at some points, differs in arguing that the two "moral premises" not only intersect but imply one another. This mutual implication is at the heart of *Lord Jim*.

6 Stein's character and Marlow's treatment of him have attracted considerable critical comment. The earliest and perhaps still most powerful is Robert Penn Warren's in "*Nostromo*", *Sewanee Review*, Vol. 39 (1951), pp. 363–91. Warren's comment on Stein's words quoted above occurs in the context of a discussion of *Nostromo* and understandably does not place them in the complex context of Stein's entire conversation or in the context of Marlow's response to Stein. Bruce Johnson (*Conrad's Models of Mind*), who has admiringly quoted Warren's comment, argues that "although Stein feels a romantic kinship with Jim, there are *moral* differences between the two men" (59). Contrary to this, my interpretation of Stein argues that the older man's actual experience suggests simply a compromise with experience, not a morally superior stance. Indeed, Jim's refusal to compromise makes for a possibility of desire, a possibility that Stein himself wishes to realize vicariously through Jim. Berthoud's discussion of Stein (*Conrad: The Major Phase*, pp. 87–89) is persuasive, but again does not take into account the matrix of contradictions within which Stein's character acquires its obscure power over us.

7 Both the character of Jewel and Marlow's response to her have been almost entirely ignored in major studies of *Lord Jim*. For instance, Guerard has said that "a characteristic mediocrity sets in with the introduction of Jewel in Chapter 28" (*Conrad the Novelist*, p. 168). Sister Mary Sullivan's essay, "Conrad's paralipses in the narration of *Lord Jim*", *Conradiana*, Vol. 10 (1978), pp. 123–40, offers some suggestive observations on the function of Jewel in *Lord Jim*.

8 That the hope was illusory Marlow admits very early in his narrative; see *Lord Jim*, p. 50.

9 See *Lord Jim*, pp. 5–7; see also Royal Roussel's discussion of this point in *The Metaphysics of Darkness: A Study in the Unity of and Development of Conrad's Fiction* (Baltimore, Md/London: Johns Hopkins University Press, 1971), pp. 81–83.

10 Jean-Paul Sartre, *Being and Nothingness: An Essay on Phenomenological Ontology*, trans. Hazel E. Barnes (New York: Washington Square Press, 1966), pp. 529–681. As Sartre explains, choice "is the foundation of all deliberation" (564). Thus, given his project to live in terms of his ideal, Jim cannot even conceive of the possibility of getting away from it, for it is only within the framework of his fundamental project that Jim's will can be efficacious.

11 See the discussion of *Heart of Darkness* by James Guetti, *The Limits of Metaphor: A*

Study of Melville, Conrad, and Faulkner (Ithaca, NY/London: Cornell University Press, 1967), pp. 46–68.

12 For a detailed analysis of this, see Watt, *Conrad in the Nineteenth Century*, pp. 281–86.

13 See Guerard, *Conrad the Novelist*, p. 146.

14 F. R. Leavis, among others, has criticized *Lord Jim*'s Patusan phase as being responsible for its failure: *The Great Tradition: George Eliot, Henry James, Joseph Conrad* (London: Chatto & Windus, 1948), p. 190. Most recently, Fredric Jameson has discussed this so-called change as "a shift between two narrative paradigms," one that Jameson argues is the result of "a structural breakdown of the older realisms, from which emerges not modernism alone, but rather two literary and cultural structures, dialectically interrelated and necessarily presupposing each other for any adequate analysis": *The Political Unconscious: Literature as a Socially Symbolic Expression* (Ithaca, NY/London: Cornell University Press, 1981), p. 207. It seems to me, however, that Jameson's reading here is the product of a strict commitment to his Marxist doctrines, for the paradigm of romance embodied by Jim's life in Patusan, far from inaugurating a radical break with Jim's life before the Patusan phase, is in fact presupposed in the first half of the novel. My reading here, with differences in emphasis, complements Tony Tanner's sensitive reading, which argues that Jim's life in Patusan has not "transcended the world of the *Patna*": *Lord Jim* (London: Edward Arnold, 1963), p. 48.

15 See Miller, "Interpretation of *Lord Jim*", for a discussion of the interplay of light and darkness in Marlow's characterization of Jim.

CHAPTER 3

1 Letter of 22 August 1903: see *Joseph Conrad: Life and Letters*, ed. G. Jean-Aubry (London: Heinemann, 1927), Vol. 1, p. 316.

2 See Conrad's *A Personal Record*, Kent Edition (New York: Doubleday, 1926), Vol. 12, pp. 98–99.

3 Albert Guerard, *Conrad the Novelist* (Cambridge, Mass.: Harvard University Press, 1958), p. 177.

4 For a discussion of genealogy and related issues, see Michel Foucault, "Nietzsche, genealogy, history", in his *Language, Counter-Memory, Practice: Selected Essays and Interviews*, trans. Donald F. Bouchard and Sherry Simon (Ithaca, NY: Cornell University Press, 1977), pp. 139–64.

5 Jeremy Hawthorn, *Joseph Conrad: Language and Fictional Self-Consciousness* (Lincoln, Neb.: University of Nebraska Press, 1979), p. 67.

6 Jacques Berthoud, *Joseph Conrad: The Major Phase* (Cambridge: Cambridge University Press, 1978), p. 117; Claire Rosenfield, *Paradise of Snakes: An Archetypal Analysis of Conrad's Political Novels* (Chicago, Ill.: University of Chicago Press, 1967), p. 66.

7   G. W. F. Hegel, *The Phenomenology of Mind*, trans. J. B. Baillie (New York: Harper & Row, 1967), esp. pp. 241−67; see also Avrom Fleishman, who says that "Nostromo is . . . directly destroyed by the contradictions between self-seeking and class consciousness" in his *Conrad's Politics: Community and Anarchy in the Fiction of Joseph Conrad* (Baltimore, Md/London: Johns Hopkins University Press, 1967), p. 175.

8   Fredric Jameson, *The Political Unconscious: Literature as a Socially Symbolic Expression* (Ithaca, NY/London: Cornell University Press, 1981), pp. 272−73.

9   My discussion in this paragraph is indebted to Albert O. Hirschman, *The Passions and the Interests: Political Argument for Capitalism before Its Triumph* (Princeton, NJ: Princeton University Press, 1977).

10 For a major study of power relations, see Michel Foucault, *Discipline and Punish: The Birth of the Prison*, trans. Alan Sheridan (New York: Random House, 1979).

11 See, for instance, Conrad's essays on political matters, such as "Autocracy and War" in his *Notes on Life and Letters* (New York: Doubleday, 1926), pt 2, pp. 83−114.

12 For a clarification of the time-scheme of *Nostromo*, see H. M. Daleski, *Joseph Conrad: The Way of Dispossession* (London: Faber, 1977), pp. 113−18; Berthoud, *Joseph Conrad*, pp. 97−101; and Juliet McLauchlan, *Conrad: 'Nostromo'* (London: Edward Arnold, 1969), pp. 9−10.

13 Friedrich Nietzsche, *The Use and Abuse of History*, trans. Adrian Collins (New York: Bobbs-Merrill, 1957).

14 For a discussion of Conrad's Schopenhauerian attitude, see John E. Saveson, "Conrad's view of primitive peoples in *Lord Jim* and *Heart of Darkness*", *Modern Fiction Studies*, Vol. 16 (1970), pp. 163−83.

15 For a rather lengthy discussion of the theme of record-keeping in order to project one's identity and a particular conception of history, see Edward W. Said, *Beginnings: Intention and Method* (New York: Basic Books, 1975), pp. 100−37. Though his reading broaches an important issue, Said places an excessive emphasis on Mitchell's place in the narrative, which is in fact complicated by the stances of Decoud, Monygham, and the impersonal narrator.

16 For instance, Robert Penn Warren, "*Nostromo*", *Sewanee Review*, Vol. 39 (1951), pp. 363−91; this is a well-known essay, reprinted as introduction to the Modern Library edition of *Nostromo* (New York: Modern Library, 1951). F. R. Leavis also says, in *The Great Tradition: George Eliot, Henry James, Joseph Conrad* (London: Chatto & Windus, 1948), that the repudiation of Decoud is essentially Conrad's repudiation of skepticism (190). Critics have disagreed over the ending of *Nostromo*. Warren argues for an affirmative vision; Guerard considers the novel to be essentially skeptical; and Irving Howe tries to reconcile the two views by saying, "Both critics seem to me right: the civil war brings capitalism and capitalism will bring civil war, progress *has* come out of chaos but it is the kind of progress that is likely to end in chaos": *Politics and the Novel* (New York: Horizon Press, 1957), p. 106.

17 Jameson, *Political Unconscious*, p. 276.

CHAPTER 4

1   Irving Howe, *Politics and the Novel* (New York: Horizon Press, 1957), pp. 95—96.

2   Albert Guerard, *Conrad the Novelist* (Cambridge, Mass.: Harvard University Press, 1958), p. 229.

3   F. R. Leavis, *The Great Tradition: George Eliot, Henry James, Joseph Conrad* (London: Chatto & Windus, 1948), p. 210.

4   J. Hillis Miller, *The Poets of Reality: Six Twentieth Century Writers* (Cambridge, Mass.: Harvard University Press, 1965), p. 58.

5   Avrom Fleishman, *Conrad's Politics: Community and Anarchy in the Fiction of Joseph Conrad* (Baltimore, Md/London: Johns Hopkins University Press, 1967), p. 188.

6   Eloise Knapp Hay, *The Political Novels of Joseph Conrad: A Critical Study* (Chicago, Ill.: University of Chicago Press, 1963), pp. 219—63; Norman Sherry, *Conrad's Western World* (Cambridge: Cambridge University Press, 1971), pp. 412—18.

7   Ian Watt, "Conrad's *Secret Agent*", *The Listener*, Vol. 83 (April 1970), pp. 474—78.

8   In his letter to Edward Garnett in October 1907, Conrad wrote, "I am no end proud to see you've spotted my poor old woman. You've got a fiendishly penetrating eye for one's most secret intentions. She *is* the heroine": *Letters from Joseph Conrad, 1895—1924*, ed. Edward Garnett (Indianapolis, Ind.: Bobbs-Merrill, 1928), p. 204.

9   For instance, H. M. Daleski, *Joseph Conrad: The Way of Dispossession* (London: Faber, 1977), p. 146; and Jacques Berthoud, *Joseph Conrad: The Major Phase* (Cambridge: Cambridge University Press, 1978), p. 142. Though my reading differs from the readings of Berthoud and Daleski, I find their discussions quite illuminating. For a fine collection of essays and background material, see Ian Watt (ed.), *Conrad: "The Secret Agent"*, Casebook series (London: Macmillan, 1973).

10 For a detailed treatment of the motif of secrecy, see Avrom Fleishman, "The symbolic world of *The Secret Agent*", *ELH*, Vol. 32 (1965), pp. 196—219; it is reprinted, in revised form, in his *Conrad's Politics*, pp. 187—214.

11 See the excellent analyses of this by Berthoud, *Joseph Conrad*, pp. 147—48 and 151—52, and Daleski, *Joseph Conrad*, pp. 145—50.

12 In his letter of 7 October 1907 to Cunninghame Graham, Conrad writes: "But I don't think I have been satirizing the revolutionary world. All these people are not revolutionaries—they are shams. As regards the Professor I did not intend to make him despicable. He is incorruptible at any rate. In making him say "madness and despair—give me that for a lever and I will move the world"—I wanted to give him a note of perfect sincerity. At the worst he is a megalomaniac of an extreme type. And every extremist is respectable." See *Joseph Conrad's Letters to R.B. Cunninghame Graham*, ed. C. T. Watts (Cambridge: Cambridge University Press, 1969), p. 170.

13 Fredric Jameson, *The Political Unconscious: Literature as a Socially Symbolic Expression* (Ithaca, NY/London: Cornell University Press, 1981), p. 202.

14 For a sensitive treatment of this theme, see David Thorburn, *Conrad's Romanticism* (New Haven, Conn.: Yale University Press, 1974).

15 For two opposed readings of this passage, which are different from my own reading here, see Berthoud, *Joseph Conrad*, p. 137, and Jeremy Hawthorn, *Joseph Conrad: Language and Fictional Self-Consciousness* (Lincoln, Neb.: University of Nebraska Press, 1979), pp. 88–89.

16 For Michel Foucault's interesting remarks on Freud and psychoanalysis, see *The Order of Things: An Archeology of the Human Sciences* (New York: Vintage, 1970), pp. 373–76.

17 Daniel R. Schwarz argues, in his *Conrad: "Almayer's Folly" to "Under Western Eyes"* (Ithaca, NY: Cornell University Press, 1980), p. 157, for an implicit moral alternative in *The Secret Agent*.

18 Karl Marx and Friedrich Engels, *The German Ideology*, large version (London: Lawrence and Wishart, 1965), pp. 316–17.

CHAPTER 5

1 Ford Madox Ford, "Tiger, Tiger", *The Bookman*, Vol. 66 (Jan 1938), p. 496.

2 Morton Dauwen Zabel's introduction to the paperback edition of *Under Western Eyes* (New York: Doubleday, 1963), pp. ix–lxi; and Tony Tanner, "Nightmare and complacency—Razumov and the Western Eye", *Critical Quarterly*, Vol. 4 (1962), pp. 197–215.

3 Irving Howe, *Politics and the Novel* (New York: Horizon Press, 1957), p. 89.

4 Albert Guerard, *Conrad the Novelist* (Cambridge, Mass.: Harvard University Press, 1958), pp. 248–53.

5 What Conrad says in his notes and letters, however, is not always consistent. In two letters to Garnett, he says "he is concerned with nothing but ideas to the exclusion of everything else": *Letters from Joseph Conrad, 1895–1924*, ed. Edward Garnett (Indianapolis, Ind.: Bobbs-Merrill, 1928), pp. 233–35.

6 Jacques Berthoud, *Joseph Conrad: The Major Phase* (Cambridge: Cambridge University Press, 1978), p. 161.

7 Avrom Fleishman, *Conrad's Politics: Community and Anarchy in the Fiction of Joseph Conrad* (Baltimore, Md/London: Johns Hopkins University Press, 1967), p. 224.

8 For a brief discussion of the parallels between Ivanovitch and Bakunin, see ibid., pp. 218–19.

9 For two subtle explorations of this, see Avrom Fleishman, "Speech and writing in *Under Western Eyes*", in Norman Sherry (ed.), *Joseph Conrad: A Commemoration* (London: Macmillan, 1976), pp. 119–28; and the second section of Frank Kermode's essay, "Secrets and narrative sequence", *Critical Inquiry* (Fall 1980). Kermode's essay strikes one at first as rather puzzling, but this is because in it

Kermode seems to me to attempt a critical reflection and analysis aimed at mediating between hermeneutics and semiotics.

10   For a discussion of this, see Marx's essay "Critique of the Gotha program", in *Marx and Engels: Basic Writings on Politics and Philosophy*, ed. Lewis S. Feuer (New York: Doubleday, 1959), pp. 112–32.

CHAPTER 6

1   See, for instance, Douglas Hewitt, *Conrad: A Reassessment* (Cambridge, Mass.: Harvard University Press, 1952), pp. 103–11; Thomas Moser, *Joseph Conrad: Achievement and Decline* (Cambridge, Mass.: Harvard University Press, 1957), pp. 116–19, 155–56 and 158–59; Albert Guerard, *Conrad the Novelist* (Cambridge, Mass.: Harvard University Press, 1958), pp. 255–61 and 272–78; and most recently R. A. Gekoski, *Conrad: The Moral World of the Novelist* (London: Paul Elek, 1978), pp. 178–81.

2   Guerard has argued most forcefully for the sentimental ethic and the decline in Conrad's later works. This ethic contains, according to Guerard, three major elements: (1) "passionate love between the sexes" in a setting of "popular romance" supplants the earlier concern "with loyalty to the community, to the brother, to one's self;" (2) "normalization" of attitude involving a "new optimism and achieved equanimity" in a "cleansed moral universe" replaces the "tragic sense of individual moral failure in a world of men" crucial to the early works; and (3) "evil and failure . . . are presumed to come from the outside rather than from within"—the heroes are innocent, immature, "incapable of significant action" and, unlike Conrad's earlier protagonists, none would conceivably commit a crime: *Conrad the Novelist*, pp. 257–58.

3   John A. Palmer, *Joseph Conrad's Fiction: A Study in Literary Growth* (Ithaca, NY: Cornell University Press, 1968), p. 196; Palmer's discussion of *Victory* (166–97) gives a very detailed account of the symbolic–allegorical structures of the novel. The allegorical reading of *Victory* was perhaps first suggested by F. R. Leavis, *The Great Tradition: George Eliot, Henry James, Joseph Conrad* (London: Chatto & Windus, 1948), esp. pp. 208–9.

4   Palmer, *Joseph Conrad's Fiction*, p. 173.

5   See, e.g., Guerard, *Conrad the Novelist*, p. 255–58.

6   The phrase is Palmer's: *Joseph Conrad's Fiction*, p. 166.

7   Moser, *Joseph Conrad*, p. 156.

8   Hewitt, *Conrad*, p. 107.

9   The following are especially suggestive in this regard: Donald Dike, "The tempest of Axel Heyst", *Nineteenth Century Fiction*, Vol. 17 (1962), pp. 95–113, and Bruce Johnson, *Conrad's Models of the Mind* (Minneapolis, Minn.: University of Minnesota Press, 1971), pp. 159–76. Dike's essay, I might add, remains closer to the allegorical reading and contributes to Palmer's expansions of that reading, whereas Johnson's reading focuses more directly on the complexities of

Conrad's narrative, a focus that seems to me central to a satisfactory response to *Victory*.

10　Guerard, *Conrad the Novelist*, p. 272.
11　ibid., p. 88.
12　ibid., p. 275.
13　Palmer, *Joseph Conrad's Fiction*, pp. 174—79.
14　See, e.g., Johnson, *Conrad's Models of the Mind*, pp. 166—69.
15　This is to remark, of course, the complex relationship that obtains between Conrad and the existentialists. For a study that makes some useful discriminations between them, see Ian Watt, "Joseph Conrad: alienation and commitment", in H. S. Davies and George Watson (eds), *The English Mind* (Cambridge: Cambridge University Press, 1964), pp. 257—78.

CONCLUSION

1　E. M. Forster, "Joseph Conrad: a note", in his *Abinger Harvest* (Harmondsworth: Penguin, 1967), p. 152.

Index